Ethnic Entrepreneurs

Ethnic Entrepreneurs

Identity and Development Politics in Latin America

Monica C. DeHart

Stanford University Press
Stanford, California

For Nayana and Ella

Stanford University Press
Stanford, California

Printed in the United States of America on acid-free, archival-quality paper

Library of Congress Cataloging-in-Publication Data
DeHart, Monica C. (Monica Christine)
Ethnic entrepreneurs : identity and development politics in Latin America / Monica C. DeHart.
p. cm.
Includes bibliographical references and index.
ISBN 978-0-8047-6933-4 (cloth : alk. paper)—ISBN 978-0-8047-6934-1 (pbk. : alk. paper)
1. Ethnicity—Latin America. 2. Economic development—Social aspects—Latin America.
3. Entrepreneurship—Social aspects—Latin America. I. Title.
F1419.A1D43 2010
305.80098—dc22
2009021944

Typeset by Bruce Lundquist in 10/14 Minion

Contents

Figures

Acknowledgments

Because research for this book unfolded over a decade-long period, it owes material and moral support to countless sources. Writing these acknowledgments thus represents an ambivalent task. On the one hand, it allows me to recognize and thank the many people who contributed to and supported this project in some way. On the other hand, this process forces me to reconcile myself to the imperfections and necessary partiality of this project, for which I alone am responsible.

Institutional support for the various phases of field research included herein was generously provided by the National Science Foundation, the U.S. Department of Education's Fulbright-Hayes fellowship, and the Inter-American Foundation, as well as Stanford University, Lewis & Clark College, and the University of Puget Sound. Language training in K'iche' was supported by a Foreign Language and Areas Studies Grant.

In terms of the work on the ground, none of it would have been possible without the long-term support, hospitality, and generosity of my many interlocutors in the various field sites where this research unfolded. In Totonicapán, the employees and community participants of CDRO were unfailing sources of orientation, information, intellectual insight, and friendship. As will be obvious in the following pages, Benjamín Son Turnil played a crucial role as both esteemed colleague and astute commentator on CDRO and the broader politics in which it was engaged. Through ongoing dialogue on the development process, Gregorio Tzoc Norato, Hilario García Toc, Arnulfo Vásquez Cuá, Jaime González, Lesbia Taló Batz, Ana Victoria García, Agustina García, and María Ramirez Tzoc were indispensable resources, fast friends, and savvy analysts of the development landscape. I owe much to their expertise, and I hope that this final product approximates their expectations and accomplishes the work that they hoped it would.

I must also thank the community members of the various Totonicapán communities in which I worked from 1995 to 2001. Although many of these collaborators must remain unnamed on these pages, they represent the reason why this work matters. The Alvarado family, especially Virgilio and Juana, were much-appreciated guides and strategic collaborators in this part of the research process. In Quetzaltenango, I owe institutional support and camaraderie to the devoted members of the Proyecto Lingüistico Quetzalteco. They accompanied me throughout many years of research, providing an important social and intellectual base. My K'iche' instructor Eduardo Elías also deserves special mention for his long years of friendship and support. Finally, members of the Galicia Meneses family continually provided a welcome, nurturing environment to which I could recede in those moments when I thought I wasn't doing research.

In the United States, I owe much gratitude to the organizers of the Digital Diaspora project, including Akhtar Badshah, who allowed me such open access to the project and welcomed my critical interpretations of it. My anthropology colleagues at Intel Corp., including Genevieve Bell and Tony Salvador in particular, were crucial to linking me to the technology side of development politics and for pushing me to articulate how it connected with the social world.

The conceptual and theoretical underpinnings of this project were also cultivated in the United States, where my ideas and methods were strengthened and honed by my amazing mentors and peers. My initial foray into anthropology was supported by Carol Smith and Charles Hale, who incited my interest in ethnography and in Guatemala and who oriented my original and subsequent travails in the field. Their initial mentorship and faith in me made all the difference in forging my intellectual commitment to anthropology. Carol Smith's continued presence in my research and thinking should be obvious in the pages that follow.

At Stanford University I benefited from an incredible set of colleagues in the Cultural and Social Anthropology Program. Kathleen Coll, Arzoo Osanloo, Anu Sharma, Bobby Vaughn, Scott Wilson, and Mei Zhan were early comrades in arms who have followed this research every step of the way and have remained essential critical commentators on my work. Consequently, their importance to my scholarly production and sanity cannot be overemphasized. At

Stanford, I also benefited from supportive intellectual godparents in the form of Ramon González-Ponciano, Bill Maurer, and Diane Nelson; they modeled how to navigate the world of academia without losing one's political compass or sense of humor. George Collier, Paulla Ebron, Akhil Gupta, and Carol Smith not only saw me through the initial stage of this research, but also taught me what counts as good scholarship, and why. Sylvia Yanagisako and Purnima Mankekar provided astute professional and scholarly insights that have been invaluable to this day; Renato Rosaldo and Mary Louise Pratt served as essential foundations for my work on Latin American and Latino crossings. Above all else, George and Jane Collier showed me what anthropology and academia could be at their best by inviting me into a world of collegiality, solidarity, and culinary delights. I am much indebted to them and hope that this research does justice to the Latin American tradition that they worked so hard to establish and nurture during their time at Stanford.

Over time, many other colleagues and friends have done me the service of engaging these ideas and/or providing constructive feedback on the actual text. My sincere thanks go to Abigail Adams, Stefan Ayora-Díaz, Stephen Collier, Jean Comaroff, Janet Finn, Edward Fischer, Melissa Fisher, Robert Goldman, Greg Grandin, Brian Hoey, Sangeeta Kamat, Denise Lawrence-Zuniga, Walter Little, Celia Lowe, Brandt Peterson, Nancy Postero, Jason Pribilsky, Suzana Sawyer, K. Sivaramakrishnan, Timothy Smith, Lynn Stephen, and Christine Walley. Central to the tasks of intellectual production, narrative construction, and also daily survival have been my stable writing group members and bosom buddies, Jennifer Hubbert and Lisa Hoffman. They have read innumerable versions of this text and imprinted themselves indelibly on the analysis in the following pages.

The arguments elaborated in this book have benefited from interlocutors in multiple conference and presentation venues. Segments of this research were presented at several American Anthropological Association panels between 2001 and 2007, as well as at the Society for North American Anthropology in Merida, Mexico, and the Guatemalan Scholars Network Conference in Nashville, Tennessee. Papers on the topics contained herein were also presented at the University of Washington, Tacoma, and the University of Puget Sound. I extend my sincere thanks to my colleagues in the Comparative Sociology, Latin American Studies, and International Political Economy programs at UPS for their helpful insights. I also thank my students who have generously read and earnestly engaged these ideas in ways that have helped me to deepen and clarify my arguments.

Earlier drafts of two of the chapters in this book were previously published. A version of Chapter Two appeared in the *Bulletin of Latin American Research* (2009), and the information in Chapter Four appeared in *Diaspora: A Journal of Transnational Studies* (2004). I owe significant thanks to Khächig Tololyan and anonymous reviewers at *Diaspora*, as well as to Leon Zamosc and Wolfgang Gabbert and anonymous reviewers at *Latin American and Caribbean Ethnic Studies* for their early feedback on the arguments further developed here. At Stanford University Press, Jennifer Helé played an essential role in supporting this project from its early stages and bringing this project to fruition. Kate Wahl and Joa Suorez also provided pivotal support throughout the production process, for which I am grateful.

Finally, I extend my sincere thanks to my family who nurtured and expressed faith not only in the completion of this long project, but also in me. Members of the DeHart, Russell, Kittilson, and Nistler clans have all provided essential moral support and untiring interest throughout the journey. Julie, Jeff, Andrea, Justin, and Jessica have been a continual source of inspiration both for this project and for other life projects. Josh, Nayana, and Ella have rejuvenated and regrounded me at every step of this process. Their curiosity, enthusiasm, and steadfast support of the "culturish" things that I do have made a world of difference.

List of Abbreviations

CAFTA	Central American Free Trade Agreement
CDRO	Cooperación para el desarrollo rural de Occidente (Cooperation for Rural Development of the West)
CIEP	Comparative Immigrant Entrepreneurship Project
FIS	Fondo de Inversión Social (Fund for Social Investment)
FOGUAVI	Fondo Guatemalteco de la Vivienda (Guatemalan Housing Fund)
FONAPAZ	Fondo Nacional para la Paz (National Fund for Peace)
HTA	hometown association
IADB	Inter-American Development Bank
ICT	information and communications technologies
IMF	International Monetary Fund
MABELI	*medicina, alimentos, belleza, limpieza* (CDRO's four product lines: medicine, health supplements, beauty, cleaning)
MERCOSUR	Mercado Comun del Sur (Common Market of the South)
NACGA	National Corn Growers Association
NAFTA	North American Free Trade Agreement
NGO	non-governmental organization
TiE	The IndUS Entrepreneurs

UN	United Nations
UNICT	United Nations Information and Communication Technologies
USAID	United States Agency for International Development

Ethnic Entrepreneurs

1 Emergent Ethnic Landscapes

IN 1996, THE KEYNOTE SPEAKER at the Inter-American Conference of Mayors in Miami, Florida, lauded a Guatemalan indigenous organization's Maya philosophy and method as a strategy from which "everybody in the development business could learn." When Mexican president Vicente Fox visited the United States in 2006, he met not only with state officials but also with leaders of Mexican migrant associations and Mexican community business leaders in four key states. He advocated for comprehensive immigration reform in the United States—a policy on which his political legacy with constituencies on both sides of the border rested. In 2007, George Bush ended his tour of Latin America by loading crates of lettuce with members of an indigenous agricultural cooperative in Guatemala. He praised its members, who partnered with Walmart to export their products to the United States, as a model of how free trade could promote development throughout the region.

Each of these encounters draws our attention to how international organizations, nation-states, non-governmental organizations, multinational corporations, and grassroots communities all converged on a familiar but refigured actor as the key to advancing development in Latin America at the turn of the millennium. This new development agent, whom I have called the *ethnic entrepreneur*, took multiple forms—including indigenous community residents, working-class migrants to the United States, and elite Latino diasporas—all of whom were seen to embody values, relationships, and forms of knowledge deemed particularly useful for the community-based, participatory development paradigm applied throughout Latin America. In a landscape marked by state decentralization, regional free trade agreements, high levels of transnational migration, and remittance-dependent national economies, the qualities imputed to ethnic actors took on a particularly strategic air. These actors were seen to embody unique local knowledge and morality, including enduring solidarity with kin and relations of mutual trust and reciprocity with fellow community members. Combined with their enterprising community-based self-development efforts, their growing technical and market-based expertise, and, especially in the case of migrants, their propensity for risk-taking, the actors defined as ethnic entrepreneurs promised more efficient, effective, and sustainable development possibilities for both their local communities and their countries of origin.

In order to understand the emergence and effects of the ethnic entrepreneur, this book traces the changing contours of development practice in Latin America with an eye toward how it has put ethnic cultural difference to work for development. First, it asks why and in what circumstances ethnic subjects have been identified as essential agents of economic development. In other words, why were rural indigenous communities that had historically been identified as regressive obstacles to national development now seen as important resources for it? What changes within these indigenous communities and also within the regional political economy in which they were embedded facilitated this transformation? Second, the book raises questions about how the mobilization of ethnic cultural identity and practice for development solidifies, challenges, or transforms the way that ethnic agents themselves perceive their own identity, their community, and their development goals. For example, how does an initiative promoting Latino community solidarity and collaboration across borders both produce and also problematize what it means to be Latino for different kinds of project participants? In examining these intersections between identity and development politics, the book posits knowledge as a crucial arena for the fashioning of both ethnic difference and its convergences with increasingly professionalized and even corporatized development sensibilities and practices. Therefore, it questions what kind of knowledge is associated with ethnic cultural difference and why that knowledge is seen to support global and regional market integration, even as it is articulated as a counterpoint to those same market structures.

The analysis is based on a multisited, longitudinal, ethnographic study of three development projects between 1995 and 2006. The projects include a self-declared ethnic development initiative pursued by a Maya indigenous organization in rural Guatemala, a United Nations–sponsored program aimed at recruiting diasporic Latinos to the task of development in Latin America, and a collaborative venture between a Maya organization and Walmart to produce spa products for global sale. Collectively, these initiatives highlight dynamic configurations of *what* constitutes ethnic difference, *who* is perceived to embody it, and *why* it is valuable for development. As such, they underscore not only how ethnic difference has been put to work for development, but also how development practice has served as an important space for defining ethnic difference. Furthermore, they draw attention to the changing meanings of entrepreneurism at work in the field of development and their relationship to ethnic subjects in particular. By looking at the distinct sensibilities and practices identified as entrepreneurial—be they opening a successful "chain" of development initiatives, migrant risk-taking and investment in "home" communities through collective remittances, or the repackaging of ethnicity as a niche commodity for global consumption—we can see how individual development practitioners, indigenous communities, and Latino migrants come to represent diverse ethnic and entrepreneurial forms. Through them, I explore the implications of different actors' efforts to mobilize ethnic difference as a tool for producing effective and moral solutions to the problem of development.

This study analyzes how these seemingly disparate actors all became visible within the space of development as a new type of subject, rather than analyzing indigenous actors and Latino migrants in terms of their relationship to specific community or state politics in Guatemala or the United States, respectively. I argue that this new subject reflected the reconceptualization of ethnic cultural difference as a productive development resource relative to neoliberal development norms such as decentralization, privatization, and self-enterprise. I focus special attention on the role that class and gender inequalities have played in shaping different actors' ability to represent the genuine forms of cultural difference assumed to constitute the ethnic entrepreneur. I argue that these forms of inequality become especially salient in light of the increased material and political stakes for asserting authentic ethnic difference within neoliberal development practices.

Indigenous community development activists that I worked with in Totonicapán, Guatemala, embodied the ethnic entrepreneur in their efforts to preserve indigenous, rural community lifestyles through a pragmatic and selective retrofitting of Maya ethnic and market-oriented development practices. They had founded the organization CDRO (Cooperation for Rural Development of the West) in 1984 with the goal of promoting local self-development through the operationalization of Maya cultural principles and practices. By the late mid-1990s, CDRO figured prominently in the Guatemalan development landscape for this innovative ethnic methodology, which included a successful microcredit network, a natural medicine production plant, and a community institution-building program. These successful ventures had positioned CDRO's indigenous leaders both as important interlocutors in state development policy and as savvy administrators of CDRO's million-dollar institutional budget.

Not limited to indigenous actors *in* Latin America, the ethnic entrepreneur could similarly be said to define both working class and professional actors associated with emigration *from* Latin America, despite their quite distinct geographic and class locations in the United States. For instance, George González, a second-generation Mexican-American technology market analyst from the western United States, was just one of the many ethnic entrepreneurs that filled the halls of the United Nations headquarters in New York during the inauguration of a Digital Diaspora for Latin America project in 2003. He and the other Latino professionals recruited to this project were presumed to embody both the market acumen and a moral obligation to "brothers and sisters" in Latin America that could be put to work for development in the region. These assumptions ostensibly linked González and the Colombian-born lawyer also seated at his table as fellow Latinos. Despite the stark contrast in the class, ethnic, and geographic positioning of González and his professional counterpart relative to their rural, indigenous Guatemalan peers, a primary assumption behind the Digital Diaspora project was that professional Latinos would have an affinity with and link up to grassroots initiatives like CDRO as part of a broader Latin American ethnic community. These assumptions raised the question of how and why ethnic difference was being put to work for development as well as how the new forms of mobilized ethnic identity resonated with different actors' definitions of identity and community.

CDRO's project provides one strategic lens through which to examine these questions because it highlights convergences between the rise of indigenous social movements in Latin America during the 1990s, concurrent processes of political and economic transformation of Latin American states, and global efforts to protect and foster indigenous rights. CDRO's efforts to mobilize an explicitly Maya K'iche' ethnic identity[1] as the foundation for development emerged in the context of a broader Maya revitalization movement in Guatemala that gained international attention with Rigoberta Menchú's 1992 reception of the Nobel Peace Prize. The Guatemalan state was in the process of signing a historic peace accord, bringing an end to thirty-six years of armed conflict. And following in the footsteps of many other Latin American countries during the 1980s, Guatemala was embarking on a process of democratization, state decentralization, and intensified trade-based development. In this context, CDRO sought not only to provide a culture-based development strategy in its affiliated K'iche' communities, but also to potentially replace the Guatemalan state as the local provider of healthcare, education, and other development services. The organization pursued this mission by pairing traditional cultural concepts such as the *pop* (woven mat)—which emphasized collectivity, reciprocity, and universality—with ambitious economic enterprises such as a regional microcredit initiative.

By 2006, however, CDRO had abandoned some of these previous, explicitly ethnic projects in order to produce a line of spa cosmetic products that it marketed globally via Walmart. This new initiative was remarkable in that the spa products bore no signs of their indigenous origins, but rather sought to accrue value within a global niche market as universal, cosmopolitan products. Through this elision, CDRO's ultimate purpose was to finance the reproduction of the rural ethnic community in the new regional free trade economy. What are we to make of this bold new venture in terms of what it says about the relationship between ethnic difference and development practice? Does the switch from more traditional ethnic products to seemingly universal ones mark a radical shift in ethnic development strategy and/or in the identity of its practitioners? Or does it simply reflect the natural evolution and culmination of CDRO's basic philosophy? In the chapters that follow, I examine CDRO's innovative ethnic methodology, its programmatic success in the rural communities, and its subsequent popularity with both the Guatemalan state and international donors in order to answer these questions and to illustrate the dynamic relationship between indigenous identity and development politics at work there.

The Digital Diaspora project provides another angle from which to discern the different forms attributed to the ethnic entrepreneur, highlighting the role that international organizations, states, and corporations played in equating transnational migrants with certain entrepreneurial qualities and capacities. The definition of ethnic difference that emerged from this initiative shaped the project's proposed division of development labor across diverse communities in the region. Organized by Seattle-based nonprofit Digital Partners and sponsored by the United Nations Information and Communication Technologies (UNICT) Task Force, the Digital Diaspora for Latin America project sought to mobilize U.S.-based Latino professionals in the communications and technology industry and connect them with technology-based, grassroots development initiatives in Latin America. Modeled after an earlier initiative that paired Indian expatriates in Silicon Valley with development projects in India, this new Digital Diaspora effort hoped to bridge a pan-Latino community in the United States to promote development in what was perceived by organizers to be that community's homeland. Its inaugural event was attended by a wide variety of actors, including Latin American engineers or lawyers newly emigrated to the United States, second- or third-generation U.S.-born Latino professionals like George Gonzalez, non-Latino industry representatives from firms like Microsoft and Verizon, and Latin American–based bureaucrats. All participants thus belonged to multiple professional and ethnic communities within the United States, as well as exhibited varying degrees of connection to Latin America. This demographic diversity was an important reflection of the initiative's basic, and ultimately erroneous, assumptions about *who* counted as Latino and *what* their relationship to Latin America was.

Taken together, the initiatives undertaken by CDRO and the Digital Diaspora provide compelling illustrations of the emergence and often contradictory effects of ethnic entrepreneurs within translocal development practices. They illuminate how diverse actors in multiple locations and with distinct relationships to Latin America were similarly reimagined as valuable development subjects vis-à-vis their ethnic difference. After all, during the 1990s neoliberal economic and political reforms held sway across Latin America, characterized by efforts to decentralize and privatize Latin American state functions in order to promote efficient and transparent market-based development. In the process, both states and international organizations moved away from developmentalist, welfare-oriented strategies that targeted ethnic actors as *objects* of aid, toward strategies that recruited diverse kinds of ethnic actors as potent *subjects* of social and economic change. Indigenous community members in Guatemala, as well as migrants and Latino professionals in the United States became visible as legitimate development agents in this context because they were seen to essentially embody the localized, participatory, and enterprising cultural forms that global development norms sought to build on and reproduce. Consequently, CDRO and the Digital Diaspora's strategic redefinition and mobilization of ethnic difference were validated by the international development industry as exemplary forms of development methodology.[2]

While I am positing the ethnic entrepreneur here as a new kind of development subject, the concept of the ethnic entrepreneur is not a new one. Indeed, a long trajectory of sociological research on immigrant communities in the United States has invoked this term to speak to the particular way that ethnic groups have organized economic relations, negotiated integration, and pursued upward mobility.[3] In summarizing this genealogy, Min Zhou (2004:1041–42) describes two dominant analytical approaches to the ethnic entrepreneur: one that focuses on "middleman minorities who trade in between a society's elite and the masses" and another that highlights the coethnic entrepreneurial activity located in immigrant neighborhood or enclaves. These approaches thus take ethnic identity as a point of departure and theorize how that ethnicity shapes the type and degree of entrepreneurism that a group exhibits. Research on Native American communities in the United States has similarly highlighted a long tradition of entrepreneurial activity oriented toward the reproduction of corporate identity groups, especially in terms of more recent successes in the gambling industry; however, these studies have often problematized the notion of ethnic identity as an appropriate frame for understanding native cultural formations (see, for example, Cattlelino 2004; Comaroff and Comaroff 2009; Perry 2006).

This study extends and complicates these other theories of entrepreneurialism among culture groups by focusing specifically on the domain of regional development practice. My analysis assumes that development policies and practices constitute important processes of identity formation and political struggle. It draws from the work of critical development theorists who have asked how development reflects a cultural formation in its own right (Escobar 1995; Ferguson 1990; Rahnema and Bawtree 1997; Sachs 1992;)[4] and who have examined how diverse actors consume, experience, appropriate, and even subvert development discourse (Bornstein 2005; Elyachar 2005b; Gupta 1998; Pigg 1997; Sharma 2008; Walley 2004). Therefore, the ethnographic analysis that follows pays special attention to the production of ethnic identity and community by diverse agents, each of which seek to appropriate the economic value that has accrued to ethnic difference for diverse corporate, national, or regional development projects. It examines the specifically translocal nature of that production process given the increasingly central role that migration has played within both community and global development strategies. Finally, it questions the multiple, contradictory ways that class and gender are invoked to explain and incite different understandings of community and who holds agency within it. This critical ethnographic approach is especially useful for understanding the nature and stakes of development policies that privileged decentralized, localized, bottom-up initiatives. From this angle, we can ascertain both how the forms of knowledge and authority that have previously been marginalized have suddenly come to the fore as valuable tools for inciting self-enterprising, self-sustaining development processes (see also Elyachar 2005a, 2005b) as well as what that new visibility means for differently situated ethnic subjects.

Decentralization and the Micropolitics of Ethnic Development

Over the last two decades, development strategies in Latin America have been defined by multilateral efforts to promote neoliberal economic reform and global market integration. Following economic shocks of the early 1980s, the economic austerity measures imposed on many Latin American states by global financial institutions like the International Monetary Fund (IMF)—policies known as structural adjustment—required major economic and political reforms, to include lowering trade barriers, promoting export-led production and foreign direct investment, reducing bureaucracy and social programs, and privatizing national industry, among other things. These economic transformations were designed to restore financial solvency, promote economic efficiency and growth, and facilitate competitive integration into the global marketplace. In many cases, their implementation was orchestrated and overseen by U.S.-educated technocrats working within the government.[5] Regional and hemispheric free trade agreements—such as the North American Free Trade Agreement (NAFTA), Central American Free Trade Agreement (CAFTA), and Common Market of the South (Mercado Comun del Sur, or MERCOSUR)[6]— were employed by Latin American states to serve as both the means and the end of regional development, such that more trade would foster greater development, and more development would be evidenced by greater trade. Indeed, both Vicente Fox's 2006 visit to the United States and President Bush's 2007 tour of Latin America sought to highlight the positive outcomes this market-oriented development strategy could offer: Fox's by accentuating the economic significance of migrant remittances and enterprise for Mexico's national development, and Bush's by showing the power of export agriculture to provide cheap food for U.S. consumers while also alleviating poverty in Latin America.

Despite their overtly economic aims, these reforms also had important political dimensions. Within individual national contexts, they prompted state divestment from the top-down developmentalist policies that had dominated the previous decades, making room for laissez-faire relationships between non-governmental organizations, grassroots groups, and international donors. Development tasks that were previously central to establishing state authority were increasingly decentralized and privatized in order to transform what were seen to be bloated, corrupt, inefficient states into more effective, manageable instruments of governance. One by one, communication industries, banking systems, public utilities, and other industries were auctioned off to foreign firms in order to promote competition and efficiency. Similarly, development project money now flowed not "down" from the state, but directly from private and multilateral funding agencies to specific local constituencies, repositioning beneficiaries as development agents and stakeholders (entities with an explicit interest in or connection to the outcome of a project). The Digital Diaspora for Latin America project I describe here—organized by nonprofit organizations, multilateral institutions, states, corporations, and individual citizens—represents an example of the increasingly decentralized, transnational, and privatized nature of development practice.

Many Latin American states touted decentralization as synonymous with a democratizing impulse that sought to strengthen civil society, cultivate transparency, and improve legitimacy at home and abroad through an emphasis on human and civil rights (see Van Cott 2000; Yashar 2004). Often, these political discourses conflated the economic accountability mandated by structural adjustment with political accountability (see, for example, *"Decentralization"* 1997). The shift toward bottom-up, community development was, therefore, explained not simply as a way of making development more efficient, but also as a process of strengthening and empowering civil society. In this way, neoliberal shifts in development repositioned the local community as a privileged site of agency, where new political and economic rationalities coalesced to produce new subjects and forms of governance.[7]

State decentralization processes in Guatemala are illustrative of the way that these economic and political reforms were intertwined.[8] Between 1996 and 2002, Guatemalan state and municipal government officials, along with civic groups, popular media, and individual communities, engaged in an ongoing debate about the terms of the state's proposed Law of Decentralization. This proposal outlined strategies for the devolution of budgetary resources and decision-making authority to the local level. The proposed shift was described in government documents as a process of increasing *poder local* (local power) denoting a transformation in not just the location, but also the nature and political effects of governance (DeHart 2003; Gálvez Borrell 1998; MacLeod 1997). One of the hot topics of debate, however, was which local institution was the most legitimate and effective agent for governance. After all, a broad constellation of departmental, municipal, and grassroots groups invoked the local community as their constituency. Therefore, organizations like CDRO competed with municipal corporations to win precious authority and resources from both the Guatemalan state and the increasing array of international sources that were to fund local development.

The privileging of the local in national development politics pivoted not just on assumptions about scale and efficiency, but also on assumptions about the nature of the community as a particular kind of political, economic, and social organization. In many ways, it conflated the concepts of local, community, and ethnic, bundling these concepts as a coherent counterpoint to Western modernity (see Gupta 1998). For example, the Inter-American Foundation—a development institution with influence throughout Latin America—saw the local community as a location set apart from the corrupting influence of the bloated state bureaucracy. As such, the community embodied innovative, unconventional orientations that derived from the distinct cultural orientations of its marginalized residents (Kleymeyer 1994:5; World Bank 1996). Given the development industry's search for more holistic, empowering, and sustainable development strategies, the local community thus represented an exciting point of departure for locating new practices rooted in cultural difference. Development projects were increasingly designed with culture in mind, seeking to mobilize local culture as an important source of "social capital" (Laurie, Andolina, and Radcliffe 2005:476; see also Elyachar 2005a).[9] Because of the way local and community were conflated with ethnic cultural difference in particular in Latin America, indigenous communities were often marked as the quintessential site of these authentic communitarian values and knowledge.[10] Accordingly, by the late 1990s, both the World Bank and other major development institutions had increasingly prioritized projects proposed by indigenous groups (Partridge and Uquillas 1996). In this way, indigenous communities emerged as ethnic entrepreneurs whose local identity, collective development strategies, and alternative cultural practices could underwrite regional development.

Many of these same assumptions about the nature and power of local communities informed the emergence of transnational migrants from Latin America as previously undervalued but now increasingly coveted development

actors. By 2005, transnational migrants from Latin America not only constituted a sizeable population within the United States, but in several cases their
remittances to communities in Latin America were substantial enough to rival
or surpass other forms of foreign aid and foreign investment (López-Córdova
and Olmedo 2005; IADB 2003 and 2008). They thus increasingly came to be
appreciated by fellow community members, states, international organizations,
and corporations as agents of lucrative, translocal social and financial networks
with the potential to finance sustainable regional development. As such, migrants illustrate yet another site in which we can see the transfer of previously
state-led, top-down, national development efforts into more diffuse, decentralized, localized, and private initiatives. Here, however, we see this process of
decentralization not in terms of the delegation of development responsibility
to community-based initiatives located *within* the boundaries of national territory, but rather as part of an effort to shift that responsibility to diverse communities spread across a transnational landscape. Migrants' capacity to occupy
and link multiple social fields was a crucial trait for development initiatives that
sought to leverage the benefits of increasing human, commodity, and capital
flows between the United States and Latin America during the late 1990s and
early 2000s.

Transnational migrants from Latin America can be seen as another formulation of the ethnic entrepreneur because of the way that the economic value they
produced in the United States was perceived to be directly linked to particular
cultural qualities, values, and practices that were rooted in communities back in
Latin America. In their burgeoning studies of migrant practices and economic
potential, international organizations like the United Nations and the World
Bank represented migrants as embedded in close-knit communities and large
families, and defined by "hard work, courage, and a willingness to take risks"
(Zlotnik 2006b:2; Burns and Mohapatra 2008). These representations naturalized migrants' entrepreneurial behavior and positioned it as a function of their
presumed ethnic difference. Recognition of these qualities by development experts indicated a shift away from seeing migrants as remitting *individuals* to
their construction as calculative risk-takers and savvy entrepreneurial agents
with the power to construct *collective* social change. These policy reformulations thus reframed the nature and significance of migrant economic practices
and social relations; what once was potentially illicit (undocumented migration), informal (individual remittances), and regressive (failing to assimilate)
now became seen as positive foundations for development.[11] Consequently,

as I describe in the chapters that follow, development initiatives increasingly focused on migrant organizations and diasporic communities in the United States as potent sources of capital and knowledge transfers for regional development in Latin America.

As an indication of their growing recognition of the entrepreneurial power of transnational migrants, many Latin American states—for example, Mexico and El Salvador—created new, more flexible forms of transnational citizenship as a way of preserving legal ties with migrants. Those legal bonds were often legitimized by invoking an enduring kinship among national citizens at home and abroad. In these reformulations, migrants were hailed as *hermanos lejanos,* or distant brethren, marked by their intrinsic ties to the local community and national family "back home" (Baker-Cristales 2004; Coutin 2007; Glick-Schiller and Fouron 2001; Landolt, Autler, and Baires 1999; Popkin 2003). This lasting cultural connection to Latin America was reiterated by migrants' positioning within U.S. society and politics where, as Latinos, they became marked as ethnic subjects seen to embody certain essentialized cultural traits that distinguished them from the white, Anglo-Saxon norms upon which a dominant U.S. cultural identity was constructed.[12] Therefore, as I discuss in Chapter Four, Latino identity politics in the United States became a matter of development policy as experts tried to appeal to migrants' diverse affiliations, often in ways that reinscribed migrants' ethnic identity. In this way, states, international development organizations, and corporations alike pursued migrants as members of specific culture groups whose moral obligations and lasting ties to Latin America could be exploited to support broader development goals.

As the foregoing regional development overview suggests, Latin America's recent development context made possible important convergences between new economic policies, forms of governing, and development subjects. These convergences wed enterprising, autonomous ethnic subjects and efficiency as both the means and ends of development success. By conflating economic and political reform, they also coupled the notions of market expansion and empowerment, allowing global capitalist development to be viewed as a moral, collective, emancipatory process. Finally, they privileged direct translocal relationships among diverse development actors, thus diminishing not only the visibility but also the responsibility of the state within national development efforts. This convergence among diverse development constituencies and interests meant that development practice offered the opportunity for new kinds of authority, participation, and recognition for previously marginalized actors, even as it potentially reinforced certain forms of inequality and produced new dilemmas.[13] Recognizing the multiplicity and ambivalence of identity-based development policies thus raises the question: How do neoliberal development norms work *through* particular kinds of subjects, forms of knowledge, and practices associated with ethnic difference? How do they build upon and reshape power relations within the ethnic community itself?

This book seeks to identify and map these shifting relations of difference, tracking their articulations and implications across a translocal development landscape. To do so, I employ two main analytical strategies throughout this book. To begin, I approach development as a contentious set of encounters in which both hegemonic and subaltern political struggles increasingly play themselves out. Development projects often function as the arena where debates among international organizations, decentralized states, and "empowered" civil society most forcefully take shape (Ferguson 2006; García 2005; Moore 2005; Paley 2001; Sawyer 2004; Sharma 2008). Consequently, rather than assuming development to be the direct reflection and/or extension of state or global neoliberal projects, I ask what kind of knowledge and practices are valued for development, why they are valued, who is assumed to possess/enact them, and what they stand to gain. Instead of taking the neoliberal aspect of these development practices for granted, this approach purposefully teases out the specific elements associated with neoliberalism, the contingent configurations they take, and the trajectories through which they are diffused (Hoffman, DeHart, and Collier 2006). In the process, I examine how state and institutional politics, corporate marketing strategies, community activism, and intracommunity authority structures have worked together within the domain of development to shape the contested conditions of recognition for ethnic subjects.

To achieve a nuanced understanding of these development encounters, I also introduce here what I call the micropolitics of development—an approach that interrogates everyday practices of and debates over ethnic identity in relation to development. Rather than merely suggesting a modification in scale so as to capture a "more local" point on some vertically organized, scalar organization of global, national, and local spaces (Ferguson and Gupta 2002), a micropolitics interrogates how already-existing inequalities—in this case class and gender differences—translate into competing ideas about and practices of ethnic authority and authenticity in relation to development. As such, it constitutes a focus on what Foucault has called a microphysics of power, tracing how power is exercised in specific strategies rather than possessed as an essential property of a given actor or institution, such as the state (Foucault 1980, 1995). For example, as ethnic difference accrues value within a development strategy, I show how development authority is invoked and performed by different types of ethnic actors. I examine the techniques and evidence brought to bear in the effort to meet shifting standards of authenticity in the eyes of local community members versus international development organizations. I also highlight how those techniques reshape the boundaries between the ethnic community, the state, and international organizations. By attending to these kinds of processes, I suggest that we can go beyond a simple appraisal of ethnic community power vis-à-vis the state or a global hegemonic neoliberalism in order to understand how new forms of knowledge and practice come together within the space of development to constitute and legitimize new subjects and forms of governing that have unstable and unequal effects for differently situated actors. This approach similarly pushes us to consider the *sites* where practices of governing and power are located. Therefore, it responds to calls for more research at the "interstices of the state, international organizations, and nongovernmental organizations" (Elyachar 2005b:94), so that we can see how these development practices take shape through and across specific bodies, spaces, and institutions.

As the micropolitics framework illustrates, development constitutes a contentious political and moral project, often defined in relationship to the question of how to live in relation to the market. Therefore, a study of development and its intersection with identity politics underlines the methodological and analytical utility of a multisited, ethnographic anthropological study that can illuminate the logic, mechanics, and implications of neoliberal development, taking into account how it works through the production of new subjects and spatial relations.

Translocality and the Remapping of Ethnic Identity

A long history of social science literature has grappled with the question of ethnic identity. In these wide-ranging debates, ethnic difference has been alternately posited as cultural essence, as historical residue, as relational difference, as minority standing, as racial marking, and as commodified object, to name just some of the contours of the broad literature encompassed by the topic. What is clear among these various strands of analysis is that, as Wolfgang Gabbert (2006:86) has noted, a great deal of confusion exists within academic uses of the idea of ethnicity, even as the idea of the ethnic community itself continues to be posited as a "ubiquitous form of social organization."[14] My goal in this book is not to examine a single group that can be defined as ethnic or even to produce an authoritative definition of what ethnic identity is, but rather to explore how ethnic difference is produced through and for development, by whom, and with what consequences.[15] In doing so, I seek to engage debates about ethnic identity that have emerged in terms of its meaning and deployment within the capitalist market, as well as in diverse disciplinary frameworks.

Reinvesting in Ethnic Difference

In their suggestively titled recent study, *Ethnicity, Inc.*, John Comaroff and Jean Comaroff explore the contemporary possibilities and problems that arise as "Identity is increasingly claimed as *property* by its living heirs, who proceed to manage it by palpably corporate means; to brand it and sell it, even to anthropologists, in self-consciously consumable terms" (2009:29; emphasis in original). They have coined the term *ethno-preneurialism* to reference the marketing of ethnic cultural difference as both a naturalized biological fact and a source of strategic economic value in the marketplace, as both a legally constituted form of personhood and a brand name (2009:28, 51). As the Comaroffs' terminology implies, the study of the changing nature, expression, and value of ethnic difference has tended to privilege the capitalist market and the realm of law, rather than the sphere of public politics, as the space where claims for cultural recognition and value are increasingly articulated. For them, this move reflects a move away from "the struggle for rights toward the world of venture capital" (2009:77). Scholarship on the mutually constitutive relationship between market activity and ethnic identity globally has reiterated this dilemma, highlighting in particular the role of ethnic industry as a crucial space that both reflects and shapes how indigenous communities are situated within the national and global political economies (Hodgson 2004; Little 2003, 2004a; Meisch 2002; Myers 2002; Nash 1993; Stephen 2005; Weismantel 2001; Wood 2008).

Similar to the above studies, this book focuses on the intersections between ethnic cultural difference and global political economy; however, it does so by examining the nature and significance of these relations within the domain of development in particular. Rather than taking ethnic identity as a point of departure for explaining the behavior of a single group that is assumed to share common cultural traits and exhibit bonds of mutual trust (Glick-Schiller, Caglar, and Guldbrandsen 2006), I ask both how ethnic difference is produced through development discourse and practice to mark certain populations as potent development agents, and how differently situated subjects within those populations debate, reconfigure, and even reject those forms of difference as the basis for their development agency.

The domain of development is an important entry point for this kind of inquiry because it serves as a site where we see highly contested engagements among local community members, states, international organizations, corporations, and non-governmental organizations, as each of these entities attempts to identify and mobilize particular formulations of ethnic difference as a source of economic value. For example, in examining CDRO's evolving projects of ethnodevelopment, I show how their dynamic formulation of Maya ethnic identity both critiques and complements the interests of the Guatemalan state and mega-retail chains like Walmart. Similarly, I demonstrate how some of CDRO rural community affiliates have challenged the authenticity of CDRO's representation of Maya culture in order to promote alternative forms of local cultural authority for development. Consequently, by examining the role of identity formation within development politics, we get a much more nuanced picture of how the marketing of ethnic difference fits within the changing forms of governance and relations of power that may work through but are not synonymous with a hegemonic capitalist market. This approach thus allows us to consider how ethnic difference figures within geopolitics, despite its apparent displacement from the realm of public politics.

Crossing Disciplinary Borders

To understand how such disparate actors as transnational migrants and indigenous communities came to be seen as similar kinds of development agents, we need a way of looking at these different actors under one lens. However, debates about the meaning of ethnic identity in the Americas in particular have largely been defined by a bifurcation between ethnic and area studies. In other words, the relationship between ethnic groups in the United States and Latin America has been examined largely through disparate disciplinary lenses (see Siu 2005; Stephen 2007), with the two regions sometimes juxtaposed against one another to emphasize the relativity of ideas of race and ethnicity.[16] Over the last decade, race and ethnic studies in the United States have responded to the reality that Hispanics or Latinos,[17] historically viewed as a minority population, are increasingly becoming a majority population and one with considerable political and social clout.[18] Furthermore, migrants' continued connections to communities in Latin America have made the analytical distinction between U.S. and Latin American ethnic studies increasingly problematic as a way to apprehend the complex social realities of groups who live their lives across multiple social fields. Instead, the question has become how to make sense of the shifting, relational, and highly contentious production of ethnic difference across multiple borders (Stephen 2007).

In the United States, Latino studies have highlighted both the social construction of ethnic identity by powerful entities like the state or the media (Dávila 2001, 2008; Oboler 1995; Rodríguez 1998) as well as the mobilization of ethnic identities as a means of challenging racial hierarchies and marginality in the United States (DeGenova and Ramos-Zayas 2003a, 2003b; see also Alcoff 1998; Padilla 1985; Rodríguez 2003; Suárez-Orozco and Páez 2001; and G. Torres 1998). As these studies show, the rise of a Latino ethnic identity imposes cultural homogeneity upon a highly diverse and stratified set of actors, even as it provides an important means of marking the experience of racialization and discrimination in the North American context that many Latinos share. Taken together, these two approaches provide a productive point of departure for thinking about the unique ways that ethnic difference is produced, mobilized, and contested within development practice for diverse political and economic ends.

In Latin America, ethnic identity has been understood primarily in relation to a dominant Hispanic, mestizo national identity. Especially in countries with a large indigenous presence (like Guatemala, Bolivia, Ecuador, and Mexico) the main axis of difference has been between indigenous and nonindigenous populations.[19] Ethnic identity has become an increasingly important subject in Latin America over the last two decades as a result of both state democratization processes and identity-based social movements.[20] The rise of indigenous political figures such as Rigoberta Menchú in Guatemala or Evo Morales in Bolivia, as well as the political struggles between indigenous groups and the state in Mexico (the Zapatistas) or between indigenous groups and private corporations in Ecuador provide just a few examples of the salience of ethnic politics in this moment (Hale 2005, 2006; García 2005; Nelson 1999; Postero 2007; Rappaport 2005; Sawyer 2004). Scholarly analyses of these phenomena reflect a long history of studies on the relationship between indigenous populations and national identity (Grandin 2000; Sieder 2002; Smith 1990b; Van Cott 2000; Warren and Jackson 2002; Yashar 2004), while also highlighting the way global human rights discourses or neoliberal development agendas have shaped the contours of contemporary ethnic politics. Like development studies, many of these analyses have stressed the subversive role of ethnic communities as "antineoliberal" forces.

How might we bridge these diverse intellectual fields and the political borders that separate them? Theories of transnational migration would seem to be ideally situated to do this work. Nonetheless, as Glick-Schiller notes, many of these transnational studies have tended to focus on ethnic groups as the central unit of analysis, thus reproducing the assumption of a homogeneous shared culture among groups under study (2005:53). For example, the social, political, and economic phenomena that define a Mexican migrant community in California are too often analyzed in terms of the ethnic community, rather than in terms of the multiple, overlapping social networks or fields of action in which the migrants might participate (Glick-Schiller, Caglar, and Guldbrandsen 2006). Furthermore, that migrant community experience frequently is invoked to represent the experience of all Mexicans in the United States. In doing so, these analyses naturalize rather than analyze the meaning of ethnic cultural difference.

This book takes another approach to examining how different types of actors were similarly identified and mobilized within the field of development based on their common identification as ethnic subjects. Following the work of Appadurai (2003), Ayora-Díaz (2007), and Zhan (2009), I use the term *translocal* in this book, rather than *transnational,* to describe the diverse cross-border encounters, relations, and politics that are invoked to define the ethnic community. Translocal, in this sense, figures not as an ontological distinction to denote "an intermediate scale of circulation conveniently nestled between the local and the global," but instead as a critical analytical stance that seeks to highlight locations and practices of interaction (Zhan 2009:8). Accordingly, I interrogate how different spatial arrangements, sociopolitical connections, and economic strategies have intersected to shape understandings and experiences of local community (Fischer and Benson 2006; Larner 2007; Ong 1999, 2006; Stephen 2007). In particular, I am interested in how shifting, heterogeneous forms of practice, knowledge, and identity become categorized and mobilized as specifically "local" in nature and, therefore, valuable for development based on the perceived cultural differences they are assumed to embody.

Ethnic cultural difference has served as an important indicator of locality within Western modernity due to its conflation with primordial, discrete spaces situated at the bottom of a vertically organized scale of global relations (Ferguson and Gupta 2002). My emphasis on translocality, therefore, attempts to bring into view the underlying assumptions and inequalities that have informed this slippage between local and ethnic. In particular, I study how the new relationships forged through transnational development strategies draw attention to the profoundly uneven and unequal effects of development across different localities, both transnationally and also within specific Latin American nations. Specifically, I problematize constructions of space and mobility that value "larger" scales of flows, which are coded as masculine and agentive in relation to "smaller" scales or spaces (like community) that are coded as feminine and stagnant (Massey 1994; Freeman 2001). These formulations of locality have an important bearing on how the ethnic community is conceived in relation to development, how development labor is divided, and who has authority over development decisions. In this way, I highlight the links and ruptures that mark the relationship among diverse locations and identities that are defined as local.

In each of the field sites discussed here, we see ethnic difference as a shifting, contentious field rather than a stable referent. Therefore, while I speak about indigenous communities and Latino professionals as both constituting "ethnic subjects," I do so to problematize the notion of ethnic difference rather than to use these two groups as emblematic of particular cultural or national communities. My analysis emphasizes the relational, structural, and strategic dimensions of identity so as to allow us to discern how ethnic difference is produced in relation to a dominant norm or unmarked category,[21] and how these norms vary according to context, the product of tense negotiation among diverse projects of subject-making. In this light, the ability to define who counts as ethnic, and why, becomes an important political question, reflecting a tense interplay between dominant social constructions and strategic self-identification on the part of ethnic subjects. I, therefore, trace how different types of actors (such as Latino professionals, male migrants, female microcredit agents, and indigenous peasants) were similarly made visible and mobilized in the field of development based on their common recognition as ethnic subjects in translocal spaces. From this angle, we can appreciate how ethnic identification, whether articulated by community members themselves (as in the case of CDRO) or by development institutions (like the United Nations) assumed both a translocal, moral commitment to coethnics and gendered forms of knowledge and practices that were compatible with neoliberal development norms.

In summary, through an examination of transnational migrants' changing role and value within regional development policy, this book focuses attention on the crosscutting spatial and social relations upon which both ethnic identity and development practice have increasingly been built. It also highlights the changing role of states, corporations, and multilateral institutions in producing local development strategies that can effectively serve national and regional development goals.

Mapping Place and Method

This book reflects a pointedly multisited ethnographic study of a new kind of translocal, entrepreneurial ethnic subject. This new subject takes diverse forms, reflecting contingent formulations of ethnic identity and entrepreneurism in different places, even as those forms pivot on similar reconceptualizations of how and why ethnic difference is valuable for development. For this reason, my methodology was crucial to the micropolitics analysis that I use throughout the book. Because my analysis does not assume ethnic identity to reside in certain actors or specific locations, it raises the question of how ethnic identity and entrepreneurism are articulated, debated, and mobilized as development strategy across diverse landscapes by different kinds of agents. Answering this question requires a methodology that is located in multiple communities, problematizes relations within those communities, and places in conversation dynamics that crosscut those communities, all with an eye toward interrogating the microphysics of power that these dynamics reflect and enact.

My research within Guatemala, while not located in a single community, was situated within a specific geographic and social space that is easily locatable on a map of Guatemala. The department, or province, of Totonicapán is located in the western highlands of Guatemala, with an estimated total population of about 314,831 residents, approximately 50,000 of whom live in the urban municipal center. The majority of the residents self-identify as Maya K'iche', reflecting their identification with a historical Maya civilization and an affiliation with the largest of Guatemala's twenty-three diverse linguistic communities.[22] Despite a well-documented commercial tradition, Totonicapán incorporates some of the most underdeveloped rural villages in the country. In many of its forty-eight "official" communities, just over half of the land is considered appropriate for cultivation, with approximately 40 percent of that land requiring terraced cultivation due to its steep inclines and uneven surfaces. Many of these residents are engaged in commercial production of textiles, woodworking and pottery, animal husbandry, agriculture, and other forms of petty commerce. By the 1990s, most communities also had significant numbers of men working abroad; the local estimates often calculated 25 percent of community males to be working in the United States.

In this way, my initial research in Guatemala was fairly conventional by anthropological standards, consisting of twenty-four months of fieldwork that included an institutional ethnography (of CDRO) and community studies of three different K'iche' communities in Totonicapán. Through interviews with institutional administrators and staff, program participants within different communities, nonaffiliated community members, state bureaucrats, and international development officials, I attempted to map how Maya culture was being mobilized as a tool for explicitly ethnic development strategies. However, as I began to investigate CDRO's newer collaborations with Walmart, additional methodological tactics were necessary. Promotional videos circulating on YouTube, corporate mission statements articulated on websites, and even a trip to my local Walmart store all became new sources of information about CDRO's latest ethnic development initiative. These new sites literally "brought home" the changing development landscape in which CDRO was operating.

The Digital Diaspora project represented a very different ethnographic terrain in that it had no single, locatable field site, but rather spanned national contexts. The digital nature of this transnational project, and also the highly dispersed, mobile professional subjects that participated in it, thus required very different research methods. With no physical headquarters, the project was constituted by a network of Latinos spread out across the United States, brought together in a series of encounters. As a virtual initiative, its only physical referents were the inaugural meeting that I attended and the offices of individual participants. Therefore, after the inaugural meeting, my research consisted of exchanging e-mails with project participants, conducting telephone interviews, monitoring the website, and collecting any publications written for or about the initiative. The virtual and especially tenuous nature of this kind of an ethnographic community was thus a methodological as well as analytical problem, forcing me to rethink the role of place, identity, and community within the project as a whole. The significance of these challenges was accentuated in 2004, when the diaspora seemed to disappear. Rather than receiving an announcement by the project's leadership, I instead began to notice a marked lack of activity and an absence of updates to the project website. I had received no new e-mail confirming the place and date of the tentatively scheduled future meetings. Furthermore, when I wrote to contacts at Digital Partners to get a revised report on the project's status, I found that the organization itself had been dissolved and that its directors had all relocated to other organizations. It thus took quite some investigative work to confirm that the project, and the field site it represented, had indeed ceased to exist. In many ways, this dilemma brought home the need for a translocal approach to the study of this subject.

Rather than erasing these methodological and analytical "problematics," the chapters that follow provide a means of reencountering the dilemmas they pose as productive processes of identity and place making. The chapters move back and forth across diverse landscapes and scales, denying a single spatial, geographic, or subject position in favor of highlighting how these differences frame the terms of the debate over what constitutes ethnic difference.

Overview of the Book

My analysis of development in Latin America unfolds as a chronological narrative to show how both grassroots and institutional formulations of ethnic identity have rearticulated with entrepreneurism in order to make distinct kinds of actors visible and valuable to neoliberal development programs. This longitudinal focus begins with ostensibly local formulations of ethnic entrepreneurism vis-à-vis the indigenous community in Latin America, moves to transnational configurations of ethnic entrepreneurism through migration, and returns full circle to the indigenous community, albeit now as a site of global commodity production and corporate identity. These three cases show successive yet simultaneous reformulations (in that one form did not necessarily replace the others) of what constitutes ethnic identity, who is seen to embody it, and how it deployed for development. As such, they illuminate how formulations of ethnic difference constitute not just changing cultural identifications, but also political and moral projects that are in conversation with the changing human, capital, and commodity flows that shape the region.

Each of these initiatives is examined as a series of encounters in which the meaning of ethnic identity and its relationship to development are actively debated by diverse actors. In these encounters, it is as much the process of negotiation that interests me as the product that emerges; I ask who the actors are, who has authority, and how that authority is embodied and expressed. Because this approach focuses on debates that illustrate contentious critiques among community members and because there is much at stake in the outcome of these debates, I have chosen to use pseudonyms for all of the Guatemalan communities and development actors I describe in the book, except where specifically noted. In this way, I seek to provide community members with a modicum of confidentiality.

I begin in Chapter Two by introducing the Cooperation for Rural Development of the West (CDRO) as an illustration of how grassroots and global development desires converged through the ethnodevelopment paradigm. Drawing on interviews with CDRO's founders and administrators, I demonstrate how the organization's strategic representations of Maya cultural difference sought to distinguish it from other Maya organizations in ways that resonated with neoliberal development priorities. To do so, I focus specifically on CDRO's use of the *pop,* or "woven mat," K'iche' ideology as a concrete tool for development. Far from representing a monolithic version of authentic Maya development practice, I show how CDRO's Maya development model has been critiqued by local community development practitioners who have perceived it as an extension of neoliberal privatization or the "branding" of culture. I explore how these critiques have attempted to reposition the relationship between capitalist entrepreneurial culture and authentic indigenous culture in order to accommodate complex, changing class relations within the Maya community.

While the ethnodevelopment paradigm tended to fetishize the local nature of indigenous communities, Chapter Three chronicles the development industry's increasing recognition of the transnational character of Latin American communities and subsequent efforts to "mainstream" migration for development. I examine how migrants come to be seen as intrinsically entrepreneurial subjects with the unique power to effect both local- and national-level development through individual and collective capital flows "back home." Drawing on materials produced by international organizations such as the United Nations, the Inter-American Development Bank, and the World Bank, I document how the essential qualities and connections ascribed to migrants shaped not only institutional and state goals for the kind of development migrants could do, but also the nature of development work to be undertaken by those left behind in "home" communities in Latin America. This chapter thus demonstrates how increasingly transnational development efforts relied on the entrepreneurialization of ethnic subjects in multiple places and in class- and gender-specific ways. Through an ethnographic portrait of one Guatemalan community, I show how this construction of the migrant-entrepreneur produced a gendered division of development labor that posited migrants as mobile, risk-taking masculine providers, and those they left behind as feminized, sedentary, passive receivers of development. Nonetheless, because of the dynamic nature of these articulations between ethnic identity and entrepreneurism, I chronicle how women's enterprising practices and knowledge of microcredit eventually resituated them at the forefront of community-based development methodology.

In Chapter Four, I trace how the development industry focus on working-class migrants and their transnational connections translated into efforts to harness the social and economic capital of an elite Latino diaspora in the United States. This chapter provides an ethnographic analysis of the Digital Diaspora for Latin America inaugural event in Washington, DC, as an especially poignant illustration of the way that ethnic difference, class, and gender come together in the space of neoliberal development. Through a study of the inaugural event, I examine the project's efforts to mobilize Latinos as transnational development agents based on their assumed ethnic particularity and connection to a Latin American homeland. I explore the intersection between global technology markets, states, class identity, and personal responsibility as these forces were brought together as foundational principles in the construction of a Latino digital diaspora.

Chapter Five examines post-CAFTA Guatemala to examine the incipient "community business model" being developed by CDRO in partnership with the multinational corporation, Walmart, as yet another articulation of ethnic entrepreneurism. Through the initiative, CDRO has encouraged rural community members to forego household corn production—a symbolic and material staple of ethnic identity—in light of the negative economic impact of regional free trade and the biofuel-food crisis on corn prices. Instead, it has encouraged them to become producers and shareholders in a venture that manufactures spa cosmetics to be sold globally by Walmart. The products' label actively elides the cosmetics' ethnic origins in favor of appealing to global consumers as a niche "natural spa" commodity. This project illustrates significant changes in the production methods and livelihoods of the rural communities, even as those changes have been implemented in order to preserve the ethnic community. As such, it demonstrates the growing importance of a corporate business model for reproducing the material base of the ethnic community—a model that, ironically, reflects a reciprocal search for ethical business practices that privilege community relations of mutual trust and accountability of the kind often attributed to the ethnic community.

Chapter Six reflects on how the dynamic articulations of ethnic identity and entrepreneurism analyzed thus far can be understood as rooted in debates over knowledge. Therefore, I explore the diverse, competing forms of knowledge, expertise, and authority that have been imputed to the ethnic entrepreneur. To this end, I revisit debates in the rural communities, both within CDRO's institutional practice and at the level of the Digital Diaspora project, in order to interrogate how the three initiatives embody and negotiate the meaning and value of different forms of knowledge in relation to formulations of ethnic identity. In particular, the chapter illustrates the complex role of rationalized, bureaucratic, and technological expertise in redefining ethnic identity. I tease out how these professionalized forms of knowledge often associated with Western, capitalist institutions have provided ethnic groups the kind of legitimacy they seek in the field of development; however, I also highlight the contentious role that they play in shifting forms of authority. Furthermore, I point to the role of local knowledge and "moral" community practices as central to redefining corporate and state practice.

In the final chapter, I return to reflect on the implications of these diverse, situated articulations of ethnic entrepreneurism. Through a reflection on the fate of these three initiatives, I examine what is at stake for the diverse array of ethnic subjects who have been recruited to the task of translocal, neoliberal development on the basis of their perceived cultural difference. I argue that an anthropology of development is crucial to unearthing the varied and uneven effects of these new subject and knowledge forms as they are located in multiple spaces. Finally, I suggest what the changing content and value of ethnic difference within development tells us about the predicaments posed by the changing regional market and the transnational flows that have come to define it.

As this overview suggests, this book provides a translocal, ethnographic analysis of the intersection between ethnic identity and development politics in Latin America. It thus offers a situated, multidimensional portrait of how distinct types of subjects in diverse locations have similarly been reimagined as development agents. In order to accomplish this task, I begin by asking: What is *ethnic* about ethnic development?

2 *Pop* or Fried Chicken?

Redefining Development and Ethnicity

IT WAS IN THE SUMMER OF 1996 that my fieldwork with the Cooperation for Rural Development of the West (Cooperación para el Desarrollo Rural de Occidente, or CDRO) took me to the organization's self-declared star community: San Pedro. Given that this trip occurred at a relatively early moment in my history of research on indigenous development projects in rural Totonicapán, I was not yet a regular visitor to San Pedro or the two other rural K'iche' communities in Totonicapán where I would come to work. Upon hearing that I had never visited San Pedro, Emilio, a CDRO program director, eagerly offered to take me to see the community hall that the organization had built there. We set off in one of CDRO's many four-wheel-drive Toyota pickups with the trademark CDRO logo—the K'iche' *pop* (woven mat) image—on the driver and passenger doors announcing our passage. Along the bumpy, two-mile drive over the mountainous landscape, Emilio lauded the many development achievements that this star community had achieved, noting that it was definitely the most advanced of all of the CDRO affiliates. Indeed, he cited the community hall that we were going to see as the best example of that progress.

"We're here," Emilio finally noted, as we pulled up to a black metal entrance gate on the right side of the road. A large, cement-block, two-storey yellow building stood behind the gate, set off by a dirt playground/parking area. I remember being impressed by the structure. From the outside, the building communicated a formal institutional persona rarely seen in the rural communities at that time. Once inside the building, however, that formality was shattered as I confronted a hall full of playing school children, whose shouts echoed off of the cement tile floors and upper balconies. After a moment of confusion, Emilio and I were greeted by an earnest-looking man in his mid-thirties who Emilio briefly introduced as Juan García, CDRO's local council president. Juan offered to take us on a tour of the building and eagerly escorted us up to the second storey, where he pointed out different rooms and offices for my benefit. Then he led us to the roof, where construction of a third storey was under way. Finally, Juan brought us back to the community council's designated meeting room, where he took a seat at the front desk, flanked by two quiet men who had also accompanied us on the tour.

Emilio politely introduced me to our hosts and explained, in Spanish, that I was a North American anthropologist studying CDRO's development program. Nodding enthusiastically throughout the introduction, Juan barely waited for his cue before addressing me. He thanked me for my visit and then launched into a description of the community hall's functions, mentioning that it hosted a primary school, a shoemaking apprentice program, a typewriting training program, and an office for the local political authorities. Judging by the glowing image that Juan presented, Emilio was not alone in considering the community hall to be CDRO's crowning development feat. Juan finished by mentioning the council's current plans and needs, most notably efforts to finance a prospective computer lab. Then he paused, leaned forward a bit, and asked, "Which international foundation did you say you represented?"

This impromptu meeting with the council members in San Pedro left no doubt in my mind why this site had become CDRO's showcase community. In addition to the monumental development feats it housed, its council members were clearly accustomed to unannounced visits from international passersby who sought a glimpse of the progress the organization had made. The 1996 signing of the Guatemalan Peace Accords, which had put an end to thirty-six years of armed conflict, unleashed a veritable flood of international development activity in the Guatemalan countryside, proliferating both the number of international aid organizations on the ground and the number of projects available for funding. Therefore, rather than an anomaly, my visit reflected an increasingly customary ritual of international visitation. These council members seemed to know all too well how important these visits were to securing new development funds. The fact that I was an anthropologist studying development initiatives, rather than a donor or aid organization representative, was a distinction of little importance to them.

Thus it was no small irony when, three years later, the same Juan García who had been our gracious tour guide sat with me in a private interview and disparagingly compared CDRO to a fast-food, fried-chicken restaurant chain whose sole interest was to expand its franchises, rather than to promote real development. He and other local critics claimed that CDRO's "ethnic" development strategies represented a savvy marketing strategy rather than an authentic Maya development method. Their critique challenged the validity of CDRO's ethnic development program and its difference from Western capitalist corporations. In particular, they implied that *pop*—a K'iche' concept meaning "woven mat" upon which CDRO's philosophy and methodology were built—was just another item on CDRO's fast-food menu. This derisive assessment provocatively raised the question of *who* CDRO represented—the indigenous community or a profit-driven corporation—and *what kind* of relationship between ethnicity and development the *pop* concept reflected.

In this chapter, I draw on the CDRO experience to explore the relationship between ethnic identity and development in Guatemala. I show how development served as an important arena for redefining ethnic identity both within the rural indigenous communities and in relationship to state and international organization development policies. I begin by examining how CDRO's self-proclaimed Maya method, based on the *pop* concept, came to be seen as a strategy compatible with the priorities of neoliberal development policy. I then analyze how the *pop* concept provided a contentious, yet productive space for competing community articulations of authentic indigenous identity and its relationship to a global capitalist culture defined by "Western" principles of entrepreneurialism and individual profit motive. Ultimately, these community debates over the meaning and authenticity of CDRO's *pop* method reflected efforts to come to terms with the contemporary privileging of ethnic cultural difference within a neoliberal development context marked by the state decentralization and privatization. They also illuminate how changing understandings of class difference and corporate capitalism were mobilized in an effort to claim ownership over community development. The ethnic entrepreneur thus emerges here as both a celebrated and a stigmatized subject, simultaneously symbolizing the value associated with ethnic difference within neoliberal development models as well as the challenges this model poses to community moral economy.[1]

*Pop*ularizing Local Development

As described in the last chapter, the global proliferation and intensification of neoliberal development policies throughout the 1990s made participative, community-based ethnic development initiatives attractive in new ways. Because of the efficient, integral, transparent methodology they were seen to support, these initiatives complemented state decentralization and privatization efforts to shift development responsibility to the lowest denominator. They marked a shift away from welfare-oriented development strategies that had positioned ethnic communities as recipients of aid, to initiatives that imagined these communities as participatory agents of self-development.[2]

In Latin America, indigenous communities in particular were privileged because of the way their community-based efforts were assumed to embody an essentially different and more holistic worldview whose conservationist, collectivist, and participatory values and practices might form an important source of social capital for development. The kind of difference that ethnic, or "local," communities came to represent within development during the 1990s was centrally defined by global human rights frameworks and their application to indigenous actors. The United Nations played a central role in this procedure vis-à-vis the International Labour Organization's Convention 169 (adopted in 1989), which set forth a global framework for indigenous peoples' rights. A United Nations working group also drafted the Declaration for the Rights of Indigenous Peoples during the Decade of the World's Indigenous Peoples (1995–2004). In 1982 the World Bank demonstrated its growing recognition of the importance of ethnic identity and rights in its Operational Manual Statement (OMS 2.34), emphasizing the need to evaluate the impact of development projects on "tribal groups." As a result of both logistical and political evaluations, this policy was eventually reconsidered and expanded to address global conversations about indigenous and human rights. Therefore, by the 1990s, the World Bank had revised not only its OMS, but also its general framework, such that "Much of the Bank's current work with indigenous peoples must be seen within this broader framework of the search for alternative strategies or models of development" (Davis 1993:14).[3]

The "ethnodevelopment" framework that emerged from this process redefined indigenous cultures as a resource for development and an important means of combating poverty and social disintegration, as well as for promoting biodiversity and conservation (Partridge and Uquillas, 1996, pars. 13, 14). The assumed close proximity between actors, the existence of a discrete "local knowledge" about resources, the homogeneity of identities, and the subsequent assumed sustainability associated with the local were considered important resources for community self-development. Consequently, rather than seeing ethnic community beliefs and practices as regressive obstacles to development, ethnodevelopment policies privileged indigenous communities as both essentially different from Western forms of social, cultural, and economic organization and also the source of knowledge that was "invaluable to the Western world" (Partridge and Uquillas, par. 16; see also Davis 2002; Kleymeyer 1994; Stavenhagen 1986; Van den berg 2003).

A quintessential example of ethnodevelopment, by the late 1990s CDRO had become one of the preeminent indigenous development organizations in Guatemala, working in over thirty-eight different indigenous communities in Totonicapán as well as seven additional municipalities, and managing an operating budget of over a million dollars (see Figures 2.1 and 2.2). Much of its success, however, derived from its unique grassroots origins. The CDRO initiative emerged in the early 1980s when indigenous community leaders from rural Totonicapán initiated a pilot project based on a methodology for "integral rural development." That venture was quickly advanced by a visit from World Vision representatives, who had come to rural Totonicapán looking to invest in an innovative, experimental community development program. In consultation with local indigenous activists and professionals, these parties went looking for the "ideal" community to support a new self-development initiative—this ideal

Figure 2.1 CDRO's main offices, Totonicapán. Source: Author, 2000.

Figure 2.2 A bird's-eye view of Totonicapán. Source: Author, 2006.

community turned out to be San Pedro. By 1984, the CDRO association was formally established in the rural Totonicapán communities with the participation of twenty-five members. These original founding members established an organizational system based on traditional Maya culture, which they envisioned as a vehicle for facilitating community self-development.

CDRO's efforts to promote a development project rooted in Maya culture explicitly sought to address indigenous development needs and interests in a way that other projects—including urban ladino insurgencies and authoritarian state development models—had not. In response to the Guatemalan state's violent repression of indigenous communities and its scorched-earth tactics of the early 1980s, CDRO publicly positioned itself as a neutral, nonpoliticized organ promoting proposals rather than protest in response to the urgent poverty of the communities.[4] Nonetheless, the founders' vision of ethnic development was necessarily shaped by the politicized context out of which CDRO emerged. Consequently, the organization's cultural projects pursued implicitly political ends, such as ethnic consciousness-raising and local autonomy. CDRO organizers drew upon Maya oral traditions, historical documents, and community customs to formulate the institution's unique vision of the Maya worldview and its relevance to the development process.

Central to this worldview was the notion of the *pop*—a K'iche' concept with dense cultural significance within the rural Totonicapán communities. According to CDRO, the woven mat referred most literally to the sacred place where K'iche' community elders would traditionally sit at ritual social gatherings. At a more symbolic level, the mat's round shape represented the cyclical, continuous notion of time and space that are held to guide K'iche' worldview. Finally, the mat's weave pointed to the interconnectedness and interdependency that characterize Maya collective traditions. Building on the *pop*'s many meanings, CDRO used the woven mat to represent the organization's development methodology, its institutional configuration, and its authentic Maya identity. In addition to using it as a concrete development strategy, CDRO graphically depicted the *pop* concept in a circular, weblike structure composed of multiple, color-coded, overlapping, and interwoven lines that serves as its organizational logo (see Figure 2.3). In this form, the *pop* icon became a ubiquitous image in the Western highlands during the 1990s, marking CDRO's numerous four-wheel drive vehicles as they traveled through the rural communities and also prominently displayed at the entrance to CDRO's administrative and training buildings.

As an organizational form, the *pop* concept reflected the numerous layers of community participation that constituted the organization. Looking at the *pop* diagram, the outermost circle represents the base communities that are connected to the community councils (depicted by the medium-size circle) and finally to specific programs such as health, infrastructure, handicrafts (represented by the inner ring of eight medium-size circles). All of the aforementioned entities participated as members of the general assembly, from which the board of directors (the center nucleus) is elected. In CDRO's graphic rendition of this structure, all of these spheres are coded vis-à-vis primary colors, both as a means of facilitating interpretation of the structure and also denoting symbolic cultural connections—such as between the human and natural worlds as well as between community members. The lines that form the weave are interpreted as diverse forms of relation and coordination that exist in the system (CDRO 1997:7).

CDRO used the woven mat trope not only to depict this unique organizational structure, but also as a representation of its development method. Specifically, CDRO mobilized the *pop* emblem to reference three main cultural tenets informing every project: total community participation, mutual support, and horizontality. In essence, these concepts referred to a development process that was to be universal, inclusive, democratic, and egalitarian, mobilizing the community as a collective protagonist of development through the promotion of

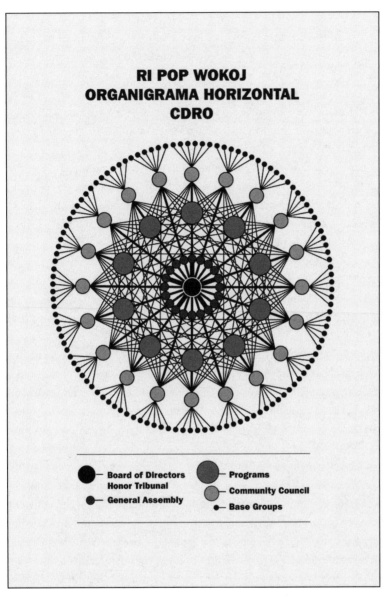

Figure 2.3 *Pop* is CDRO's indigenous philosophy, organizational structure, and institutional logo. Source: Association CDRO. Revised for publication with permission.

reciprocity and equilibrium. It should be noted that this egalitarian formulation was in contrast to other scholarly interpretations that identified the *pop* as a hierarchical symbol of kingship or elite privilege (Freidel, Kerr, and Everton 1995; Robicsek 1983; Schele, Miller, and Kerr 1986; Tedlock 1985). However, CDRO's reformulation was very much in line with revisionist articulations of culture and history promoted by Maya activists that sought to redefine the Maya peoples' relationship to Guatemalan society and history (see, for example, Warren 1998; Montejo 2005).

The *pop* organizational scheme reflects CDRO's three main principles vis-à-vis multiple levels of representation and authority, interconnected to form a complex system of checks and balances. Specific individual and group interests are balanced at the community council level, encouraging total participation and mutual support. Representatives from the community councils are elected to serve on CDRO's Board of Directors, thus maintaining "community" control over the development process, even at the municipal level; however, two-year service terms ensure that these representatives go right back to working at the community level, applying their experience for the greater good rather than toward individual social or economic advancement.

CDRO also incorporated the *pop* concept into one of its more provocative projects, a modern financial operation known as Banco Pop. This microcredit network was designed to operate in CDRO affiliate communities, providing needed capital to struggling household businesses. Rather than reflecting a conventional microcredit program, however, Banco Pop was uniquely designed to meet the K'iche' communities' specific needs. First, CDRO provided each community with a communal capital fund that was complementary with the indigenous tradition of communal instead of private property. Community members were able to access credit from this fund without requisite collateral by relying on the cultural concept of mutual support; consequently, the community became collectively responsible for the loan, with each member co-guaranteeing the debt.[5] The success of the system thus pivoted on cooperation and interdependency among all parties, fostering mutual support in all of its interactions. Equality was also promoted by progressively figured interest rates for the loans, such that community actors with a longer and more solid financial history would pay higher rates while poorer community members would pay less. If an individual or group defaulted, their integrity, honor, and prestige within the community would serve as a leverage point for coercing compliance. Additionally, each community managed and administered its own financial re-

sources; therefore, community members gained access not only to added capital, but also to important accounting and management skills. All business was
conducted in the communities and in K'iche' so as to accommodate the low
literacy rates within the rural population. Within the Banco Pop project, then,
the *pop* concept served as both the starting point and the end goal.

As these descriptions of its method suggest, CDRO's initiative represented
an innovative effort to convert indigenous traditions into development practice
and, thereby, to cultivate alternative forms of modernity for the rural K'iche'
communities. This was indeed how supporters of CDRO's method interpreted
its contribution. However, despite the organization's articulation of traditional
Maya culture as method and end point of its development efforts, CDRO's
goals were clearly not antithetical to global capitalist ideals; indeed, in many
ways it promoted them. For instance, by reinforcing collective over individual
risk/gain, Banco Pop allowed community members to place some conditions
on their participation in the market and to mitigate some of its negative consequences. Nonetheless, it simultaneously extended and deepened the role of
modern financial institutions within the rural landscape. Therefore, rather
than undermining or opposing Western capitalist practices, CDRO's ethnic development selectively appropriated and retrofitted them for community use.
This strategy was in line with CDRO's administrators' stated desire to follow
the example of Japan—a case that they felt reflected a successful effort to mod-
ernize through non-Western traditions, even as those traditions were oriented
toward integration into a global market economy. It was also a reflection of
Totonicapán's exceptional history of local ethnic entrepreneurism and petty
commodity production for regional markets, a point to which I will return.
Therefore, the *pop* symbol wove together more than simply the threads of Maya
cosmology and community development practice; as I will discuss in the next
section, it also reflected the convergence between neoliberal political economic
values and indigenous cultural difference. For this reason, CDRO can be seen
to embody the ambivalent, but potent combination of authentic difference and
entrepreneurial sensibility that defines the ethnic entrepreneur.

Community Development Convergences

The participative, community-driven development model embodied by the
multivalent *pop* symbol resonated easily with the market-oriented, decentralized development policies that characterized the global development industry
during the late 1990s (see also World Bank 1996). On the surface, therefore, the

concurrent reconceptualization of the indigenous community actors as development agents or "stakeholders" suited CDRO's grassroots project as much as it did the state agencies charged with devolving development tasks. This shift toward privileging local development strategies was especially pronounced in Guatemala, where military violence and human rights abuses against the populace during the 1980s promulgated a wide variety of direct, transnational connections among international humanitarian groups and grassroots communities within Guatemala.[6] As the civil conflict ended and a process of national reconstruction began, these translocal relationships between aid organizations and grassroots communities proliferated and intensified to the point that it became a running joke among people with whom I spoke that "everyone and his brother" was involved in some *proyecto* (project) or was running his own non-governmental organization.[7]

In this context, CDRO's bottom-up, social enterprise development efforts were held in special favor by foreign donors (especially from Scandinavia, Holland, and Canada) because of the compelling way that they spoke to both economic development and humanitarian priorities. Specifically, CDRO's initiative was community based and culturally appropriate, promoting participation, sustainability, transparency, and equality—principles touted by global development. It was also rationally organized, empirically evaluated (vis-à-vis budgetary audit procedures), locally managed, and complementary with market incorporation.

These convergences between CDRO's organizing principles and global development norms allowed the organization to become a poster child for indigenous development in Guatemala, spawning an interest in extending CDRO's model to other nonindigenous community organizations. Accordingly, in 1998, CDRO proposed a regionalization project that aspired to use the CDRO woven mat methodology as a template for self-development initiatives among nonindigenous community organizations across seven departments of Western Guatemala (CDRO 1998). Working in collaboration with a consortium of international foundations, non-governmental organizations, government bureaucrats, local research organizations, and other development groups, the venture sought to universalize CDRO's bottom-up, culturally specific development model. In this way, the unique principles of the *pop* concept would be put to work to fulfill one of the primary principles of development industry: that development projects be modular and reproducible.[8] Despite the eventual failure of the proposed regionalization project to proceed, CDRO's achievements in *pop*ularizing a regional ethnic development model were nonetheless highly productive in terms of increasing CDRO's visibility and legitimacy. Indeed, at a CDRO general assembly in July, 1998, Guatemala's then-Secretary of State, Gustavo Porras, went so far as to cite CDRO as "a pioneer" and "a model" in its efforts to forge new relations between civil society and the state.

CDRO's complementarity with state and international development goals was, of course, not entirely mutually beneficial. Because self-development strategies were directly correlated with transformations in global capitalism, many critics have noted that local governance and local development came into favor as global strategies at just the moment that state support for those processes was dissolving. Consequently, rather than marking new opportunities for enfranchisement or citizenship, the rise of "participation" as a central development priority effectively shifted the burden of development to the poor (Annis and Hakim 1988; Keating 2003; Paley 2001; Rahnema 1992; Reilly 1995). Furthermore, as we will see in the Digital Diaspora initiative (Chapter Four), this approach privileged the market, rather than state politics, as the primary arena for recognition and involvement. For these reasons, the ascendancy of community development and sustainability as industry buzzwords might be seen as an effort not so much to sustain natural resources as it was to sustain neoliberal conditions favorable to production for the market.

For CDRO however, neoliberal development norms that privileged the local community enabled an opportunity to increase indigenous political and cultural autonomy over local development decision making, even as they required the organization to independently seek the material means to support that effort. CDRO pursued its organization's autonomy through financial independence—working hard to diminish its dependency on external funding—as well as program expansion and sustainability. Due to the diligence and creativity with which it approached this problem, by 2006 only 40 percent of CDRO's budget was derived from external sources; the remainder came from program-generated income.[9]

Nonetheless, the need to woo support from both state and international development agencies indelibly shaped the organization's labors. As evidence of its awareness of the importance of public image and diplomacy, between 1996 and 2000, CDRO promoted "inter-institutional relations" as a primary focus of its community development programs. Through this training, CDRO hoped to augment the ability of its affiliate communities to effectively promote themselves and campaign for resources in an increasingly competitive development market. In this market, one's visibility and legitimacy as a development agent rested not only on one's methodology or efficacy—such as the ability to produce local, efficient, enterprising, market-oriented practices—but also on a group's identity. Therefore, both CDRO and its community affiliates' successful self-promotion in the national and international development arena also pivoted on their representations of indigenous authenticity, now seen as an important vehicle for the above-mentioned development values.

Development through Difference

The *pop* method proved attractive to the international development industry not only because of the way it embodied community-based, participatory, local development principles that aligned with neoliberal values of decentralization, and market-based modernization, but also because of its explicitly ethnic roots. Indeed, during the late 1990s CDRO's *pop* became a veritable global commodity. At the 1996 Inter-American Conference of Mayors in Miami, Charles Reilly, a former Peace Corps director and Inter-American Development Bank representative used his closing speech to single out CDRO and the *pop* concept as the most promising example of local governance:

> Of course, highland Guatemala is not Asuncion, Buenos Aires, Kingston, New York, Quebec, Rio de Janeiro, Santiago de Chile, or even Guatemala City. But the mayors of those cities and thousands of other towns and everyone in the development business might learn something from the *Pop*. . . . Because universal policies are seldom universal, they are supplemented by "targeted" policies. CDRO, with its woven mat, is far ahead of us. Inspired by the ancient Mayan document *Pop Wuj*,[10] it insists that advancement requires that "no group be left behind." This highland organization weaves together interdependent villages, towns, and representatives in an extraordinary social, economic, and political tapestry rooted in Mayan culture. That single sphere, woven from the many threads of polity, economy, and society to form a pattern of local development, was for me the compelling message from Miami. (Reilly 1997:7)

As Reilly's quote reveals, the appeal of the *pop* symbol obtained from its ancient origins and the holistic, egalitarian, participative alternative they represented. In other words, it was exactly the *pop* model's ethnic particularity that made it a strategy from which "everyone in the development industry might learn."

Reilly's praise is reflective of how state and global development paradigms of the 1990s had come to value indigenous knowledge and community development strategies as part of the rubric of "ethnodevelopment." Given this global focus on indigenous culture and knowledge, there was much at stake—in terms of both recognition and resources—in establishing one's authentic ethnic difference. In this context, CDRO's *pop* logo not only identified the organization as an effective, participative *community* initiative, but also affirmed CDRO's cultural authority as a legitimate *Maya* organization. Using the *pop* concept, CDRO sought to communicate the central role that indigenous knowledge played in defining CDRO's development method and goals.

An example of the particular representational strategies CDRO utilized to project its ethnic authenticity can be found in the organization's 1995 promotional brochure, *Saq Tzij* (The Truth). This document was one of several that prominently displayed the *pop* logo and explicitly defined the organizational framework and cultural principles that it represented. The legend that accompanied the *pop* organigram explains the color coding of the diagram in the following way:

> The color green reflects hope and nature for the Maya people. Yellow symbolises corn, its principle nutrient. Blue reminds us of the immensity of the sky and the oceans. Red means life and carries with it the memory of the martyrdom and the suffering of the people through history. White symbolises purity and peace. (CDRO 1995:6)

In this explanation, CDRO showed the colors and shapes of its logo to be coded with cultural meanings that are part of a rich, local K'iche' worldview and history. Not simply a catchy institutional logo to mark company cars, the woven mat is depicted as an authentic Maya symbol, denoting an essential relationship to nature and a history of discrimination. By embodying Maya cosmology and culture in this very literal way, CDRO thus sought to use the *pop* symbol to validate the organization's organic ethnic identity.

However, CDRO's efforts to substantiate its Maya roots were not limited to associating itself with the *pop* concept and attributing to it an essential cultural logic; the organization also asserted its legitimacy by contrasting itself to the perceived antithesis of indigeneity—namely, the West. CDRO's general advisor, Benjamín Son Turnil (not a pseudonym), provided an eloquent example of this type of self-representation in a story he related to me about a visit to a neighboring Maya organization during the mid-1990s.

> One day I went to visit a non-governmental organization in Chimaltenango. The name of the organization was written in Kaqchikel, and upon entering the

office, I saw a desk covered with *típica* (indigenous) fabric, there were expressions from the *Popol Wuj* . . . everything appeared to be indigenous. But when I spoke with the director, I encountered an administration that was eminently Western, capitalist. So the external was indigenous, but the internal was not. What that approach communicates is that the only valuable thing we have is something that can be photocopied. This isn't right because in the rural communities I've found many ideas about how to manage emergency situations, how to mutually support one another, how to attend to problems of public welfare, how to help each other with production, how to administer resources. . . . We are throwing away the most substantial part of our culture, and we're orienting ourselves toward the past without trying to confront the present.

Son Turnil's story reflects how grassroots indigenous organizations struggled to define the terms of Mayaness in a context characterized by multiple and often competing formulations of Maya culture—a point well documented by anthropologists studying Maya mobilization (Bastos and Camus 1993; Fischer and Brown 1996; Nelson 1999; Warren 1998).[11] Son Turnil established his own authenticity by making an essential distinction between Mayan and Western institutions and ways of knowing. Indeed, in that example, he critiqued the Mayan artifacts he encountered as cultural commodities and evidence of Western capitalism rather than as proof of an authentic indigenous identity. For Son Turnil, an essential indigenous subjectivity was evidenced by persuasive interpretations and appropriate application of traditional Maya knowledge rather than simple display of cultural artifacts. This authentic disposition was a product of one's embeddedness in Maya community life, where K'iche' language, calendrics, and *traje* (traditional clothing) operated as lived practice, rather than cultural relic. He endorsed CDRO's version of Maya culture by forefronting the alternative forms of social welfare, production, and administration of resources they offered for the Maya communities. In his words, the value of these forms of cultural difference derived as much from their essential ethnic origins as they did from their practical efficacy and applicability as development practice.

There was nothing especially novel about CDRO's efforts to position Maya culture in opposition to Western traditions; indeed, the notion of ethnic difference hinges on that very distinction (Chatterjee 1993; Brass 1991). Furthermore, a long history of Maya community studies has illustrated indigenous efforts to distinguish Maya cultural essence from "foreign" and/or colonial Guatemalan national culture.[12] CDRO differentiated between the two cultural spaces by juxtaposing a unique Maya moral economy defined by collective property and mutual support against the private property and individual accumulation of Western society (see also Montejo 2004). However, CDRO's mobilization of this dichotomy is unique in the way that it highlighted the legitimacy and efficacy of specifically Maya approaches to development and modernity within the neoliberal context. In other words, CDRO framed Maya culture as a different and more useful means of achieving development within the rural communities. Development institutions like the World Bank attributed value to this integral approach and, to the extent that they saw it as an intrinsic property of indigenous culture, privileged indigenous development methods (Partridge and Uquillas 1996; Martinez and Bannon 1997). Indeed, it was exactly this holistic development approach that Charles Reilly praised in his glowing assessment of the CDRO project.

Therefore, while CDRO's program used the *pop* ideology to mark its ethnic authenticity and distance from Western capitalism, its goal was to promote modernity and development that would be complementary to it. As Appadurai notes, notions of culture and development have often been juxtaposed to one another such that culture represents a kind of "pastness"—custom or tradition—while development is seen in terms of the future—plans, hopes, goals. "Thus, from the start, culture is opposed to development as tradition is opposed to newness and habit to calculation" (2004:60). Challenging this configuration, Son Turnil's appraisal of the most significant aspect of Maya culture portrayed it not as some remnant of the past, but rather as a powerful tool for the future. His critique of the neighboring Kaqchikel organization challenged that organization's reliance on Maya cultural relics as a way to mask Western ways of doing development. By contrast, CDRO's forward-looking *pop* method strategically wed local culture and modern, scientific technologies within all of its initiatives (CDRO 1995, 1997).

It was the particular combination of ethnic difference and its systematization into a coherent development program that allowed Son Turnil to represent this vision as an authentic and authoritative source of ethnic difference endorsed by both state and global development institutions. From this angle, Son Turnil's critique was not just a claim on the modern, but an attempt to redefine indigeneity through the accepted terms of localization and efficiency that characterized neoliberal forms of governance. Furthermore, because of the primacy of the indigenous community within those practices of governance, there was much more at stake, both within the Mayan community and beyond, in authoritative assertions of authentic indigenous knowledge.

The organization's ethnic particularity thus explains CDRO's international success rather than detracts from it, as it was exactly this ethnic difference that made the ethnic entrepreneur visible and productive in relation to a variety of other development agents (like the state). Therefore, when CDRO embarked on plans to build a regional training center in 1999, the center's blueprints were admired by Spain's Queen Sofia, who visited CDRO during her trip through Guatemala. When CDRO's training center was completed a year later, its inaugural event was attended by the Spanish ambassador to Guatemala and representatives from the United Nations, the Inter-American Foundation, and the Soros Foundation. The Guatemalan government also validated the CDRO method, awarding the organization its National Order of the Guatemalan Cultural Patrimony award in 2000. The *pop* method's notoriety in these instances reflected both national and international interest in alternatives to conventional, state-centered development methods.

However, the same qualities that made CDRO attractive to global development agencies produced problems for CDRO's local cultural authority. As I discuss below, CDRO and its council members in San Pedro (the site of my initial introduction to CDRO's "success") eventually came into conflict over whether the *pop* concept—per CDRO's formulation—could be considered a legitimate example of Maya culture. In these debates, community members presented a clear picture of how neoliberal state policies infused local understandings of the development process. Specifically, these community affiliates questioned the perceived links between the replicable development model proposed by CDRO and neoliberal economic practices such as corporate franchise expansion, foreign investment, and privatization that they feared aspired to usurp communal resources and erase community agency. For its detractors, CDRO's *pop* method thus became a vehicle for critiquing both class inequality and neoliberal reforms within the space of the ethnic community.

Fried Chicken or *Pop*?

In the Totonicapán community where the *pop* method had perhaps proven most successful, it also served as a point of contention among local organizers. In many ways, it was the *pop*'s fame as an innovative community development model that was responsible for creating these tensions between CDRO and a few of its community affiliates in San Pedro. San Pedro council members challenged the authenticity of CDRO's ethnic development program, calling it more of a global marketing strategy than a reflection of legitimate community ideals. Their critiques demonstrated the powerful role that the space of neoliberal development had come to play in mediating community politics and class positions in rural Guatemala.

I got a glimpse of these tensions firsthand when I went to interview Juan García at his home in San Pedro on a rainy June day in 1999. By this time, Juan had retired from the community council president post that he had occupied when he led me and Emilio on a tour of San Pedro's community hall several years prior. Now, although he remained active in the community council, he had changed his tune about CDRO considerably. We sat in a storeroom located just off the main production room of his large house. While we talked, I watched his four employees stretch printed cotton-polyester fabric over long worktables, preparing to make the polo shirts that Juan—a successful merchant—sold in markets throughout central and eastern Guatemala. Juan shifted back and forth on his makeshift chair (a bundle of freshly sewn and packaged shirts) while he talked about the council's work, but when I asked Juan about his relationship with CDRO, he became visibly agitated:

> CDRO is like Pollo Campero [the Guatemalan equivalent of Kentucky Fried Chicken]. CDRO found a good business and went out looking how to expand without thinking about the problems it might cause. CDRO comes to the communities and constructs an organizational framework but doesn't resolve the problems of the communities, and thus leaves them in an awkward state of confusion. Our village succeeded because it took the opportunity and knew how to get ahead, but even so it lacked the resources to do everything it wanted.

This provocative analogy between CDRO and Pollo Campero immediately struck me. After all, Juan—a quintessential ethnic entrepreneur in his own right—was accusing CDRO of having a capitalist mentality that equated development with "good business." He was accusing CDRO of seeing its affiliates as nothing more than franchisees. These were strong charges given Totonicapeños' history of ethnic and class solidarity (Smith 1984, 1990a). In this context, Juan's critique essentially impugned CDRO for failing to abide by the terms of traditional ethnic solidarity. This critique was made even more paradoxical because of the way that it misconstrued CDRO's method and goals. Indeed, CDRO's entire program was oriented toward promoting community *self*-development and the revival of local Maya culture, rather than imposing development from above. More ironically still, CDRO had represented Juan's community as its star example.

When I asked another San Pedro council member—who, notably, was also a successful merchant—about how CDRO was using Maya culture, he corroborated Juan's critique, responding, "Oh, that's just how CDRO paints the organizations for the gringos."

These local assessments of the *pop* method should look suspiciously familiar. After all, by talking about the "community" versus the "Western capitalist," Juan and his colleague were repeating the distinction that CDRO itself had used to validate its own vision of authentic Maya culture; however, in the council members' critique, *CDRO* itself was the organization charged with being nothing more than an "eminently Western capitalist" institution.

In thinking about the meaning of these labels—community versus capitalist—it is important to situate them in relation to Smith's study (1984, 1988, 1990a) of Totonicapán's long history of petty capitalist production for regional markets and the central role that commerce has played in Totonicapeño ethnic identity since the nineteenth century. Community and capitalism had certainly not been mutually exclusive in recent history. What is more, many of the community council members like Juan García were part of a fairly wealthy local merchant class who sold products to larger urban and national markets. Consequently, their use of the capitalist critique must be seen in strategic terms.

On the one hand, the council members' critique of CDRO sought to reduce the *pop* method to nothing more than a marketing strategy so that council members could then highlight their own individual contributions to San Pedro's development. In their eyes, it was not the franchisor, but rather the local franchisee that actually made things happen. Given the way local communities had been repositioned as protagonists of self-development by both global participatory development paradigms and CDRO's specific indigenous development platform, it was only right that council members should take credit for the remarkable development progress made, starting with the impressive community hall that I had first toured with Juan many years prior. In this way, council members attributed to themselves the enterprising subjectivity that was implied by their redefinition as "stakeholders" within neoliberal development policies.

On the other hand, these council member critiques of CDRO's capitalist mentality went beyond just writing off CDRO as the responsible party for development; they also hoped to distinguish local council members as more moral and authentically indigenous development actors. In this sense, the council members were reproducing the difference between local ethnic and global capitalist moral economies that both CDRO and admiring development officials had made before them. In this case, council members like Juan did so by eliding their own class privilege in order to accentuate CDRO's professional class status and the exploitative capitalist logic that it was presumed to reflect. He and the other council members downplayed their own entrepreneurial identities in order to stress the overriding "fact" of their ethnic authenticity in relation to CDRO.

According to council members, CDRO employees' semiprofessional status, international travel experience, and fixed salary distinguished them as a local professional class relative to their community counterparts. This class difference was exacerbated by rumors that "CDRO employees' salaries come in dollars." The idea of dollared salaries and the sight of CDRO administrators driving brand-new, four-wheel-drive vehicles emblazoned with the *pop* logo contributed to community perceptions of CDRO as a different kind of capitalist than the historically peasant tradition from which the organization emerged. I use *peasant* here not to reference a particular relation to production or objective class, but rather as Collier (1994) and Kearney (1996) have done, to denote a particular form of rural social and political identity. In the case of Totonicapán, this identity was directly linked to a particular ethnic content, such that community members defined themselves in terms of a single "Indian" class that was distinguishable both from ladinos and from members of other indigenous communities (Smith 1990a:215; see also Smith 1988). Therefore, council members' efforts to stigmatize CDRO employees as members of an elite economic and social class had the effect of immediately distancing them from community ethnic identity. In their eyes, the *pop* "brand name" on the car doors not only lacked symbolic meaning, it also marked vehicle occupants as corporate managers rather than community members.

By singling out CDRO as an encroaching capitalist entrepreneur, council members also deflected critiques that they themselves constituted an exploitative capitalist elite. As successful merchants and powerful members of the local community council, Juan and his counterparts had come to control significant resources within the community, not least of which was the impressive community hall building and the development programs it housed. This put them at odds with elected local authorities—members of the civil-religious hierarchy—who had political and moral authority, but few material resources at their disposal (see Chapter Six). Ironically, members of the local political structure challenged the council's authority over development resources by charging that Juan and his crew were essentially trying to privatize communal goods. The fact that the council had undergone a process of legal incorporation without first notifying community members of its plans had heightened fears that the council itself wanted to be a corporation in the capitalist sense of the word.

In the context of state privatization of industry and services throughout Guatemala, the threatened privatization of public goods was unfortunately a threat all too real for community members. Indeed, many Totonicapeños complained that privatization of basic services such as electricity had brought price gouging and irregularity rather than the improved efficiency and lower prices promised by competition. Therefore, as the council began to look more and more like a corporation itself, community members feared the imminent sale of their community property to the highest bidder. In an effort to neutralize these fears, council members like Juan aimed to redraw the community's boundaries, repositioning themselves firmly within the community moral tradition and identifying CDRO as the predatory capitalist. In doing so, they attempted to reinstitute themselves as more authentic ethnic actors and averted critiques that *they* were the entrepreneurs working on behalf of global capital.

It was, nonetheless, no surprise to San Pedro community members that by 2006 Juan and his fellow council members had come to embody the same kind of dubious capitalist that they had accused CDRO of being. Instead of continuing to affiliate with CDRO, these merchants formed their own development organization that increasingly prioritized the financial security of its members rather than of the community at large. For a time, the council continued to meet in the San Pedro community hall, inviting CDRO officials and community members to an annual assembly where they would document and assess their development efforts. The tipping point occurred when these council members decided not to hold their annual assembly in the community hall that I had visited, but rather at a retreat organized exclusively for the council directors in a resort off the shores of touristy Lake Atitlán. This change of venue quite literally communicated the council members' distance from the indigenous community. After that point, the group rented a private office in the municipal town center and conducted their activities as a private corporation—not as a representative of the organized community. Ironically, their urban outpost was situated directly over a block of the town square occupied by a row of independent, mobile fried-chicken vendors.

Grounding Ethnic Difference

This chapter has explored the concrete implications of the ethnodevelopment paradigm in terms of its effects on grassroots development initiatives in Guatemala. In that context, I have argued that development served as an especially productive and controversial arena for the articulation of authentic ethnic identity. Because of the value attached to indigenous difference as a powerful tool for local community development, I have shown how both CDRO and its council members in San Pedro sought to position themselves as legitimate community development agents vis-à-vis competing formulations of authentic Maya culture. CDRO's *pop* concept became the focus of this contest, simultaneously projected as the essence of Maya cosmology and collectivism on the one hand and critiqued as a manifestation of neoliberal corporate expansion and privatization on the other. In other words, based on one's social positioning, the *pop* emblem was seen either as an organic embodiment of Maya culture or as a fried-chicken franchise logo, marketed for gringo consumers. I have argued that it was the particular convergence between neoliberal development norms and the way indigenous culture was repositioned as a vehicle for it that made these multiple interpretations of the *pop* idea viable and meaningful, both within and beyond the K'iche' community in which they were situated.

As the dichotomous readings of the *pop* model make clear, corporate encroachment on community development resources shaped the contours of this debate over the relationship between ethnicity and development. In the encounters I have described, residents attributed "capitalist" mentalities to those members of the community who seemed to have the economic power and connections that would allow them to usurp and privatize communal goods and property. Therefore, while Totonicapeño identity and economic practices had long been defined by production for the market, "capitalist" operated here as a code for the individual profit motive imputed to those groups or institutions whose communal affiliation and morality were in question. Rather than signaling a mutually exclusive relationship between indigenous development and capitalist market integration, critiques of community capitalists thus highlighted the strategic and contingent way class identity figured in these articulations of indigenous authenticity. While class identity in Totonicapán had historically been conflated with ethnic identity (Smith 1984, 1988, 1990a), the mobilization of class difference in debates between CDRO and the council members—in terms of salaried professionals versus independent merchants, for example—shows how community development operated as an important arena for critiquing growing inequality within the indigenous community.

These changing class differences were significant not only for the perceived threat they presented to ethnic solidarity, but also because of the heightened stakes introduced by community-based development models. After all, as many recent studies of indigenous politics in Latin America have indicated, culture-based development policies have introduced new conditions for ethnic community recognition and agency, such that not all formulations of indigeneity are considered equal.[13] Consequently, the ability to occupy the moral high ground associated with authentic indigenous authority translated into the ability to procure development resources and status beyond the community—a fact evidenced by CDRO's notoriety within international circles. To the extent that it was unclear whether a group or institution reflected a Maya initiative or an "eminently Western capitalist" logic, this context gave new and dubious meaning to the notion of the *corporate* community, highlighting slippages in the legal, social, and economic connotations associated with the term.[14] Therefore, in order to claim legitimacy within the community, both CDRO and the council attempted to distinguish their respective authenticity by virtue of "internal" qualities, rather than "external" cultural trappings or economic class markers. CDRO used the *pop* symbol to graphically depict its horizontal organizational structure, its holistic approach, and its culturally specific development goals— qualities that might not be self-evident in light of its savvy institutional politics and market-oriented financial enterprises. For council members, however, CDRO's *pop* logo and method reflected unconvincing representations of Maya culture, masking a strategic marketing campaign and salaried professionals under the surface.

By highlighting the situated and strategic nature of these representations of indigeneity, I do not seek to reduce indigenous identification to a purely constructed or instrumentalist phenomenon.[15] As I discuss further in Chapter Six, in the context of neoliberal development models, authoritative representations of indigenous identity were subject not only to global development validation, but also to local community ratification. Therefore, CDRO's early success was as contingent upon its ability to design community programs that built on and resonated with the everyday lived practices of Maya culture within its constituent communities as it was upon its compatibility with neoliberal development norms. Neoliberal policies, and the ensuing fears of the privatization of community resources that they provoked, shaped the daily idiom of authenticity and provided a frame for understanding the nature and stakes of class inequalities within the community. This market framework set the terms for how to distinguish moral, legitimate community members from encroaching capitalists. Consequently, the *pop* method's ability to draw international celebrity status as an authentic grassroots development solution, while simultaneously being analogous to a fast-food restaurant chain looking for franchise expansion, highlights the complex way that neoliberal development trends relocated and resignified ethnic and class difference within the rural indigenous landscape.

3 Remapping and Remitting Development

VICENTE FOX'S 2006 VISIT to Mexican migrant organizations in the United States was indicative of the important place that migrants had come to occupy in the Mexican economy and national politics. By that time, migrants had become Mexico's largest and most profitable export, with their remittances totaling more than either international development assistance or foreign direct investment (see IADB 2003; López-Córdova and Olmedo 2005). Consequently, Mexico had much at stake in the continued ability of its citizens to remain in the United States and to provide a steady flow of money to Mexico.[1] Not restricted to Mexico alone, in 2007 Latin American emigrants collectively produced remittances of an estimated $59.9 billion (Ratha, et al. 2008). Thus, for President Fox and many of his Latin American counterparts, transnational migrants were recognized as potent economic agents who could effectively produce national and regional development from the ground up. Indeed, it was the combination of migrants' absence from their nation of origin, their continued connection to coethnic kin "at home," and their unique risk-taking, calculative traits that made them idealized ethnic entrepreneurs.

> Migration is an ideal means of promoting co-development, that is, the co-
> ordinated or concerted improvement of economic and social conditions at
> both origin and destination based on the complementarity between the two.
> Migration plays a positive role by providing the workers to satisfy the labor
> demand in advanced economies and in the dynamic developing economies
> while at the same time reducing unemployment and underemployment in
> countries of origin and, in the process, generating remittances, savings and

know-how for the benefit of the latter. (United Nations General Assembly 2005:22)

As the passage above suggests, at the turn of the millennium governments and international organizations expressed an increasing appreciation for the potential economic benefits of transnational migration and cultivated efforts to harness migrants' productive potential for development. Since 2000, institutions such as the Inter-American Development Bank, the World Bank, and the United Nations—the largest and most important development institutions in Latin America—have commissioned numerous studies, organized conferences, and financed projects to measure and eventually "leverage" remittances for development.[2] The United Nations' "High-Level Dialogue on International Migration and Development" in 2006 brought together representatives from over one hundred countries to debate different dimensions of migration policy and their relationship to the UN's Millennium Development Goals. This dialogue culminated in calls to "mainstream migration" into development policy (Khalifa 2006) and spawned a consultative body, the Global Forum on Migration and Development, to continue work on these issues. The High-Level Dialogue and associated initiatives evidenced how development agencies and states alike had come to see migration as a central feature of global development policy and national economic development.

Recent statistics demonstrate why migration has become so important to development. By 2005, international migrants numbered 191 million, with the United States hosting one in every five migrants (United Nations 2005:12). Of those foreign-born U.S. residents, 47.2 percent were of Hispanic/Latino origin (U.S. Census 2006). Mexican migrants composed a third of this number, constituting the largest source of migrants to the United States. Among the other Latin American countries (representing about one-fifth of total migration numbers to the United States), Central American countries such as El Salvador and Guatemala have been the most prominent contributors. As migration emerged as an important development issue globally, these migration patterns from Latin America and the significant capital flows they produced thus made Latinos important for development in the region in new ways.

To better understand these cross-border development dynamics, this chapter explores the relationship between transnational migration and development in Latin America during the late 1990s and early 2000s. In the previous chapter I described how global development practice had privileged participatory, community-based initiatives such as CDRO's; however, by the mid-1990s, both states and international organizations alike had come to realize the impact of migration not just locally on communities like San Pedro, but also on national economies more generally. This chapter thus focuses on how transnational migrants, alongside their indigenous counterparts, came to be seen by states and multilateral development institutions as potent development agents who could be personally entrusted with developing communities throughout Latin America.

In what follows, I explore three dimensions of the migration-development nexus. First, I examine the new development work that migrants were recruited to do. Second, I argue that this work relied on the entrepreneurialization of both migrant subjects and also community members left behind. Third, by looking at both sides of the migration process, I show how this entrepreneurialization reflected gender- and class-specific processes. Throughout the chapter, I present an ethnographic study of one rural Maya community in Guatemala, Santa Cecilia, as suggestive of how these processes have unfolded on the ground. This case presents the experience of migrants from rural Guatemalan communities who go to Houston, often as undocumented, unskilled labor, to work as agricultural laborers, dishwashers, gardeners, and the like. In the next chapter, I turn attention to another class of migrant—the professional Latino working in the information technology and communication industries. The juxtaposition of these two types of ethnic entrepreneur highlights similarities in what these distinct migrant populations were presumed to offer for development, as well as the gender and class assumptions on which migrants' subjectivity were based.

Sending Development Home

The migratory flows between Latin America and the United States are long-standing; however, contemporary flows have been distinguished in several ways. Large-scale movement of both legal and unauthorized migrants into the United States from Latin America essentially began in the 1970s in response to violent dictatorships in South America and in the 1980s as a result of violent civil conflicts in Nicaragua, El Salvador, and Guatemala. According to many observers, these violent circumstances meant that migrants of this period moved north without plans of taking up permanent residence in the United States. The continued and even mounting arrival of Latin American migrants during the latter half of the 1990s, therefore, seemed to imply different migratory dynamics. After all, by this time peace agreements had been signed in both El Salvador and Guatemala, Nicaragua had achieved a democratic transfer of power, and Mexico had begun to pursue a diplomatic (rather than simply military) solution to the Zapatista uprising in Chiapas. It was, instead, heightened economic instability, underemployment, rising costs, and decreasing state support for basic services and industries—changes that many attributed to neoliberal state reforms across Latin America and the implementation of regional free trade agreements such as NAFTA—that were identified as producing increasing migrant flows northward during this period. Noting the brutal effects of these reforms on unemployment rates, labor relations, and social security throughout Latin America during the late 1980s, Catherine Elton (2006:1) has argued that "the very entities now celebrating migrant remittances as a remedy for underdevelopment prescribed and promoted policies that created the conditions for increased emigration" from Latin America in the first place. The search for new economic opportunities abroad happened alongside a deepening of social ties to the United States by already-established migrants who, in many cases, never did return home and had expanded social networks that facilitated new migration (Coutin 2007; Hamilton and Stoltz-Chinchilla 2001; Smith 2006).

While these economic and social explanations might seem to distinguish earlier flows as political (and, thereby, forced) and later flows as economically driven (and, thereby, voluntary), it is important to note the complex structural forces at work in producing migration. Despite the end of civil war in Central America and the transition to democratic regimes throughout much of Latin America, residents of the region continued to experience intense economic and physical insecurity that have manifested in increasing poverty and brutal violence, associated in part with growing illicit economies. In places like Colombia, armed conflict between rebel and government forces has remained intractable, flamed in part by failed U.S. drug policy in the region. Therefore, "the structural roots of civil conflicts and of emigration are still in place" (Menjívar 2006:228), and rather than an end to civil conflict, many Latin American countries have experienced an intensification of structural violence over the last decade, albeit in more diffuse forms than past state violence (Caldeira 2000; Goldstein 2004; Holston 2008; Offit 2008; Payne 2000). Migrants' departure must be understood as intimately related to this structural violence.

On the ground, one does not have to look far to appreciate both the poverty fueling migration and the impact transnational migration has produced. When I began work in Santa Cecilia—a small, rural K'iche' community of about 3,500 residents located on the western boundary of Totonicapán—in 1998, the community was considered poor and underdeveloped by all accounts. The average monthly income of most community residents was approximately US$70—an amount insufficient to provide for the average seven-person household. The vast majority of residents remaining in the community engaged in small-scale agriculture and animal husbandry to supplement the production of textiles for local highlands markets.[3] Santa Cecilia had a painfully low literacy rate (30 per cent) and no local facilities for postprimary education. The community had no community hall—a common staple in the center of most rural communities—no health clinic, and no local office to house its local authorities. Furthermore, it had not associated itself with any local development initiatives, such as CDRO's, to advance its development status.

While Santa Cecilia lacked these traditional signs of material wealth, it was simultaneously marked by the proliferation of new structures on the landscape. Santa Cecilia and other rural communities like it throughout Latin America were increasingly characterized by the steady outflow of community men who sought temporary employment in the United States, often as undocumented labor, while women stayed in the village.[4] As a testament to men's labors abroad, Santa Cecilia was marked by a growing number of brand-new, two-story cement-block houses that lined both sides of the dirt road running through the middle of the hamlet. These towering structures bore little resemblance to the modest adobe houses marred by peeling paint and a few tiny win-

Figure 3.1 Transnational monuments to upward mobility, Totonicapán.
Source: Author.

dows that covered most of the rural landscape. They were instead burgeoning edifices, adorned by ornate stucco bordering and detailed wrought-iron work around the doors and large windows. Columns of rebar jutting up from the roof proudly declared ambitious plans for future construction by distant family members, implying a literal upward mobility driven by "new money" sent home by men laboring abroad.

As Figure 3.1 suggests, remittances represent the most concrete manifestation of migrants' potential power to enact development. Indeed, given that 2008 migrant remittances to Latin America and the Caribbean were estimated to total $69.2 billion, these transnational flows now amount to the largest source of income for the top recipient nations,[5] surpassing foreign aid and foreign investment (IADB 2008,2009; López-Córdova and Olmedo 2005:2). At the macro level, these remittances have been touted as an important means of shoring up a nation's credit worthiness, providing foreign currency to prevent balance of payment crises and thus serving as an essential form of insurance in the face of economic downturns or natural disasters (Kapur 2004:7; López-Córdova and Olmedo 2005). At the micro level, remittances have been credited with alleviating household poverty, financing new infrastructure construction, supplying crucial social services, and providing an important source of private capital for local enterprise.

Recognition of the development possibilities enabled by these private capital flows has led some development experts to suggest that remittances have become the "new development mantra." As Devesh Kapur (2004:7) notes in his study of migration for the United Nations Conference on Trade and Development:

> Remittances strike the right cognitive chords. They fit in with a communitarian, "third way" approach and exemplify the principle of self-help. People from poor countries can just migrate and send back money that not only helps their families, but their countries as well. Immigrants, rather than governments, then become the biggest provider of "foreign aid."

As this quote implies, migrants' popularity within development policy came not only from recognition of their ability to contribute materially to development, but also from an appreciation of how they might enact local, privatized, "self-help" strategies in particular.[6] Rather than operating as part of a nationally orchestrated program, migrants were seen as capable of effecting development through the aggregate impact of their autonomous, individual efforts. By simply responding to demand within the international labor markets, migrants would become key agents of a laissez-faire development model that would ideally supplant other forms of foreign aid.

And yet, up until recently, development experts and scholars alike have struggled to fully understand the contours and mechanics of these private transfers. A 2001 study of remittance senders sponsored by the Inter-American Development Bank revealed that 69 percent of Latin American migrants living in the United States sent an average of $200 seven times per year to family members in their home country (IADB 2001). A Pew Hispanic Center study also noted significant differences in remittance patterns based on migrants' nationality, the circumstances producing migration in the first place, and length of time in the United States (Waldinger 2007). Therefore, despite the argument that remittances were a reliable source of development capital, many studies have noted the unevenness of remittance effects on individual household poverty and overall community development (Caglar 2006; Elton 2006; Kapur 2004; Waldinger, Popkin, and Aquiles Magana 2007).

Both the power and the politics of remittances were easily evidenced in the Santa Cecilia where, for residents, remittances were both a lifeline, subsidizing household consumption needs, and also a responsibility. Lucia, an industrious forty-year-old mother of five who ran a local storefront provides a telling example. Since her brother's migration to Houston eight years prior, she had also been assigned the task of overseeing construction of her brother's home, financed by remittances he sent from abroad. She often commented how difficult it was to make sure that the construction remained true to her brother's wishes and to ensure that the money was wisely spent, so as to guarantee that his investment would approximate his dreams. Would these windows be right? Was this contractor overcharging her? The task required constant managerial vigilance and precise bookkeeping. Yet she fulfilled this duty both out of filial obligation to her brother and also in order to benefit from the small additional allowance he sent to compensate her efforts on his behalf. Her experience thus begins to suggest how development practice has produced an entrepreneurialization of migrants and the community members they have left behind, albeit in class- and gender-specific ways.

From Remitting Migrants to Ethnic Entrepreneurs

Migrants came into view as valuable development agents not only based on their individual or collective capacity to send money home, but also because of assumptions about the kind of subjects they represented. The prototypical migrant subject pursued by governments and international development institutions alike embodied a valuable combination of individual risk taking and enduring connections to family and community, presumably reflective of a certain ethnic and class background. Additionally, his mobility and productivity abroad were engendered by an assumed paternal masculinity (despite the fact that, since 2000, women account for approximately 50 percent of migrants globally) (UN-INSTRAW 2006; UN General Assembly 2006). By virtue of this construction, migrants were perceived to bridge diverse types of local/moral and expert/technical knowledge (Chapter Six). Based on these qualities, development policies increasingly posited migrants as entrepreneurial subjects whose development tasks included providing private capital investments for their home community and remitting essential financial know-how to peers. These entrepreneurial acts would be oriented not only toward economic development, but also toward reproducing the ethnic community and ethnic identity.

In examining migrant subjectivity, my analysis builds on a long history of research on the relationship between migration and entrepreneurship that extends across the fields of sociology, geography, economics, and anthropology. Despite their broad disciplinary scope, these previous studies have been organized around what I see to be three main questions. The earliest group of studies took up the question of immigrant entrepreneurism as a means of evaluating the possibility of immigrant assimilation in the United States. From Cubans in Miami to Koreans in Los Angeles, these studies examined how ethnic economies (defined by a high number of coethnic employers and employees) and ethnic enclaves (locational clusters of firms with coethnic employer/employees) served to promote or prevent economic mobility and social integration into U.S. society (see Halter 1995; Light 1972; Light and Bonacich 1988; Portes and Bach 1985; Zhou 2004). Another vector of research focused on particular communities' predisposition for entrepreneurial activity based on those groups' perceived "cultural comparative advantage" vis-à-vis a cultural ethos or values deemed compatible with entrepreneurism. This line of inquiry encompasses studies that investigate stereotypes of Jews' propensity for self-enterprise or Chinese affinity for commerce, cases in which migration has functioned as a manifestation of this essentialist business orientation (Geertz 1963; Sombart 1951; Wong 1987).[7] Finally, over the last decade, many studies have focused on the transnational dimensions of entrepreneurism not only in the United States, but globally. These studies have analyzed the structure and mechanics of cross-border social networks, especially in terms of globalization and multiculturalism. Ultimately, they have been interested in how migrants live their lives in multiple social fields simultaneously, rather than simply pursuing assimilation in the United States (Itzigsohn et al. 1999; Landolt, Autler, and Baires 1999; Levitt 2001; Levitt and Jaworsky 2007; Ong 1999; Rouse 1991).

As a result of this new interest in transnationalism in particular, sociologist Alejandro Portes and other members of the Comparative Immigrant Entrepreneurship Project (CIEP) have collaborated to distinguish the contours of transnational entrepreneurism from more conventional forms of ethnic entrepreneurism in the United States as well as from more basic transnational activities, such as sending remittances or casual resale of U.S.-purchased goods in the homeland.[8] This line of research has focused on how to classify the kind of entrepreneurism practiced by migrants in terms of geographic scale and the social networks it involves.

While my analysis benefits from the insights produced by these studies, my focus is on migrant subjectivity and its implications for development. Specifically, I am interested in the assumption by development experts that, in many places, migrants are more likely to be entrepreneurial than natives. Therefore, it is the particular dispositions, practices, and sensibilities attributed to migrants—rather than their objective labor status—that concerns me here. Among the reasons given for the assertion of migrant entrepreneurism, Hania Zlotnik, the director of Population Studies for the UN Department of Economic and Social Affairs, claims that migrants offer "hard work, courage, and a willingness to take risks in order to succeed," as evidenced by their willingness to migrate in the first place (Zlotnik 2006b:2; see also Burns and Mohapatra 2008). Buttressing these qualities, migrants have access to more sources of labor vis-à-vis their large, unified family units, and can draw on community solidarity to more easily access credit (Zlotnik 2006a). This portrait posits risk taking, large families, and communities as defining qualities of migrant subjectivity, thus presenting a view of migrants frequently repeated in studies of ethnic enterprises in the United States and validated by development experts (see Zhou 2004; UN General Assembly 2006).[9] This ethnic "othering" is naturalized by the tendency to view national territory as coextensive with cultural identity, such that migrants are, "by definition, culturally and socially different because they originated in other national territories; natives, by this same logic, became a homogeneous whole" (Glick-Schiller, Caglar, and Guldbrandsen 2006:613).

Ironically then, while ethnic difference—as manifest in high immigrant-population growth rates, language retention, and cultural insularity—have frequently figured as central issues in political debates over immigration (see Huntington 2004), these same essentialized qualities—large families, cohesive communities—have been identified here as making migrants favorably predisposed toward entrepreneurism and, thus, valuable development agents.

This migrant-entrepreneur prototype not only eschews the complexity of migrant diversity more generally, it also ascribes to migrants a subjectivity born of a specific ethnic and class background.[10] Zlotnik's characterization of migrant entrepreneurship (which takes as its case study Turkish migrants to Germany) imputes to migrants in general the enduring solidarity and collective identity historically associated with ethnic and working-class communities in particular. Migrants are perceived as poor, adventurous, morally obligated to kin back home, and socially embedded in a cohesive, even ethnic, community. It is, therefore, the combination of the migrant's personal daring, cultural values, and collective baggage (such as their connection to kin) that become the foundation for successful entrepreneurship and translocal development. Rather than structural conditions defining an individual's propensity for migration, both the act of migration and its economic potential are seen as reflections of individual or group attributes. Exemplifying this perspective, the Secretary General of the UN provocatively declared to the General Assembly: "Migration is a courageous expression of an *individual's will* to overcome adversity and live a better life. Over the past decade, globalization has increased the number of people with the desire and capacity to move to other places" (UN Secretary General 2006; emphasis added). For these kinds of subjects, experts at institutions like the UN have promoted migration as a means of producing development in "sending" and "receiving" countries based on the largely unskilled labor these migrants could provide (see quote at the beginning of this chapter). Moreover, migration-based development has been lauded as a means of reproducing, rather than debilitating social community. Interestingly, these efforts to stimulate knowledge and capital flows among migrants are distinct from development conversations about the problem of "brain drain," or the emigration of highly educated professionals out of the developing world (Chapter Four). Whereas development experts and state officials alike had universally lamented the loss of development potential reflected by brain drain, the migration-development nexus discussed in this chapter clearly speaks to a different class of migrant.

This institutional view of migrants' entrepreneurship departs dramatically from some community members' perceptions of migrants, evidencing not only the ethnic and class assumptions at work, but also the gendered dynamics behind migration and development. When I asked one group of women in Santa Cecilia about how migration had shaped the community, they noted that some male migrants stay away for just a few years, returning to live in the cement-block houses and drive the pickups that they have purchased abroad. Others, however, increasingly stay in the United States, sending remittances to their parents, wives, and children in Santa Cecilia. One somewhat despondent young wife whose husband had been in Houston for the last six years noted wryly: "The men say, 'Why should I go back? It's just the same dirt and road. . . . I'm better off here [in the States].'"

As this comment suggests, for at least some community members in Houston, Santa Cecilia's dirt road represented the physical community as a place that was not only spatially distant, but also temporally backward compared to modern U.S. living conditions. The narrative accentuated the community's lack of vital productive opportunities—no development, no modernity, just dirt and road—and thus justified migration on the basis of the need to go elsewhere to pursue economically productive enterprises. In doing so, the narrative repositioned the community as nothing more than a space of social reproduction and a destination for remittances rather than a place of production in and of itself.

Commentaries like these highlight not only the class roots of the migrant subject, but also the gendered nature of his construction. The negative views of the road expressed by Santa Cecilia residents provide an example of how "migrant groups' identities are . . . produced within place-based contexts of power relations and 'community' politics that shape and are shaped by the gender-differentiated possibilities of migration and ethnicity" (Silvey 2006:70). Therefore, the privileging of transnational migrants as potent entrepreneurial agents with special development capabilities has been premised not only on migrants' economic practices, but also on their gendered construction and positioning within the space of development. Through a micropolitics approach, we can see how these gender subjects shape development on both sides of the migration-development nexus—namely, male entrepreneurial subjects that do development work abroad and also female entrepreneurs that increasingly do development work at home.

The mobile, agentive male and the sedentary, feminized local community have been prevalent tropes in studies of transnational migration and global development, especially in relation to ethnically marked populations. For example, Siu (2005:102) notes how migration among diasporic Chinese was primarily a male endeavor, in that "the majority of migrants were men and migration was encouraged, even expected of men to fulfill their role as providers for the family and as the means to achieve upward social mobility." A respected, older woman from one of Totonicapán's smaller rural communities reiterated this gendered relationship between migration and development one day during an informal women's meeting: "We are supposed to stay home, take care of the house, the kids, the animals, the milpa[11] . . . that's fine. But we can't get by like that. We need more income and more productive strategies that we can pursue from the home."[12]

Feminist geographers like Doreen Massey have noted how these patterns reflect gendered geographies of power (Mahler and Pessar 2001) in the contemporary globalized world:

> It is interesting to note how frequently the characterization of place as home comes from those who have left, and it would be fascinating to explore how often this characterization is framed around those who—perforce—stayed behind; and how often the former was male, setting out to discover and change the world, and the latter female, most particularly a mother, assigned the role of personifying a place that did not change. (Massey 1994:166–67)

This view elides the feminization of migration, not only in terms of the rising number of women migrating but also in terms of migrant women's increasing role as the main economic breadwinners for their households (UN-INSTRAW 2006:1; see also Sassen 1999); indeed, the predominance of female migrant labor globally has certainly shifted historical gendered stereotypes of the migrant subject. Nonetheless, Massey's insights draw our attention to how migrant mobility has been gendered and, in the case of the rural villages in which I worked, had come to be assigned masculine and even paternal qualities. This gendered construction of migration has shaped the contours of current transnational development paradigms on both sides of the border and introduced into development projects a broad range of actors as active collaborators.

Given the perceived entrepreneurial quality of migrant subjects, the role of development policy as laid out by the World Bank, IADB, and United Nations has been simply to promote translocal connections that enable migrants to pass on both the private capital and also the business knowledge that they have accrued in order to effect development. To this end, multilateral institutions, banks, corporations, and states have all come to work together as important stakeholders in this fluid, transnational development equation. One area where we can see this multilateral coordination at work is in the formalization of transnational money transfers. Both the U.S. government and various Latin American governments have advocated for "reduc[ing] the cost of transfers . . . to promote a greater role by banks and other financial institutions in an industry currently dominated by wire transfer firms" (Orozco 2004b:1). The Mexican government in particular has collaborated with Wells Fargo and Bank of America to allow its citizens to open U.S. bank accounts with a *matricula consular*, or Mexican national identification card, that it grants through its consular agencies in the United States. The Central Reserve Bank of El Salvador authorized Salvadoran banks with U.S. branches to serve as remittance agencies (Landolt, Autler, and Baires 1999:295). In response to these policies and targeted marketing by U.S. banks, Latinos had opened 400,000 new bank accounts by 2004 (Orozco 2004b:3). While this kind of collaboration reflects a desire to lower the cost of transfers, formalize remittances, and thus maximize their development potential, it also reflects an express interest in getting migrants in the door of the banks so that those institutions can sign them up for other financial products. As such, it reveals a growing awareness by banks of the profit potential of individual migrants as consumers of a variety of financial services.

In addition to the new role assigned to banks, transnational development practice has also redefined the role of individual states. Based on the collaborative, rather than authoritative, role that they play within these projects, states increasingly act as coordinators of private, transnational development investment rather than as the primary agent of national development (see also Larner 2007; Glick-Schiller and Fouron 2001). Indeed, where states have historically been the main recipient of foreign aid, in these translocal initiatives it is their own migrant-citizens to whom they must appeal for development funds. Consequently, state efforts to generate financing from migrants often include a package of projects that could be designed by multiple actors working together (Popkin 2003:361), a point I explore in more depth below. The new relationship emerging between states and migrant communities thus reflects more than just efforts to leverage the economic potential of migrant contributions; it also highlights more diffuse and dynamic state forms, as well as new practices of governance.[13]

In addition to efforts to facilitate and leverage *individual* migrant transfers, transnational development initiatives have increasingly looked to collaborative relationships with migrant organizations, a form most visibly exemplified by hometown associations (HTAs). While reflecting a variety of types, HTAs are essentially "entities formed by immigrants who seek to support their places of origin, maintain relationships with local communities, and retain a sense of community as they adjust to life in the United States" (Orozco 2006:5–6, 2004a, 2003). And while HTAs have been documented in the United States since the mid-1800s (Moya 2005; Caglar 2006), contemporary Latino diasporas and their civic associations in the United States, in particular, have received special attention over the last decade because of the interest in the economic and political potential of their development impact in home communities in Latin America (Orozco 2003, 2004a, 2006; Baker-Cristales 2004; Coutin 2007; Popkin 2003, 2005).[14]

Scholars note that Salvadoran, Mexican, and Guatemalan HTAs in California were often born out of recreational soccer leagues (Waldinger, Popkin, and Aquiles Magana 2007; Popkin 2005). Providing an important social network for migrants abroad to recreate and network, these HTAs began to sponsor community festivals and provide desperately needed relief following natural disasters back home. As part of their philanthropic mission, HTAs have since supported human capital development in their home communities, supplying educational and medical resources as well as student scholarships. Furthermore, they have increasingly been involved in fostering private enterprises within their home communities; indeed, scholars have tracked HTAs' transition from philanthropic exercises to more infrastructural and entrepreneurial development. HTAs thus function more and more as local development agencies for both state and multinational agencies (Caglar 2006:8).

Because of HTAs' potential for mobilizing large amounts of private capital and reinforcing national identity among migrant-citizens, Latin American states have pursued innovative policies to enhance HTA development potential, both abroad and in their countries of origin. As Waldinger, Popkin, and Aquiles Magana (2007:844) note: "From the standpoint of development agencies, the prospect that immigrant associational activity in the developed world could leverage capital *and* participation for stay-at-homes in the development world seems worth the gamble, as evidenced by a rapidly expanding portfolio of research and programme development grants."

On the economic front, states such as Mexico have encouraged private capital flows by enabling foreign currency holdings and instituting matching-funds programs[15] as incentives for HTA investment in local development projects. The Salvadoran state has agreed to reduce tariffs on machinery imports brought in by migrants to set up new businesses in their home communities. Other state-supported economic incentives have included subsidizing new migrant-formed enterprises in immigrant hometowns or issuing "diaspora bonds" through which migrants directly invest in the economic health of their home country (López-Córdova and Olmedo 2005; Ketkar and Ratha 2007). On the political front, states like Mexico and Guatemala have pursued such strategies as enabling dual citizenship and allowing citizens abroad to vote in home-country elections. In the case of Guatemala and El Salvador, these state efforts have even included lobbying the United States for asylum rights on behalf of their citizens in the hope of keeping lucrative migrant remittances flowing (see Coutin 2007; Popkin 2003).

Efforts to capitalize on translocal migrant entrepreneurism have involved stimulating an exchange not only of money or goods, but also of knowledge across borders. To this end, Vice Minister of Work, Social Affairs and Equal Chances at the United Nations, Kastriot Sulko, has highlighted the important role migrants must play in expanding financial know-how and market acumen: "Civil society organizations, including migrant organizations, could also play an important role by promoting financial counseling among migrating families as well as advice and support for entrepreneurship. Access to such support was a means of leveraging the benefits of remittances for development" (Sulko 2006:2).

Interestingly, development experts have imbued this knowledge transfer not only with the power to effect development in the sending countries, but also as a "training ground" for new waves of migrants and a means of contributing to the "cohesion of the community" (Zlotnik 2006a:5). Therefore, according to these institutional approaches, migrant entrepreneurship is to be perceived as part of an essentialized feedback loop, in which a natural entrepreneurial disposition on the part of the individual migrant is supported by community and family connections that make possible more entrepreneurial activities that, in turn, reinforce community cohesion.

As this brief overview of transnational development strategies suggests, efforts to tap into migrants' development potential pivot on certain gendered and classed understandings of migration and remittances. The subjective qualities associated with migrant development work have profound impacts not only on migrants, but also on the development work done by community members that remain at home. For example, part of the institutional power differentials between HTAs and their "home" communities can include gender inequalities between migrant organizations—defined by high levels of male membership and leadership (Waldinger, Popkin, and Aquiles Magana 2007; Popkin 2005)—and the feminized communities and community residents that have been left behind.[16] Consequently, in what follows, I return to Santa Cecilia to explore how those community members who do not migrate become increasingly entrepreneurialized as a result of the way their development work is transformed through others' migration.

New In-Roads to Development

For some in Santa Cecilia, the unchanging dirt road and the lack of productive development initiatives reflected a feminized space of lack relative to the active, mobile, and productive male migrants abroad. This gendered configuration of people and place was further accentuated by Maya cultural norms that posited indigenous women as traditional bearers of culture and reinforcers of community moral codes (Smith 1995).[17]

Women's central role in reproducing both the cultural boundaries of the local community and the material foundations of community life has had important implications for how they are positioned within the space of development. Especially to the extent that the community was perceived and experienced as a place lacking in productive, income-generating options, women's own productive potential and development agency has been effectively erased.[18] Critiquing this dynamic in her genealogy of local community development in Santa Cecilia, Catalina Tzoc, an important community organizer, was quick to note that her community could not boast any real development because "the donor agencies leave us." She thus attributed the lack of concrete developments to the mobility and flightiness of the funding institutions, rather than to any lack of interest or agency on the part of the community.

In their daily practices and discourse, Santa Cecilia women sought to contest the prevalent notion of the community as a static place of lack. Indeed, my initial inquiries into community development with an assiduous group of women were quickly transformed into a conversation about the possibilities for collaborating on a new project they had been formulating. As part of that collaboration, these women described for me cases within the community in which women's development experiences were remembered as much for their accomplishments as they were for the challenges they posed to women's authority as development agents. Their experiences illustrated the different ways that development has been done in the wake of transnational migration, highlighting the ambivalent openings that this context has produced for women's leadership in development projects.

One example of women's work as development agents was illustrated by a successful stove project that several Santa Cecilia women proudly recounted to me. This project exemplified how postconflict development dynamics in Guatemala and the rise of transnational migration from these particular communities had opened up new opportunities for women to do local development work. The project was advertised on a prominent blue-and-yellow sign that stood along the entrance to Santa Cecilia's main road, just off its intersection with the Pan-American Highway. Responsible for introducing 383 "improved stoves" to the community, the initiative reflected the enthusiastic international humanitarian and development assistance that followed the signing of the 1996 Peace Accords.[19] The sign was located in front of the house of the woman who organized the project—Catalina Tzoc. Impressed by the magnitude of the initiative, I sought her out to investigate this singular process of community organization, expecting to hear an important tale of development in this place defined by its absence. Her story provided insight into the micropolitics of local development in Santa Cecilia, illuminating how women became protagonists of development in the absence of male peers, but also how their newfound authority was challenged by men who were left behind.

Catalina is a vivacious, energetic woman in her fifties whose deeply wrinkled face attested more to her frequent smiling than her age. She boasted a long history of involvement with community projects ranging from an animal husbandry initiative to a state-sponsored sewing course to her current role as a literacy teacher for community women. She was clearly someone who actively sought out new opportunities. When I asked her about the stove project, she proudly described how her organization of forty women had created it. The women had gone around from house to house to promote the project and to sign up over three hundred potential beneficiaries. But the results had not been immediate; it took five years from the date of the original proposal for the delivery of the stoves to occur. While Catalina lauded her group for keeping the faith during that time, she noted with frustration how a community engineer, Manuel, and his followers, had tried to "take over" the project. His efforts, and

Catalina's critique of them, echoed narratives that posited male migrants as entrepreneurial protagonists of local development:

> He went to [the donor agency] and looked up the project, which was referenced by number. He informed the people [at the agency] that the project had been abandoned by the original community group. He took over the project and went around collecting Q43 [US$7] from every potential beneficiary, saying that *he* was going to be the one to bring the stoves.

One of the women who had participated in the stove project recounted the confusion that this struggle for leadership caused for the beneficiaries within the community.

> Manuel's group came around saying that they were going to submit a proposal for stoves. . . . He said that we had to sign up on his list. I wasn't sure which list was the "true" list [Manuel's or Catalina's], so I signed up on his as well. When he went to solicit the project, there were two proposals from the same community with the same list of beneficiaries.

When Catalina heard what was happening, she went to the donor agency and complained that she and her group were still actively involved with the project. The agency demanded a clarification as to who was in charge of the project, and Catalina and Manuel fought over rights to it. Eventually Catalina emerged as the rightful project president when Manuel ceded his claims to the project and apologized. However, as Catalina narrated these events to me, it was clear that the resentment caused by Manuel's attempted usurpation had not entirely abated. Indeed, her narrative emphasized how the new flow of people and money reflected by migration and remittances had affected subjectivity on both sides of the equation. The way Catalina told the story accentuated how gendered notions of development authority had shaped who donor organizations and fellow community members deemed to be legitimate project leaders. Much of her pride emanated from the satisfaction of knowing that she and a group of fellow community *women* had brought this project to fruition. Her frustration with Manuel, who she singled out as both a man and an engineer, shed light on how a changing gendered division of labor was increasingly redefining community development politics in the wake of transnational migration.

As part of a dwindling pool of community males, Manuel's efforts reflect the growing importance of local development initiatives as a space for asserting masculine authority. With other community males working abroad, asserting leadership over local development became especially important to preserving Manuel's masculinity. The fact that both local residents and also the donors were left questioning who was the rightful project leader implies that his assertion of male authority provided a confusing and potentially compelling challenge to Catalina's efforts. Therefore, although the stove project succeeded in mobilizing ambitious female community activists and in providing them with valuable leadership opportunities, it also highlighted the tenuousness of women's authority within development projects and the pressure on community males to stake a claim in development politics. By examining the micropolitics of development practice, we can see how gendered, ethnic, and class configurations of development and migration become central to positioning people within the space of development.

Nonetheless, the gendered division of development that emerged in Santa Cecilia was constantly in tension with changing global development practices.[20] The same forces responsible for positioning Santa Cecilia's female residents as passive, "lacking" development subjects in the mid-1990s and then as tenuous development leaders in the late 1990s, made women in similar communities visible as idealized, efficient, and moral economic agents during the early 2000s. This visibility was underscored by a 2006 Guatemalan newspaper article titled "Women Entrepreneurs." The article included an interview with Lesbia Taló, an indigenous woman from Totonicapán and the general manager of CDRO's newest development enterprise (a line of spa products sold through Walmart, described in Chapter Five). Contrasting her managerial experience within the new enterprise with the "submissive housewife" stereotype of Maya women that she claims existed previously, she noted, "I remember five years ago, I went to talk to a community and men wouldn't pay attention to me. . . . Today, I am going to the same community and they not only listen to me, but are taking interest in our approaches" (cited in Cordero 2006).

To further elaborate on the nature of this shift in development agency, in Chapter Six I detail how poor women, and especially those "left behind" by migration, have become the primary target of international and community-level initiatives that seek to foment local enterprise through microfinance and microenterprise. The gendered division of labor that I described in this chapter, which posited men as mobile economic producers and women as sedentary social reproducers, is often invoked by microcredit supporters as the reason why women are better borrowers: ironically, in these cases, it is both women's rootedness in the community, where few income-generating opportunities are presumed to exist, and their long experience with managing household resources that make them especially effective entrepreneurial subjects. Therefore, exactly because of their relative underdevelopment and immobility relative to community males, women have been identified as development authorities in their own right, especially in the field of microfinance.

Shifting Development Landscapes

In this chapter, I have described the increasing institutional appreciation for migration as a development tool with benefits for individual households, local communities, national economies, and even the global system. Rather than diverging entirely from the kind of local, participatory development practices defined in Chapter Two, I have argued that migration-centered development practices have sought to build on migration as a vehicle for translocal, private, self-managed development flows. While in the last chapter I described how community initiatives such as CDRO's became visible because of the convergence between *local*, ethnic organizing principles and neoliberal rationalities, here, too, migrants become visible as powerful development actors, based on their ability to enact private *translocal* development. Similar to indigenous communities that preceded them, migrants and those left behind went from being perceived as manifestations of *under*development to being recognized as exemplary agents of regional development.

Interestingly, this inclusion of migrants as positive agents of change was justified not only in terms of the mutual economic benefits that migration provided, but also in terms of emancipatory cultural politics. In other words, just as CDRO's ethnic initiatives were portrayed as innovative alternatives to Western-influenced development strategies of the past, Kapur's analysis indicates how remittances were seen to represent "third-way," communitarian endeavors. Framing translocal, remittance-based development strategies in this way elided the shift of development responsibility from the state onto civil society, reflected by migrants' replacement of government as "the biggest provider of foreign aid" (see also Elton 2006). Instead, this shift is equated with empowerment and autonomy for local communities, especially to the extent that migration-based development strategies promoted the ascendance of women "back home" into prestigious new roles as entrepreneurial development agents.

In the next chapter, I turn to the Digital Diaspora project for Latin America in order to explore how this interest in mainstreaming migration has been operationalized in relation to a different class of migrant, namely the Latino professional. The Digital Diaspora project provides a vivid example of how states, corporations, and multilateral institutions have collaborated to capitalize on migrants' perceived essential connection to Latin America in order to harness remittances and market know-how to the task of regional development. Like their migrant counterparts described in this chapter, diasporic professionals who were recruited for the Digital Diaspora project were seen to embody a productive, "masculine" source of development knowledge, technology, and money relative to their "home" communities and kin in Latin America. As such, the Digital Diaspora project must be seen as part of a larger effort to organize and institutionalize relationships with the diasporic elite and the financial and technological flows on which they are based (Larner 2007:340).

"Hermano Entrepreneur!"

Constructing a Latino Diaspora across the Digital Divide

ON A BALMY SEPTEMBER MORNING IN 2003, I arrived at the United Nations headquarters in New York to attend the launching of an innovative development initiative. This invitation-only event was advertised as a novel effort to promote "the achievement of the Millennium Development Goals through mobilizing the technological, entrepreneurial, and professional expertise and resources of Diaspora networks."[1] Based on the successful experience of an Indian initiative in 2000, followed by a project for Africa commencing in 2002, this newest so-called Digital Diaspora project had its sights set on Latin America and the Caribbean. In an effort to bridge the technology gap—referred to here as the "digital divide"—between North and South, the program aspired to increase the direct flow of knowledge and resources between U.S.-based Latino entrepreneurs and community development projects in Latin America. The kick-off event was to be attended by a diverse array of business executives, diplomats, consultants, non-governmental organization representatives, and information technology experts as well as a handful of academics with an interest in building this initiative from the ground up.

I came to the meeting with the dual interest of commencing research on the proposed development plan and encountering the pan-Latino diaspora through which the project was to be enacted. As a blonde-haired, blue-eyed Mexican-American from California, I was more than familiar with the complexity of Latino identity politics and, thus, should not have been surprised by the lack of "physical evidence" of such a Latino community at the event. Nonetheless, I was taken aback when less than half of the attendees appeared to be Latinos; abundant instead were non-Latino representatives from Microsoft,

Verizon, Intel, and various other technology and communications companies. My puzzlement grew when program organizers confirmed my demographic assessment of the Latino absence. Where was the Latino diaspora, I wondered? More important still, what did the absence of Latinos at this inaugural event imply about the presumed identities and relationships upon which this new project was founded?

While the previous chapter described the transnationalization of development practice in response to increasing levels of migration to the United States, this chapter analyzes the Digital Diaspora for Latin America project to illustrate how global development agencies sought to build upon ethnic identity, in particular, as a tool for translocal, neoliberal development strategy. Through an ethnographic analysis of the inaugural event, I show how the Digital Diaspora initiative attempted to harness elite expatriate knowledge and capital for regional development. This transfer was justified through the invocation of individual responsibility, social enterprise, and postnational economic and technological integration. While the project was framed as an effort to reconnect Latinos with their brethren in Latin America, I examine how states, private corporations, and multilateral institutions like the United Nations shaped the project and what they stood to gain from its mobilization of these new ethnic entrepreneurs.

The Digital Diaspora project organizers appealed to a preconstituted Latino diaspora as the point of departure for this initiative; indeed, this diaspora was the pool from which they hoped to recruit Latino elites for regional development. I detail how organizers drew on assumed filial obligations among coethnics and the emancipatory potential of market expansion to highlight moral links among diasporic subjects. This approach elided the production of "Latino" as a reflection of U.S. cultural politics and effaced the ongoing importance of class and national identities within Latino identity politics. Therefore, my analysis of the inaugural event illuminates how, rather than simply mobilizing a preexisting population, the project *constructed* a Latino diaspora tied to a postnational Latin American homeland.

In what follows, I provide a brief background on the Digital Diaspora phenomenon to reveal its philosophical and institutional underpinnings. I highlight the constitutive role of overlapping networks of expert knowledge, neoliberal rationalities, and diasporic identities in constructing transnational technology-based development initiatives. I show how these networks, identities, and technologies were mobilized as a potential way of bridging the digital divide.

The Digital Diaspora Concept

The Digital Diaspora networks were the product of a series of initiatives created by a Seattle-based development organization, Digital Partners, and the United Nations Information and Communication Technologies (UNICT) Task Force. They reflected a growing international focus on technology as a crucial measure of and tool for addressing development inequalities globally.[2] Originally, the Digital Diaspora projects at issue here sought to "bring together qualified members of the Diaspora—high-tech professionals, entrepreneurs, and business leaders—into a network with their counterparts in order to promote ICT-for-development initiatives in their home country" (UNICT n.d.:10). The goal of these initiatives was to capitalize on the technological expertise and humanitarian impulse of diasporic professional communities in the United States in order to address what many saw as a proliferating technology gap between those with access to crucial information technologies and those without. This technology gap became defined as the "digital divide," and while the notion is now often used to reference technology gaps between many different types of constituencies (among class and ethnic groups in the United States, for example), the Digital Diaspora projects in particular arose out the desire to address the chasm between the United States and developing nations specifically (see Figure 4.1).[3]

Figure 4.1 The "real" digital divide.
Source: *Chris Sattlberger/Panos Pictures.* Printed with permission.

The Digital Diaspora projects were modeled after the IndUS Entrepreneurs (TiE) network—a partnership of South Asian technology industry professionals who organized a nonprofit organization in 1994 to foster entrepreneurship and development throughout the Indian diaspora. That specific initiative attempted to build upon the "mix of a Silicon Valley culture of economic value creation through entrepreneurship and the ancient Indian tradition of Guru/Chela (or Teacher/Disciple) relationship."[4] The project thus mobilized identities born of a specific cultural context yet refashioned through a professional class culture and identity forged in the United States. Through these hybrid positions, the TiE venture hoped to provide mentoring and knowledge exchange between U.S. and Indian communities rather than simply charity. Digital Partners helped to mobilize a digital diaspora project for India in 2000 that built off of this template and tried to institutionalize its efforts on an even broader scale. The India-diaspora initiative and those that followed hoped to apply the successful two-way network method to other communities in order to promote "guidance and insight to make the [development] process sustainable."[5]

The first such project sponsored by the UN was the Digital Diaspora Network for Africa. This initiative emerged out of a series of serendipitous encounters between Digital Partners' CEO, Akhtar Badshah (not a pseudonym), and Ghanaian entrepreneur, John Boateng. The trajectories of these two men and the coincidental nature of their encounter are worth elaborating on, as they are illustrative of the way the Africa and, subsequently, the Latin America Digital Diaspora projects took shape. They also point to the importance of overlapping global networks of expertise and postcolonial identity politics as constitutive forces in diasporic development, a point to which I return in Chapter Six.

Akhtar Badshah was born in Bombay, India, and worked as an architect in both India and Sri Lanka before receiving his doctorate from the Massachusetts Institute of Technology. After teaching at MIT for several years, he entered the field of community development and went on to work with numerous nonprofits (such as Digital Partners) even as he published on issues of development, sustainability, and information technologies. He has served on advisory boards for various international development initiatives including World Links India, World Corp., Teachers without Borders, and Datamation Foundation India, and he has consulted for the likes of USAID and the Rockefeller Foundation. However, his energies are primarily focused on his role as Senior Executive Director of Microsoft's Community Affairs Division. This history makes Badshah an internationally known development expert both within the nonprofit community and also within the larger development and corporate institutional environments.

John Boateng, born in Ghana and a U.S. citizen, received his degree in electrical engineering from an Ivy League college and worked with several large U.S. corporations in the aerospace industry before founding his own company, Africast.com—a "transaction-based service provider to the Global Africa marketplace" offering e-commerce and dynamic media services. The lead header on the Africast webpage frames these services as part of an intimate personal relationship between diasporans and their homeland, reading, "Connecting Africa worldwide. Visit your home country . . . Ghana, Nigeria, Kenya. . . ."[6]

Badshah recounted for me how he and Boateng met coincidentally in Harvard Square after both had gotten lost while looking for a nearby conference that they were to attend. Upon realizing their common plight, the two men went to have coffee and chat. It was during that conversation and several subsequent talks that the Digital Diaspora project began to take form. Badshah recalls telling Boateng of his ideas for the project and noting, "But we don't have a champion." Boateng cinched the deal by responding, "I will be your champion." Badshah and Boateng enlisted a group of interested individuals "who were connected to networks" to construct the Africa project. They also recruited the UN—initially to support the inaugural meeting, but with the hope of receiving long-term funding—as it had shown great interest in the India project.

Both Badshah and Boateng's individual trajectories as well as the circumstances of their collaboration reveal the kinds of transnational networks and expertise upon which the Digital Diaspora project hoped to build. As cosmopolitan development experts these men embodied the deep diasporic connections, the technical knowledge, the market acumen, and the philanthropic impulse that the diaspora projects sought to mobilize as the foundation for transnational development. Importantly, this combination of attributes implied not just the technical know-how needed to serve as effective agents of transnational development, but also a particular kind of subject—namely, a gendered subject who reflected both the masculine domains of ICT, finance, and business services as well as a moral disposition toward development as work that could be "championed" by each of them as individuals.[7] As the Latin American case will later demonstrate, the existence of a project "champion," like Boateng, turned out to be a crucial catalyst for the project's consolidation.

The Africa project commenced in 2002 with the recognition of the new challenge constituted by working with a continent rather than a single country, as had been the Indian case. This move toward a continental or regional project signaled a shift in orientation away from the historic emphasis on nation-states as the primary objects of development interventions; instead, it redefined development expertise and solutions relative to a different kind of development object, identified not by political boundaries but rather by the capacity for connectivity. The regional challenge was exacerbated in this instance by the absence of a strong technology background within the African expatriate community; however, the combination of UN support, an enthusiasm for information and communication technologies (ICT) solutions, and dynamic "champions"— like Boateng—with strong ties to their respective countries of origin made this project attractive.[8]

Digital Partners and the UNICT Task Force launched a Caribbean initiative in 2003; however, this project never really got off the ground. Therefore, when the possibility of a project for Latin America was raised, the project organizers proposed a joint initiative for Latin America and the Caribbean that would attempt to synergize relevant efforts in both areas. Badshah recalls that his organization was receiving increasing numbers of applications for projects in Latin America. This influx stimulated a desire on the part of Digital Partners to find people who could give both time and resources to projects that would confront computer illiteracy and the lack of access to ICT as "increasingly powerful obstacle[s] to the economic, civic and political development of the region."[9] Representatives from several Latin American states also expressed an interest in making the project a reality.

In 2003, after the successful meeting of the African diaspora, Digital Partners and the UNICT Task Force sponsored an inaugural event for Latin America and the Caribbean. Due in part to Digital Partners' newness to the Latino context and also due to the rapidity with which this event was put together, the list of invitees to the event was not crafted with a well-established list of people in mind; rather, the recruitment efforts "worked through a kind of snowball process that identified a somewhat random network of individuals, industries, academics" who could come together and talk about the project (personal communication, Akhtar Badshah). The snowball process in many ways assumed the existence of a preconstituted network of Latino professionals; its task was then simply to tap into this network. I was linked in as a result of my connection to a team of anthropologists at Intel Corporation who were studying the social dimensions of technology.[10] A research project I had recently conducted for Intel on the interface between social practices and information technology in

Latin America garnered me an invitation to participate in the Digital Diaspora opening event (DeHart 2002).

Inaugurating the Diaspora and Identifying "Us"

The inaugural event at the UN headquarters was divided into two different kinds of encounters. The first consisted of a series of panel presentations by diplomats, technology industry representatives, and expatriate leaders. The goal of these panels was ostensibly to share experience and inspire collective action on the part of the attendees. The second part of the day was devoted to working in small groups on case studies in the hopes of hammering out crucial issues that the project should address. Both of these activities provided unique insights into the tensions undergirding the project's working definition of the Latino diaspora.

The morning's activities took place in one of the large, arch-shaped UN meeting halls, with all of the attendants seated facing a stage with podium and cloth-draped table. As the room filled, successive waves of diplomats and development experts made opening speeches, followed by panels organized around diverse perspectives on the relationship between ICT and development in the region. Interestingly, despite the fact that this event was organized for the Latino diaspora, the majority of the talks were presented in English.

At several points throughout the morning, I could not resist the temptation of fiddling with the multilingual headphone system in front of me in order to listen in on the Spanish translation of the talks. The translator's Castilian, delivered with a thick Madrid accent, brought an ironic smile to my face, the European inflection seeming strangely out of place.[11] However, as I pondered this irony I began to ask myself what kind of Spanish accent would have sounded appropriate in this context. Had I expected to hear a Mexican dialect? A Venezuelan accent? While Spanish language has been cited as a common unifying principle among Latinos, it is also a basic means of distinguishing among them (Suárez-Orozco and Páez 2001:7; DeGenova and Ramos-Zayas 2003b:7; Bedolla 2005).[12] Therefore, the lack of a universal Latino dialect was not just a linguistic distraction on my part, but rather a core issue for this project in particular and for a changing American sociopolitical landscape more generally. In other words, it was the ambiguity surrounding the idea of *Latino*—who was included in that term and what kind of relationship to diverse U.S. and Latin American communities that person embodied—that both enabled and problematized the concept of a Latino diaspora as a potent transnational development agent.

Basic assumptions about who constituted the Latino community were immediately illustrated by the notable introductory remarks of project organizer Akhtar Badshah of Digital Partners. He introduced his interest in the Latin America project by noting, "Many of us who live in the U.S. and come from other countries, have supported family or village through our advancements here. Information technology will help us to do that more efficiently." Badshah mentioned that this could happen through both the transfer of knowledge, what he called "mindshare" and the use of that knowledge to generate resources and effect policy change. He spoke eloquently of the power of both individuals and a collective to effect change, noting that the group must "harness the power of the network." His charisma was palpable and clearly one of the driving forces behind this initiative. Nonetheless, his comments immediately prefigured some of the important ways that neoliberal rationalities had shaped this project: first, in terms of a coherent transnational community—framed as "us"—that was connected to Latin America by virtue of moral obligations; and second, by the injunction to harness the power of the "network"—a concept that conflated the development possibilities of Internet connectivity with that of the diasporic transnational community itself.

Badshah's appeal to "us" was followed by another entreatment to the vaguely defined yet presumably intimate transnational community of Latino professionals. In a video by José Maria Figueres-Olsen, the former president of Costa Rica and, since 2000, managing director of the World Economic Forum and special representative to the UNICT Advisory Group, further marked this exchange as a friendly dialogue among community members, explicitly directing his remarks at "those of us who have come out of Latin America." Figueres stated that "many of our brothers and sisters" would benefit from the information with which "we" are blessed. The route through which this would occur would require, among other things, that "all of us who are professionals donate our time to development," creating a multifaceted network through which technology would be the "conductive arm of development."

At several points during Figueres's and subsequent presentations, I found myself looking around the room to sense how these personal appeals were resonating with the very mixed group present. What did these supplications to "us" in the name of "our brothers and sisters back home" mean to the many non-Latino technology industry representatives here? How would his comments sit with others, like me, whose academic and personal identities and interests had apparently landed them smack in the middle of an intense recruitment process? Most other attendees that I observed were listening earnestly to the speakers and seemed nonplussed by these invocations of community and migration, processes to which they may or may not have felt connected. Others were clearly busy networking and would frequently move to speak to other participants, exchanging business cards and handshakes. Perhaps more telling than the reactions of those present, however, was the apparent absence of the powerful Latino diaspora toward whom the event was geared. Why had those invoked by the notion of "us" not materialized in a critical mass at this event?

In order to answer these questions, we must do more than simply examine the contours of the Digital Diaspora project discourse; rather, we need to explore the broader global context in which it was embedded. In many ways the working definition of *Latino* employed by this project—as a coherent cultural identity derived directly from Latin America—played upon the U.S. media constructions of Latinos as a homogeneous consumer group or niche (Dávila 2001:1–4, 2008; Waterston 2006). This vision contradicted the production of Latino as a social category forged within the history of U.S. civil rights politics.[13] Furthermore, it elided the lingering importance of both class and national identities in structuring relationships both within the U.S. Latino community and between that community and Latin America.[14] Consequently, in the next sections, I ask how the context of neoliberal development and regional economic integration facilitated and in fact incited some of the ambiguity surrounding the Latino concept by both redefining development as a translocal, collective project of self-care and reconfiguring Latin America as a postnational homeland.

Moral Markets

As noted in Chapter One, development strategies in Latin America since the 1980s have been defined by multilateral efforts to promote neoliberal economic reform and global market integration. While these efforts seemed to diminish the role of the state as the primary agent of national development, I argue throughout the book that they simply repositioned the state in relation to other potential development actors and reinscribed state power through new forms of governance.[15] As we saw in Chapters Two and Three, this transformation included the devolution of state development responsibility to local constituencies, like CDRO, as well as to migrant-citizens abroad. These state efforts sought to work through the autonomous actions of translocal actors in order to make development more flexible, efficient, and ultimately lucrative.

Ethnic communities' participation in these development endeavors was promoted as empowerment, even as this new form of inclusion was conceived in terms of access to and participation in the market, rather than legitimacy and voice within state politics. As I show here, these shifts in development practice produced a reterritorialized vision of regional development that relied on mobile, masculine, professional subjects and the ostensibly liberatory potential of technology to effect development.

In the case of the Digital Diaspora project in particular, we can see how these rationalities informed the initiative's conceptualization of why and how Latinos constituted the ideal constituency to bridge the "digital divide." First, the project reframed development as a moral endeavor that was the personal responsibility of individual diaspora members, rather than the state. As political theorists such as Burchell (1994), Dean (1999), Gordon (1991), and Rose (1991, 1996, 1999) have noted, this move is characteristic of neoliberal rationalities that promote responsibilization, autonomization, and self-enterprise as central features of neoliberal governmentality. This framework allows for the repositioning of development subjects as "stakeholders," tied to the process of development through new definitions of morality and self-care. Importantly, although neoliberal rationalities often reference the individual as the focus of self-care, this subject is also interchangeable with collective forms such as the family or the community:

> The neo-liberal forms of government . . . characteristically develop indirect techniques for leading and controlling individuals without at the same time being responsible for them. The strategy of rendering individual subjects "responsible" (and also collectives, such as families, associations, etc.) entails shifting the responsibility for social risks such as illness, unemployment, poverty, etc. and for life in society into the domain for which the individual is responsible and transforming it into a problem of "self-care." The key feature of neo-liberal rationality is the congruence it endeavors to achieve between a responsible and moral individual and an economic rational actor. (Lemke 2001a:201)

Digital Diaspora project organizers validated this reallocation of the responsibility for development self-care on the basis of the perceived filial relationship among diasporic Latinos as coethnics. As I described in Chapter Three, within development policy migrants were frequently perceived in essentialized terms that attributed to them certain ethnic, gender, and class characteristics, including large families and cohesive community connections. By invoking their disadvantaged brethren, or *hermanos* in Latin America, the Digital Diaspora project called upon diasporic individuals to be morally accountable for the development fate of their less fortunate kin. Their appeal echoed language deployed by Latin American states in their efforts to recruit migrant-citizens to the project of national development by referring to them as *hermanos lejanos*, or distant brothers (Coutin 2007; Glick-Schiller and Fouron 2001; Landolt, Autler, and Baires 1999; Levitt 2001). This incitement to obligation appealed to the mobile, masculine migrant with a responsibility to support family and lacking community back home. Recall Figueres's entreaties to the Latino diaspora, worded as "those of us who have come out of Latin America" where "many of our brothers and sisters" would benefit from the information with which "we" are blessed. The subject who could fulfill this call to action affirmed himself as both a successful professional with valuable knowledge and connections to share, as well as a respectable, responsible provider.

The Digital Diaspora organizers further affirmed the moral nature of the development project by conflating development's economic and social effects, linking market expansion to social justice. Take for example, opening comments at the inaugural event by Sarbuland Khan, an economist with the UN Economic and Social Affairs (ECOSOC). Khan noted that this project would work for "the construction of a universal participative global information society network." He asked the gathering to ponder how this project could encourage "the public sector to draw on private sector creativity to cultivate market expansion and social justice." His speech redefined market expansion as complementary to or even enabling of new forms of participation and justice. This connection made sense because of the neoliberal assumption that participation and inclusion could be achieved through market consumption, rather than political agency (Lemke 2001b). This convergence between entrepreneurism and ethics allowed the leaders of the project to reposition individual Latinos as well as a collective Latino diaspora as personally responsible, morally compelled, and collectively capable of enacting regional development.

The slippage between moral and economic goals also provided the many non-Latino technology and telecommunication industry representatives involved with a way to justify their own collaboration in this project despite their lack of organic ties to Latin America. After all, this call echoed the coupling of moral and profit-seeking agendas as mutually compatible goals within corporate social responsibility and corporate citizenship frameworks, a convergence

I discuss in more detail in Chapter Five. Therefore, by providing new possibilities for technology consumption, corporate representatives at this conference would be contributing to new opportunities for both social and corporate
enfranchisement.[16]

Postnational Homelands

In addition to recognizing and mobilizing Latino professionals as powerful
new development agents, the Digital Diaspora project's efforts also pivoted
on a relocation of Latin America itself. Rather than emphasizing national or
subnational links as the source of Latino identity and, thus, the target of development interventions, the Digital Diaspora project reframed Latin America
as a collective diasporic homeland. No longer simply Mexicans, Colombians,
or Chileans, project participants were hailed as Latinos who identified with a
singular, continental homeland. Consequently, at the heart of this project was
the reconception and virtual remapping of Latin America as a coherent, unified
regional development object.[17]

The idea of a unified Latin American, or pan-American, identity has a long
historical life within Latin America. During the regional independence movements against Spain in the early nineteenth-century, Simón Bolívar hoped to
unite Southern Cone nations under a single Latin American republic.[18] Later,
Cuban nationalist and writer Jose Martí wrote about "Our America" as a pan-
American political and social space forged out of colonial oppression and racial
miscegenation. In the twentieth century, Che Guevara imagined a unified Latin
America as part of an international socialist movement. Despite their diverse
historical and political contexts, each of these formulations promoted a singular regional identity as part of a critical, and even revolutionary, postcolonial
political project. While Latin American nations shared some cultural legacies,
what ultimately defined them was a common history of threats to their political
autonomy and economic integrity, frequently from an imperial United States.
Therefore, regional identification was as much about an oppositional stance as
it was about cultural identification and a sense of belonging within the region.

What I find interesting and specifically neoliberal about the Digital Diaspora's remapping of Latin America is the way that it appealed to not just a transnational or translocal Latino community, but ultimately a postnational one.
By superseding national and even communal identities, ICT-informed development was to provide a platform for regional and thus global connectivity.
Building on an increasingly naturalized reality of hemispheric consolidation

through regional free trade alliances like North American Free Trade Agreement (NAFTA), the Central American Free Trade Agreement (CAFTA), MERCOSUR, and the Free Trade Agreement of the Americas (FTAA), this definition of Latin America assumed a transnational field uninterrupted by national borders or loyalties. Positioning itself in regional terms allowed the project to speak of free flows of knowledge, capital, and innovation between Latin America and the United States in a way that elided the role that diverse national, class, or ethnic distinctions might play in structuring those flows. The gaping "digital divide" between the United States and Latin America was the only real border that mattered here. And, contrary to previous formulations of pan–Latin American solidarity, that divide symbolized less of a geopolitical boundary than an obstacle to the market.

The production of a collective Latin American homeland for this project, then, was not significant simply for the way that it brought into view new development actors and remapped borders; it was also significant for what it erased—namely, states and private industry. This project's framing of postnational development possibilities worked to elide the ongoing involvement of states and also the profit potential of expanding Latin American markets for ICT products. Even as this project highlighted the ostensive withdrawal of the state from the realm of development, the fact that this event was sponsored by the United Nations—the official international organization of nation-states—and supported by Latin American state representatives demonstrated the ongoing agency and influence of the state in shaping neoliberal development strategies. By mobilizing new types of development subjects—Latino elites—Latin American states sought to bridge not only a technology gap between North and Central/South America, but also the gap in national development left by neoliberal economic policies.

This shift represents a concrete example of what Caglar has called the "rescaling" of state activity. Organizationally, this process refers to the transformation from a rigid bureaucratic hierarchy to "situational ties that work through emergent spaces of regionalism and zones" (2006:11). Operationally, this rescaling translates into institutionally and geographically differentiated forms of state intervention and activity that disrupt the illusion of a homogeneous, unified state actor or space. Especially in the context of regional free trade and the cross-border flows of people, commodities, and capital that define it, states thus play an important role in establishing new patterns of uneven spatial development in their efforts to enhance the competitiveness of specific "zones" (2006:11). In the case of transnational development projects described in the previous chapter, this kind of state rescaling included local government management of migrant investments procured through community-to-community private development initiatives. As a result of this state repositioning, remittance-rich, well-organized municipalities could attract more capital and reproduce their relative economic wealth compared to poorer neighbors, thus fostering uneven processes of development across the national landscape (Elton 2006). In the case of the Digital Diaspora, rescaling could be seen in the recruitment of pan-Latino professionals, who need not be migrant-citizens of one's own nation in order to support regional development. It was also evident in the collaborative relations established with multinational partners such as Verizon or Microsoft to create regional zones of connectivity, rather than national communications infrastructure. These characteristics of state rescaling sought to make development the business of individuals and the market, rather than a national project of the state. Therefore, postnational, privatized, and market-based development initiatives like the Digital Diaspora accentuated the new managerial function of the state and its diffuse manifestations within development practice.

The ongoing presence of states within diasporic development initiatives was actively and somewhat ironically made clear at the end of the first part of the inaugural event. At noon, the event's transition from the plenary meeting to group roundtables was expedited due to the imminent arrival of President George Bush at the United Nations. Project organizers abruptly ended the panel presentations still in process and quickly shepherded us upstairs ahead of schedule. The sudden change in plan, our hosts explained, was to avoid being quarantined in the plenary hall for an extended period while President Bush and his security entourage passed through the building. This logistical dilemma provided a poignant, if somewhat comical, reminder that rather than replacing the state, transnational diasporic development efforts were designed to complement the neoliberal state's more mobile, flexible character, even following in its footsteps.

While the above explains the neoliberal premises behind the project, what remains to be explained is how this reformulation of development as a moral and regional diasporic project resonated with the extremely heterogeneous constituency recruited for the Digital Diaspora project. Who constituted the elusive Latino "us" that was personally responsible for the region? And how would this project inspire them to social action? In the following section, I return to the Digital Diaspora inaugural event to explore the contradictions that emerged from the identity politics proposed by this project.

Locating Latinos

One of the central problems with the Digital Diaspora project was its effort to mobilize a particular configuration of ethnic identity borne of cultural politics in the United States for the purpose of global capital development. Framing "Latino" in this way ignored the importance of class and race relations in the United States as an important means of structuring what it means to be Latino.[19] It also ignored the ongoing importance of national identity and local community as the most salient forms of belonging within diasporic configurations.[20] Therefore, by employing "Latino" to classify a very heterogeneous group of professionals (who may or may not have identified with that term) and to recruit their development participation in Latin America, the Digital Diaspora project erased the complex, situated, and highly politicized nature of Latino identity in favor of working with what organizers saw as a coherent, essentialized cultural identity and, thus, consumer market constituted by an organic relationship to Latin America. More snapshots from the conference demonstrate why.

For the second half of the inaugural event, all of the nearly two hundred participants were to begin collective work on actual case studies and program planning. In an elegant dining room overlooking downtown New York City, we took our seats around tables of approximately ten seats, each marked with a name tag. The tables were organized to facilitate interaction among a variety of participant types for a lunch breakout session. Dining somewhat hurriedly on chicken, we were put to work according to explicit instructions:

> The vision for this session is to offer the participants a glimpse of some of the ground-breaking ways technology is currently being deployed to address education, gender and entrepreneurship issues in Latin America and the Caribbean. Then to generate a discussion around a needs assessment for the cases . . . , resources available . . . and an action plan for implementing solutions. (Conference handout)

To my mind, the interesting part of this assignment was the following injunction, which immediately brought the problem of identity to the fore:

> Since the meeting's attendees come from a diverse background of cultures, education, and professional experience, this session should offer innovative and

fresh perspectives on development and the role *we can all play* in this revolutionary age of information technology. . . . We hope this will act as a catalyst for people to begin to brainstorm ways *they* can contribute whether it is creating a mentorship program, social venture fund, information databases, in-kind donation clearing facility, etc. The result of the session should be a list of ideas of how *this diaspora community* can contribute to the advancement of Latin America and the Caribbean. (Conference handout; emphasis added)

The noted diversity of attendees was immediately evident at my table, where I was joined by venture capitalists, Web designers, another university professor, a technology industry researcher, a nonprofit organizer, and a representative from the Organization of American States. In addition to its professional variety, the group also represented a range of ethnic identities, including African American, South Asian, European American, and two self-identified Latinos— myself and a Colombia-born, U.S.-educated lawyer/technocrat. Immediately, therefore, the way the instructions were worded created some confusion. About whom were we speaking? For whom were we planning? What role were "we" supposed to play in this process? This confusion necessarily structured the kinds of responses we had to the case studies we reviewed. As we discussed possible recommendations for how to expand inner-city Internet kiosks in Rio de Janeiro or women's handicrafts enterprises in rural Mexico, we found ourselves asking questions about the *kind* of Latino diaspora to which these projects might be connected. Were we talking about communities comprised of working-class circuit migrants? Professional networks composed solely of expatriates or also including second- or third-generation Chicano/Latinos? Did all of these constituencies constitute part of one Latino diaspora or many diasporas?

The problem of how to define the Latino diaspora continued to manifest itself during the remainder of the Digital Diaspora event. As the various working groups came together after lunch to share results of their interactions and brainstorm next steps, it was clear that little in the way of concrete recommendations had resulted from the breakout session. If anything, the groups' efforts seemed to have generated more questions than answers. For example, the leaders acknowledged the difficulty their groups had had in effectively debating these issues and the ultimate impossibility of producing a formal policy statement at this juncture. Individual conference participants reiterated their confusion about who the main patrons and beneficiaries of these projects would be and how they were positioned within a larger transnational Latino community.

Furthermore, they questioned how the recruitment of information technology to these development projects would address diverse development needs. As one group representative noted, "Where are the grassroots groups to speak to their needs?" Her intervention acknowledged that, even if this conference were to effectively represent the professional end of the Latino diaspora (which clearly it had not), no true analysis of the diaspora could be performed without a perspective from the other end of the transnational community spectrum. Apparently, the heart of the Latino diaspora lay elsewhere.

Badshah moved to wrap up the meeting by noting the selection of an advisory board to see the project through to the next step.[21] The newly appointed board included a majority of Latinos (mostly executives with communications and investment firms), as well as non-Latino representatives from the technology industry. Heading up that board was to be George González, a Latino entrepreneur from the southwestern United States with a history of executive positions within the entertainment industry and the business world in addition to his current role as partner in a Latino communications consulting firm that advises Fortune 500 companies on identifying sustainable and profitable market opportunities for the private sector in emerging Latin American markets and helping structure those partnerships. González's entrepreneurial background was paired with ties to Washington through his previous position as a liaison to the U.S. Department of Commerce. One of the chief selling points of González's selection as head of the board was his leadership role in organizing the communication industry's "premier" conferences. On the surface these experiences and affiliations appeared to mark González as an appropriate choice; after all, his prominence within Latin media and marketing identified him as part of the most influential forces within the Latino business community.[22] Furthermore, like Badshah, he represented an actor embedded in diverse networks with cross-sectoral expertise. Nonetheless, his selection brought to the fore some of the central tensions over Latino identity and diaspora that this project encountered.

For instance, despite González's important connections to the U.S. government and the Latino business community, his apparent lack of connections with Latin American states and grassroots communities would, according to some, prove to be an important obstacle to the project's future progress. González's activism on the part of the U.S. Latino community—including a "No Latino left behind" campaign—had primarily been oriented toward influencing U.S. state policy rather than on grassroots innovations in Latin America. In many ways, this work had been focused on closing a different "digital divide" than the one highlighted by this project—namely, a technology gap between ethnic and class groups within the United States. Furthermore, his work in Latin America had been focused on helping U.S. companies exploit new international markets. Consequently, while he was the only one to present himself as the "champion" of the Latin America Digital Diaspora project, his own Latino identity and politics represented a very different relationship to Latin America than the one the project assumed.[23]

At the end of the event, Badshah got up to deliver a final compelling plea to all of the conference attendees to essentially dig into their pocketbooks and begin the work necessary to get this project off the ground. The goal at this point was to set up a social venture fund to support the development of entrepreneurial activities that use ICT. Badshah noted that at the Africa Diaspora inauguration, once one person wrote a check, others came forward until there were start-up funds for the Web portal.[24] An awkward silence and uncomfortable physical squirming followed Badshah's appeals here. No one jumped up from the group to publicly write that first check. It was as if everyone assumed that he was speaking to someone else; and in some ways that was exactly true. Nobody felt implicated by the kind of personal, moral obligation that Badshah and the other leaders hoped to instill. One might say that the gaping divide here was cultural rather than technological.

In the year that followed the inaugural event, the Digital Diaspora dissipated rather than developed. Within six months, plans for a second conference in Mexico City were shelved indefinitely and the project website produced none of the promised social networking tools or announcements of new proposals.[25] When I made contact with some of the project's founders at Digital Partners in 2004, I was told that the project had, for all intents and purposes, been abandoned. Badshah had left Digital Partners to work with Microsoft, and Digital Partners had itself become a part of the Grameen Bank, thus removing an important organizational force behind the Diaspora project. The UN had failed to step up to sponsor further project goals, as had been hoped, and given the lack of individual donations at the inauguration, the initiative was left with no material base. Finally, some of the participants involved had reportedly taken up diasporic development projects with their own countries of origin in place of continuing to pursue development for Latin America as a whole.

Building on the Digital Diaspora experience, diasporic development strategies that have emerged in its wake have tended to privilege country-specific initiatives. The Diaspora Knowledge Networks projects started in 2005 by UNESCO reflects one example of this second-generation enterprise. Like the Digital Diaspora initiatives before them, these projects have sought to tap into the technical and practical business experience of expatriate professionals by providing public and private spaces online for networking, with the assumption that these interactions would lead to the articulation of concrete development projects (see also Larner 2007). However, reflecting the lessons learned from the Digital Diaspora for Latin America, these projects have worked from the ground up, identifying professionals who were "successfully integrated into the working world of a receiving country" and who also maintained a "commitment to work for the well-being of their country of origin" (UNESCO n.d.). I will return to the Digital Knowledge Networks (DKN) projects in Chapter Six to discuss how they have used diaspora networks to manage knowledge and to structure knowing organizations.

Deconstructing the Diaspora

The Digital Diaspora inaugural event reveals important tensions within this project's efforts to mobilize Latino identity for transnational technology-based development strategies. These tensions emerged from erroneous assumptions about who Latinos are and how they are, or are not, connected to Latin America. On the one hand, a lack of critical reflection on the part of project organizers and UN sponsors might explain why the Digital Diaspora project failed to connect with the Latino community that it had hoped to recruit; however, rather than simply cultural blunders, these equivocations also reveal salient dynamics of transnational development strategies more generally. Principally, despite the emphasis on bottom-up, participatory, local strategies as the centerpiece of neoliberal development practice, this project demonstrated the important role that states, corporations, and multilateral institutions played in defining ethnic difference. It also illustrates how their efforts were shaped by neoliberal principles of individual responsibility, social enterprise, and postnational economic integration.

The Diaspora project framed Latino identity as a diasporic byproduct of Latin America, imagined as a singular cultural and economic entity institutionalized in the global market.[26] This erroneous understanding of Latino identity was, in many ways, the product of U.S. media constructions that have repeatedly invoked *Latinidad* as a generic, cultural formation consolidated through Spanish language that could serve as the basis for a coherent consumer base.[27]

This construction pivots on the notion of a Latin monoculture that transcends ethnic, class, national, or racial background, as well as North-South political borders. Latin America, conceptualized as a unified postnational space characterized by cultural homogeneity, market integration, and technological underdevelopment provided project organizers with what appeared to be a potent justification for cultivating moral and material linkages between U.S.-based Latino elites and their brethren back home in Latin America. The Digital Diaspora project hoped to harness this perceived Latino monoculture as the basis for regional development.

While Latino identity is certainly forged in conversation with Latin America, thinking of it only in terms of those geographical roots misses the historical contentiousness and subversiveness of this identity.[28] The Latino concept embodies a long historical conversation about a politically and culturally unified Latin America; however, as taken up by Bolívar, Martí, and Guevara, that conversation has reflected a pointedly anticolonial and anti-imperial project. In many ways echoing this emancipatory, postcolonial discourse, Latino identity politics in the United States reflects an explicit effort to create cultural citizenship for Latinos as a subaltern population in the United States.[29] "Latino" is, thus, a U.S. invention rather than some natural, preexisting regional category. As Eduardo Mendieta (1998:47) has poignantly commented, "For us, 'Hispanic' and 'Latino' are not a fate but a quest, a choice, even an alternative. . . . We learn to think of ourselves through these imposed categories." The affirmation of Latino identity is, therefore, part of a cultural politics that has sought to construct the terms of the Latino community's own identity in an inclusive way (rather than having it defined for them in a pejorative way) that integrates various racial, national-origin, and language groups. Consequently, Latino identity has emerged out of a struggle for social, political, and economic equality without assimilation to a dominant U.S. culture or homogenization into a singular Hispanic identity (Rosaldo 1994:57; Flores and Benmayor 1996:15).

Ironically, because of their class status, the Latino professionals recruited to this project were not the kind who would necessarily identify with this kind of subaltern identity. The IndUS Entrepreneurs South Asian technology professionals—described at the beginning of the chapter as the prototype for the Digital Diaspora project—provided one example of how national identity can be cultivated through professional class status abroad and then harnessed to provide a powerful transnational development platform. Yet, in the case of the Latino professionals, professional class status in the United States has provoked some diverse identifications. On the one hand, middle- and upper-middle-class Latinos have tended to embrace the term "Hispanic" to a greater degree than "Latino," a move associated with a more assimilationist and politically conservative identity in the United States (Alcoff 2005:395; Waterston 2006). On the other hand, upper-class, cosmopolitan professionals have tended, at least in some cultural spheres, to reinforce national identity as a way of distinguishing themselves from ethnic minority status within the United States (Dávila 1999:188–89). As an example of this latter tendency, after presenting an earlier version of this chapter at an academic conference, a member of the audience approached me to discuss my work. She noted that her father—a Mexican professional living and working in Silicon Valley—would never identify as a Latino but rather would always identify himself to his North American counterparts as a Mexican national. In his case, class status structured the choice for nationalist, rather than ethnic, identification. Therefore, it is not clear that Digital Diaspora organizers could have captured the kind of professionals they hoped through the rubric of a Latino diaspora in the first place. Indeed, many of the project's assumptions about what defined the Latino diaspora seem to have derived from perceptions of an essentialized migrant subject with very different class and ethnic identifications (see Chapter Three).

Another contradiction in the Digital Diaspora's formulation of Latino identity is evident in the kinds of transnational linkages it imagined as essential to this diasporic community. The fact that Latino identity emerged as a product of U.S. identity politics certainly does not diminish what are for many Latinos deeply felt and regularly reproduced connections to family and community in Latin America. Indeed, those intense forms of belonging often motivate and structure ongoing translocal connections with migrants' places of origin. However, the assumption of diasporic connections as an essential feature of Latino identity ignores the varied circumstances that prompted peoples' migration in the first place (for example, fleeing political persecution or civil war versus seeking economic opportunity) and that produce diverse relationships to migrants' place of origin in the present. Additionally, it ignores the vast differences in the sociopolitical circumstances in which migrants find themselves within the United States (Waldinger, Popkin, and Aquiles Magana 2007). As Glick-Schiller, Caglar, and Guldbrandsen (2006:614) have argued, the overriding focus on ethnic communities within studies of transnationalism has obscured the various other configurations of social networks in which migrants participate "that include but are not limited to ethnic pathways." Therefore, the

Digital Diaspora project efforts to promote a regional, postnational development solution necessarily elided the heterogeneity of Latino identity and the
diverse relationships to Latin America it reflected.

Joining both aspects of this analysis, we can see that Latinos' connections
to local and/or national communities outside the United States did not ensure their automatic identification with a broader pan-ethnic Latino diaspora
within the United States, and might even have worked against it. In many ways,
the consolidation of "Latino" as a cogent cultural and political identity within
the United States remains tenuous as a result of the resilience of those same
translocal identifications and obligations, as well as the diverse class positions
along which they are stratified.[30] While some scholars are optimistic about the
possibilities for increasing affiliation with a pan-ethnic Latino identity and its
potential political impact, others are more skeptical about the possibility of
transcending these differences.[31] As Dávila (2001:8–9) notes:

> The homogenization of a heterogeneous population into a single "Latino" mar-
> ket, for instance, while increasing the visibility of Latino populations coincides
> with larger processes of partial containment and recognition of ethnic differ-
> ences that are at play in other spheres of contemporary U.S. society, such as
> political and social and cultural policies; in fact, it is an intrinsic component of
> such processes.

Therefore, locating the Latino ethnic entrepreneur turned out to be a much
more challenging and potentially fraught prospect than the Digital Diaspora
organizers had imagined.

Through its effort to capture and mobilize expatriate elites as vital stakeholders in transnational development, the Digital Diaspora project illustrates
the new forms of subject formation and transnational governance instituted
by neoliberal development strategies. On the surface, the project would seem
to evidence the diminution of state power as the authoritative agent of international development policy; however, the Digital Diaspora's attempts to
recruit diasporic elites to the task of development under the banner of their assumed ethnic affinities demonstrate states' ongoing interest and rescaled activity in translocal development practice. In this way, the initiative mirrors other
diaspora strategies described by Larner (2007:342), in which "Internationally
mobile individuals are actively articulating themselves to state processes, and
in turn both they and state processes are being rearticulated." Therefore, when
we imagine the recruitment process that this entailed, we can imagine the "*mi*

hermano!" appeal coming not so much from Latin American grassroots communities calling their Latino brethren home, as from state technocrats hoping to entreat their fellow-class peers to bridge the gap not only between North and South, but also between public and private development responsibilities.

The Digital Diaspora project has illustrated how new institutional development strategies have connected states, multinational corporations, and Latino professionals as partners in regional development efforts. In the next chapter, I explore an emergent collaborative enterprise between CDRO, in Guatemala, and Walmart, to examine the search for more profitable means of reproducing the ethnic community in the context of regional free trade. In doing so, I highlight convergences between corporate ethics and ethnic community practice as these processes come together in the space of development.

5 Welcome to Walmart!

Corn and the New Community Business Model

SOOTHING PIANO MUSIC PLAYS as the scene opens onto a woman soaking in a large sunken bathtub situated in the middle of a modern, smartly decorated bathroom. The fair-complexioned, slender woman with her hair pulled back in a bun reclines deep in the soapsuds with her eyes closed, beaming in a state of indulgent repose. As the relaxing music continues, the woman sits up and reaches over to a product located on the tub rim; the camera zooms in on a small, crème-colored, cosmetic container, on which only the brand name MABELI is visible. The woman brings the open container to her face and inhales deeply the scent of the product, smiling with obvious delight. She then proceeds to languorously apply the product to her arms and legs in a slow show of sensual pleasure. As the camera recedes, she lounges back into the tub, rests her head back on the rim, and sinks into a blissful state of relaxation. The background shifts to a botanical frame, filled with aloe and fern leaves over which the brand name MABELI is superimposed.

The promotional video described above was produced by Guatemala's National Competitiveness Program (PRONACOM) as part of a series showcasing domestic "Examples of Competitiveness" in 2005. Ostensibly geared toward both aspiring entrepreneurs and potential investors, the video moves from this picturesque opening to present a young indigenous woman, Lesbia Taló, the general manager of the cosmetics company MABELI. Over the course of the video, Taló (clearly distinguished from the woman in the opening scene by her use of indigenous *traje*, or traditional clothing) and a cast of other K'iche' community residents of Totonicapán proceed to tell the story behind MABELI. From their positions as native healers or agricultural producers, these community members describe how indigenous appreciation of the natural world and the healing properties of native plants can provide both an effective product for consumers, as well as a powerful source of rural development.

The MABELI line of products, I was surprised to discover during my 2006 visit to Totonicapán, was one of CDRO's newest projects. In many ways this project was indicative of CDRO's growth from a nascent community institution to a preeminent indigenous development enterprise, lauded by the Guatemalan state and foreign donors alike for its innovative efforts to operationalize Maya culture as a tool for development (see Chapter Two). Nonetheless, the new venture immediately raised questions about whether MABELI was a culmination of CDRO's longtime efforts, or a new strategy entirely. As administrator after administrator told me, CDRO had signed a contract with Walmart to globally distribute this exclusive line of spa cosmetic products that the CDRO communities had developed (see Figure 5.1). What is more, CDRO's director mentioned nonchalantly, in contrast to its earlier development efforts CDRO had decided not to advertise these products as indigenous in origin or as tied to a particular ethnic development initiative. This decision was based on market research that demonstrated that the source of the product did not matter to the product's prospective global consumer base; what mattered, instead, were

Figure 5.1 MABELI's Spa Products. Moisturizing Lotion inspired by "The purity of the forest" (*pureza del bosque*). Source: MABELI. Printed with permission.

the particular organic properties the cosmetics were to embody and the way those properties spoke to specific consumer lifestyles.

CDRO's spa cosmetic enterprise was not remarkable because it was CDRO's first commercial initiative nor because it reflected a radical departure from the historical modes of production that have defined Totonicapán's regional economy. Instead, it built on CDRO's innovative history of market-oriented development strategies, as well as a long tradition of petty commerce within these indigenous communities. Nonetheless, this strategy did displace the central role of commercial enterprise and household corn production as the joint material foundations of ethnic identity. Therefore, what was unique about this current initiative was the way it reflected an important shift in how ethnic cultural difference and the place of corn articulated as the centerpieces of community development strategy. As such, it represents yet another instance and configuration of the ethnic entrepreneur as an agent of local development.

This chapter thus seeks to illuminate how shifts in the commodity landscape have provoked new deployments of ethnic difference that sought to distance themselves from past efforts to package that difference as a marketing strategy. In particular, it tracks the transition from internationally sanctioned development strategies, which fetishized authentic ethnic difference as a privileged resource for development, to CDRO's Walmart initiative, which emphasizes the fungibility of new forms of ethnic subjects and products. This shift is rooted in a reconceptualization of community development as an entrepreneurial venture oriented toward the production of cosmopolitan, *nonethnically marked* commodities for the global marketplace. CDRO's experience thus showcases a turn to "value-added," universally recognized niche products as a means of relocating the rural ethnic community within the new regional free trade economy and its corresponding human, capital, and commodity flows. That turn brings into focus convergences between CDRO's corporate development model and other emergent forms of obligation and specificity in global economic life.

Enterprising Ethnicity

For CDRO, development has always been about translating indigenous knowledge and community practices into cultural revitalization, political empowerment, and economic profits. As described in Chapter Two, when the organization was formed by a group of indigenous community activists during the early 1980s, its goal was to operationalize Maya culture into a tangible resource for development. Specifically, the founding members elaborated a methodology for development that both reflected and built upon the rural community lifestyle its residents embodied. This lifestyle was characterized by high levels of poverty and illiteracy, as well as a long history of commercial production for regional markets. This lifestyle also involved the maintenance of visible markers of local K'iche' identity, such as women's use of traditional clothing, K'iche' language use, and household corn production, among other things. Drawing on the historically rooted cultural norms represented by the K'iche' *pop*, or "woven mat," image—that is, a universal, interwoven, egalitarian social fabric—CDRO sought to enable local, participative, and self-sustaining development processes. Yet it also actively sought engagement with the global market, in ways that I describe below.

Over the next two decades, CDRO's initiative quickly took hold, evolving into an impressive network of community councils held together by a sophisticated organizational system, a successful set of targeted programs (health, infrastructure, women's issues, and so on), and a well-developed local banking system. Especially during the late 1990s—when the Guatemalan state was struggling to resolve the thirty-year civil conflict and comply with international lending institution guidelines for more efficient governance, and international donors were interested in supporting indigenous, community-based initiatives—CDRO's program offered a development solution that was attractive to everyone.

The creation of an exclusive spa product was, therefore, simply the newest in a long line of CDRO's local development experiments. First, there was Totofrutas, a line of natural jams produced by a women's cooperative from CDRO affiliate communities. That initiative mobilized women's entrepreneurial skills and fruit products from the community to produce an explicitly ethnic item for consumption. The very label of the jam indicated both the place of origin (Totonicapán) and the fact that the jam was produced by a Maya women's cooperative. This formulation positioned both the jam and its female manufacturers as local goods rooted in a tradition of agricultural and cultural production. Over time, unfortunately, the initiative fell apart due to poor internal organization, inefficient production methods, and high overhead costs.

In the late 1990s, CDRO developed a traditional medicine production facility in an effort to cultivate native plants renowned for their cultural and medicinal applications. The organization leased a piece of land and built a modern processing plant to technically transform these goods into rationalized products for local and international sale. While the advertised efficacy of these medicinal products was in part attributed to the modern, sanitary production process from which they were rendered, the medicines were prominently marked as local products whose healing properties and economic value were authenticated by their place in a traditional indigenous healing repertoire. Despite its local popularity, this line of products failed to meet international food and drug standards and was thus unable to achieve its international export aspirations.

As these early experiments suggest, commercial production for the market was nothing new for these communities. In fact, both of CDRO's prior enterprises built upon Totonicapán's long history of petty commerce and participation in regional markets—a history characterized by both a strong tradition of ethnic community solidarity and high levels of community stratification (see Chapter Two) (see Figure 5.2).[1] Smith (1990a:210), for example, described how, in the late 1970s, a fair number of households "could be considered 'petty capitalist' in that they hired wage labor regularly in order to produce commodities for sale in a market with the aim of enlarging their enterprises." Interestingly, however, local entrepreneurs insisted on hiring community peers for all commercial labor needs, rather than drawing on labor from outside of the community, even though that "outside" labor may have been less expensive. While this practice did not diminish inequalities among community members—in

Figure 5.2 Totonicapán's commercial center. Source: Author, 1998.

fact, it built upon long-entrenched and well-recognized material differences—
it did perform the important role of naturalizing commercial production as a
central tenet of indigenous community social and economic life. Furthermore,
it reproduced a philosophy of cultural unity relative to nonethnic others, and
that philosophy worked to sustain the moral and territorial boundaries of the
rural community.[2] Consequently, participation in the market has been central
to reproducing both class and ethnic differences in this region.

People of Corn

This long history of petty commerce within the K'iche' communities has generally complemented a rural Maya way of life centrally grounded in milpa—the
household production of maize that operates as the symbolic and substantive
staple of Maya cultural community life (see Fischer and Benson 2006; Figure 5.3). The Maya are credited with domesticating corn and, since precolonial
times, they have considered growing corn to be a sacred duty. The intimate link
between Maya identity and corn was made explicit in such Maya origin stories
as the sacred text, *Popol Vuh*,[3] which designates the Maya as *hombres de maiz*, or
people of corn. According to this text, the first Mayan people were made of corn
dough, and corn thus symbolizes "the spirit of creation" (Montejo 2005:47):
"The yellowness of humanity came to be when they were made. . . . Their flesh

Figure 5.3 Reimagining the milpa. Source: Author, 1998.

was merely yellow ears of maize and white ears of maize. Mere food were the legs and arms of humanity, of our first fathers" (Christensen 2007:195). Consequently, corn production has operated as the principle terrain for the production of ethnic forms of personhood and place, even as it has long been coupled with commercial enterprises in the market.

Nonetheless, the cultural and economic meaning of corn has been subject to important recent changes. For example, during a much-publicized stop on George Bush's 2007 tour of Latin America, the then-U.S. president loaded crates of lettuce and presented a brief speech at an indigenous agricultural cooperative near Tecpán, Guatemala. The cooperative provided a strategic backdrop for the president's visit because it reflected a successful vegetable-export business that, building on USAID seed money, was now marketing its produce to Walmart Central America. Bush singled out Mariano Canu, one of the cooperative's founders, as an example of how U.S.-backed trade could help better the lives of the poor. Describing his livelihood to reporters, Canu noted that he still maintains the Maya tradition of planting corn for his subsistence and of caring for the earth in accordance with Maya cosmology but added, "you can't get by on corn alone."

Importantly, Canu's representations locate a Maya ethnic identity in continued corn production; yet Canu simultaneously seeks to reproduce the value of that lifestyle through economic enterpreneurism.[4] Throughout this book, I have used the term *ethnic entrepreneur* to describe how agents like Canu and CDRO have reconfigured and mobilized ethnic cultural difference as a productive development resource deployed alternately to complement and contest the place of ethnic actors and communities within a changing regional political economy. Specifically, I have argued that these ethnic actors accrued new value through their ability to translate rural indigenous culture, with its assumed communal, participatory, sustainable, and egalitarian character, into social and economic forms that had value in the development industry vis-à-vis their resonance with neoliberal norms of decentralization, privatization, and entrepreneurialism. In other words, it was exactly CDRO's ethnic identity, and the subject forms and material practices that this identity was assumed to encompass, that was validated by the international development industry as an exemplary form of development methodology. Importantly, this form relied specifically on externalized projections of authentic ethnic difference (such as the *pop*) and their deployment in local markets as their source of value.

CDRO's new spa line, however, draws our attention to shifting articulations of ethnic difference within the regional free trade economy; as such, it reflects changing configurations of entrepreneurism and ethnic difference for development. Instead of seeking to mobilize ethnic difference as the cornerstone of new commercial initiatives that bear explicit marks of their indigenous origins, CDRO's spa products sought to professionalize and maximize the organization's entrepreneurial potential as a way of sustaining indigenous community life (see also Comaroff and Comaroff 2009). This strategy displaced the central role of corn in the production of Maya subjects and sought instead to ensure a material base for the reproduction of ethnic selves through commensurability in the global marketplace. While the shift appears to be a stark one, I argue that this new development strategy does not reflect radical shifts in the underlying forms of personhood and place that inform it; instead, the territorial space of community continues to be the moral ground for the production of ethnic subjects, even as that community identity is rearticulated in the production process. Nonetheless, like the Digital Diaspora project before it (Chapter Four), CDRO's efforts highlight important convergences between the ethnic entrepreneur and global practices of corporate responsibility and social entrepreneurship that wed collective forms of social obligation and economic profit seeking in the market.

Expanding Commodity Landscapes

Global corn markets have changed dramatically over the last decade, and these changes have produced important effects on rural community livelihoods and ethnic identity in much of Mesoamerica. Beginning in 1994 with the inauguration of the North American Free Trade Alliance (NAFTA) and continuing through the 2005 ratification of the Central American Free Trade Agreement (CAFTA-DR), regional free trade has come to define the economic landscape in which CDRO and its community affiliates operate.

Therefore, while corn plays a starring role as a global food and energy source (Pollan 2006), it has become an increasingly fallow enterprise for indigenous community members. CDRO's decision to partner with Walmart must be seen in terms of these important changes in the global corn market, and in terms of Maya communities' growing need to procure cash to buy ever-more-expensive foreign corn rather than produce it at home. This new reality has thus accounted for important shifts in the way ethnic difference was packaged and circulated within the global market as a development good, as well as for the way CDRO's members sought to reproduce the ethnic community.

The 1994 implementation of NAFTA between the United States and Mexico provoked extreme disturbances in Mexico's rural agricultural sector, especially in the field of small-scale corn production. Inexpensive American corn, buttressed by major farm subsidies, flooded the local market and produced a 70 percent decline in the value of local corn and the subsequent dislocation of many rural small-scale farmers. Tellingly, while by 2005 the area of corn harvested had expanded and the productivity had risen, the number of corn farmers in Mexico had declined (Office of the United States Trade Representative 2005). Moreover, complaints by local farmers exposed the fact that NAFTA-imported corn introduced genetically modified breeds of corn into the local landscape. Consequently, the corn production that did continue does so under the threat of invasion by genetically modified corn strains that destroy local crops (see Ross 2004). Therefore, for many Mexican farmers, NAFTA signaled an end to local corn production, a rise in tortilla prices, and a significant threat to the country's food and biosecurity, all of which had an important impact on rural community identities.

Negotiators for the next generation of regional free trade agreements—CAFTA—took these lessons from the Mexican case to heart. In Guatemala and El Salvador, this meant campaigning for special protections for "sensitive commodities" like white and yellow corn, which are often produced by subsistence farmers and serve as a staple of domestic consumption.[5] These efforts procured some concessions from regional free trade policies, ensuring a gradual rollback of quotas on these products over the course of fifteen years. Even with this compromise, U.S. grain exports to the region were expected to increase substantially (Jurenas 2006:10).[6] For this reason, one study noted that "The National Corn Growers Association (NCGA) viewed the DR-CAFTA as creating new export opportunities for U.S. corn farmers and locking in the current U.S. market share in the region. It expects the agreement to stimulate U.S. exports of corn co-products" (Jurenas 2006:14). Furthermore, World Bank experts acknowledged that CAFTA member states "would, in the aggregate, gain little from this agreement . . . since almost all exports to the U.S. market would continue to benefit from duty-free access that they already receive under U.S. trade preference programs" (Jurenas 2006:23).

More than simply enhancing the market share of North American corn growers, CAFTA's new regional free trade alliance created new vulnerability for Central American small farmers. Studies of Guatemala, in particular, showed that CAFTA would have negative impacts on households designated as net corn producers, with more positive outcomes in the form of lower prices accruing only to net corn-consuming households (Jaramillo and Lederman 2005:133; see also Barraud and Calfat 2006). Indeed, some forecasts issued a more force-ful warning: "With more than 60 per cent of the low mean vulnerable rural households predicted to be negatively affected by CAFTA, strong attention needs to be directed at the area. The two crops which probably need the most attention are maize and bovine meat" (Portner 2003).

From the beginning, therefore, the new regional trade reality was struc-tured to offer "significant market opportunities" for U.S. producers over the long run, with the biggest costs being born by small farmers. True to this di-agnosis, since its inception CAFTA has ushered in a rise of U.S. agricultural products (including corn byproducts), a tripling of U.S. foreign investment (Murphy 2007:1), and a transition to nontraditional export agriculture. These changes have negatively impacted the Guatemalan food economy, with house-hold corn farmers, such as those associated with CDRO in Totonicapán, espe-cially hard hit.

The more recent focus on corn within the global biofuel and food crisis has further reshaped the tenuous economic landscape in which Mayan farmers are operating. Specifically, farmers experienced an increase in cheap corn im-ports in the first years of CAFTA, followed by a sharp decline in those imports and a correspondent rise in prices in 2008 (see Foreign Agricultural Service 2007). According to a report conducted by the World Bank in 2008, global food prices were driven up as much as 75 percent by the diversion of grains away from food for fuel, "with over a third of US corn now used to produce ethanol" (Chakrabortty 2008). When asked whether U.S. corn production was contrib-uting to the crisis, U.S. Secretary of Agriculture Ed Schafer noted:

> We have done such amazing things in increasing yields in this country that while our ethanol process is taking up some percentage of the corn production, at the same time, *we're increasing our exports of corn . . . We're increasing all the traditional markets for corn, as well as putting [it in] ethanol.* (emphasis added)

Therefore, despite firm assurances about the increasing global market for corn, Maya farmers experienced an erratic and ultimately negative relation to corn imports in terms of their impact on local food markets (Rosenberg 2007). For local producers, increasing import volume made corn more difficult to sell in the regional market. For both producers and consumers, increasing prices made corn more expensive to buy. Together, these changes undermined rural

Maya residents' ability to rely on corn as the centerpiece of rural subsistence production and consumption.[7]

Household farmers' ability to adjust to these global market changes was exacerbated by growing local challenges to corn production as well. The unequal effects of regional trade arrangements were intensified by generations of progressive fragmentation of small farmsteads into plots too small to provide for full employment or to yield an income sufficient to sustain a minimal standard of living for a single household. What little cultivable land remained in this mountainous, heavily forested region has been increasingly degraded by the intense farming to which it has been subjected. Finally, local farmers complained that changing climatological conditions had made harvests even more unpredictable. Therefore, it has been the combined effect of local and global dynamics that is responsible for the notable ebb in both the physical and economic viability of corn as a household staple.

U.S. policymakers, like Schafer, see free trade agreements and corn's fate within them as a positive source of both U.S. domestic growth and development abroad. When asked about the implications of U.S. trade policy for global food production, Schafer replied that the goal was simply to have more countries reproduce North American production models:

> What we need to do globally is to help other nations increase their yields to match the United States. We need farm-to-market roads. We need water-system increases, hybrid crops, good animal husbandry. The increased demand across the world is higher and unless we make huge investments in productivity in countries that haven't done so in the past, then people are going to start going hungry. (Cited in Montagne 2008)

Proponents of free trade have reiterated a familiar modernization refrain in their assessment of these developments, envisioning small farmers' predicament less as a problem and more as a necessary step forward, or even opportunity.[8] John Murphy, vice president of International Affairs of the U.S. Chamber of Commerce and executive vice president of the Association of American Chambers of Commerce in Latin America, makes this point somewhat callously in his appraisal of CAFTA's effects two years on:

> It is critical to recall that subsistence agriculture is not a development strategy. No one in the salons of Washington should wax romantic about the hardscrabble life of these subsistence farmers . . . The path forward for Central American

or Dominican subsistence agriculture isn't to freeze their conditions in time. Their conditions are bad. The path forward is to present them with new opportunities. To that end, DR-CAFTA creates vast new markets for Central American farm goods. (Murphy 2007:5)

George W. Bush (2007) made this same case in describing his encounter with Maya agricultural producers, like Mariano Canu, after his Latin American tour:

> Laura and I were recently in Guatemala. We went to a small village and saw what can happen when markets are open for local entrepreneurs. In this case, we met some farmers who for years had struggled to survive, worked hard just to put food on the table for their families by growing corn and beans. That's all they were able to do. It's a hard way to make a living, growing corn and beans. When we negotiated the trade agreement called the CAFTA-DR, which opened up new markets for Guatemalan farmers, *the entrepreneurial spirit came forth.* There are entrepreneurs all over the world, if just given a chance, they can succeed. (emphasis added)

As these statements make clear, architects of regional free trade envisioned this new economic landscape as an emancipatory space for small farmers who they saw as shackled by subsistence production. Indeed, Bush's comment imbues indigenous rural subjects with latent entrepreneurial qualities that could serve to transform the territorial space of agricultural production into a site of lucrative economic value. In doing so, he echoes Digital Diaspora organizers who ascribed to Latino professionals the power to transform Latin America into a site of postnational social entrepreneurship (Chapter Four). Despite Guatemalan indigenous communities' long history of petty commerce and participation in the market, Bush's vision maps a changing economic environment wherein all development roads lead away from corn.

The Corporate Community

Businesses like Walmart have played an important facilitating role in this transition, bringing together new producers and consumers through retail outlet empires. As the largest grocery retailer in both the United States and Central America (Warner 2006; Walmart 2008a), Walmart definitely has a corner on the market, serving as the main arena through which Guatemalan producers find North American consumers. Indeed, in several new development initiatives Walmart has paired up with USAID, non-governmental organizations like Mercy Corps, and local grassroots organizations to help small-scale farmers "move from traditional corn and beans production to demand-driven production to supply major retailers like Walmart Central America" (Walmart 2008b). Walmart's expansive business vision and search for low prices has fueled and shaped these new initiatives; indeed, Central American agricultural markets constitute important vehicles of Walmart's campaign to expand its selection of inexpensive organic produce and other previously "niche" products (like Fair Trade coffee) to upper-class North American consumers. Walmart's efforts to support the transition from corn to nontraditional export crops can thus definitely be read as an effort to buttress the supply for nontraditional export crops. As Walmart's own promotional materials suggest:

> By offering funds, technical support and market information, we help the farmers grow high quality, competitively priced produce that can be sold at our stores or other retailers in the formal market place. Through these programs, we work with farmers around the country, generating income for hundreds of families and helping to improve overall quality of life in the region. (Walmart 2008a)

In this light, the incorporation of small-scale farmers into export agriculture is not so much development aid, as it is a form of investment. Accordingly, Walmart's Local Development director in Guatemala described CDRO's new spa cosmetics line as "an example to reproduce because its creators neither depend on nor hope for charity from the government, the international community, NGOs or a particular business" (cited in Ballasteros-Coronel 2006). This sentiment is echoed in the idea that the program "increases the likelihood that all actors—producers, buyers, distributors, and consumers—are winners" (Walmart 2008b). Therefore, while Walmart might be perceived as an exploitative behemoth by critics worldwide, it presented itself to organizations like CDRO as not only the obvious choice for new development opportunities in a post-CAFTA landscape, but also a socially responsible one, with the community's interests at heart.

CDRO's collaboration with Walmart thus serves as more than just an indicator of the challenges posed to ethnic community development by regional free trade or as a cautionary tale against exploitation by Walmart; instead, CDRO's new enterprise highlights important convergences between the formulation of ethnic entrepreneurism and other emerging configurations of trust, cooperation, and profit in global economic life. Particularly, they draw our attention to the fact that CDRO's corporate venture occurred at the same moment that Western-based multinational businesses had increasingly turned to a corporate responsibility model. In other words, just as we see CDRO eliding the ethnic particularity of its commodities and assuming the identity of a corporation in order to reproduce the ethnic community, we also see corporations like Walmart increasingly aligning themselves with community and invoking ethical norms such as social responsibility and citizenship in order to reproduce their economic enterprises. Slippages between corporate and ethnic projects thus highlight the entanglement of corporate forms, community morality, and profit-seeking activities in contemporary development practice. In this entanglement, I argue that we can see the emergence of a situated form of moral reasoning or "regime of living" that seeks to act as a "possible guide to action" (Collier and Lakoff 2005:23) in regard to the problem of development in the new CAFTA/NAFTA free trade global economy.

The notion that "companies should accompany the pursuit of profit with good citizenship" is a business management theory that, despite a long history, has gained increasing strength over the past decade (Sadler 2004:852). As companies have sought to neutralize mounting allegations of labor violations, environmental degradation, and other manifestations of the reckless pursuit of profit worldwide, many firms have touted a "triple bottom line" to highlight their attention to economic, social, and environmental concerns. Accordingly, corporate citizenship (CC), corporate social responsibility, social enterprise, and fair trade all represent diverse formulations of business theory and practice that attempt to reconcile social and economic concerns in order to make business more ethical and responsible, albeit while remaining profitable. Therefore, while companies have long engaged in philanthropic work *alongside* their profit-making ventures, what is different in these current formulations is that social responsibility is integrated into the actual profit-making activities in order to make them more sustainable over the long run. As such, social responsibility efforts evidence the "diffuse patterns of corporate community morality" (Sadler 2004:858) that have come to define corporate behavior in the context of transnational production and consumption chains.

North American and British experiences have served as leading global practices informing other regional efforts of corporate citizenship (Zadek 2001:32). Nonetheless, the meaning of corporate citizenship varies widely across regions and corporate types, highlighting different configurations of obligation and accountability within corporate management practice. In Latin America in particular, scholars have identified political democratization and anticorruption efforts, along with the increasing privatization and free trade orientation of Latin American economies as shaping the push for increasing transparency, accountability, and social investments on the part of businesses in the region (Puppim de Oliveira 2006:17; see also Schmidheiny 2006). We see examples of these reformulations of corporate social responsibility in debates over the compensation practices employed by pharmaceutical companies harvesting local knowledge and plant species from Mexico and the Amazonian regions (M. Brown 2003; Hayden 2003; Peterson 2001). The environmental and labor policies of extractive industries such as mining and oil have also been subject to critique and thus reform, both in terms of firm accountability to the local communities in which they work, as well as their production of sustainable, "clean" commodities for sale in the global market (Sawyer 2004). In these examples, "good" business is posited as simultaneously good for development and good for the environment, promoting mutual benefits for all.

The corporate turn toward an "ethics of stewardship" and "social responsibility" has, therefore, repositioned businesses as one of many invested entities— or stakeholders—in local development and, consequently, as positive agents of social, economic, and environmental change. As noted above, Walmart has certainly represented its work with Central American farmers in this way, and CDRO's willingness to work with Walmart further acknowledges the centrality of private-sector actors as necessary, if not desirable, development partners.[9] The participation of telecommunications corporations in the Digital Diaspora project that I described in Chapter Four provides another clear example of the emergent and often ambiguous role of the private sector as a moral, transnational development agent. In that project, telecommunications industry involvement was articulated in philanthropic and technical terms, despite clear recognition that expanding regional technology markets meant good business for corporate sponsors. Highlighting the contradiction (rather than complementarity) inherent in the coupling of corporate morality and profit seeking, geographer Sunley (1999:2199) notes:

> More radical interpretations of stakeholding have used the metaphor to argue for a thorough process of inclusive and participatory democratization throughout civil society and public institutions . . . At the same time, however, the business origins of the metaphor mean that it frequently carries assumptions and priorities which are incommensurate with these more radical calls and it

is doubtful that it provides a coherent framework for a more communitarian local economic development.

In essence, corporate citizenship here implies a process that "seeks to capture stakeholders' loyalty by ever more surgical interventions that align profitable opportunities with their social identities and underlying values" (Zadek 2001:29). Rather than a purely philanthropic gesture, then, corporate morality frameworks reflect the increasing pressure on businesses—by both regulators and diverse constituencies—to articulate a social conscience in order to maintain market shares. Given this drive for profit, corporate participation in development may work against collective projects of social justice and equitable development. The question in this particular case thus becomes: How does CDRO's corporate strategy converge with emergent forms of obligation practiced by business, and what does that convergence tell us about the way ethnic identity and entrepreneurism are coming together in the space of development in this contemporary moment?

The Community Business Model:
New Articulations of Identity and Community

CDRO's director imagined the new spa products not simply as an isolated source of profits, but rather as integrated facets of a new *modelo empresarial comunitario* (community business model). At its heart, this model sought to conserve local ecology, to increase economic income, and to ensure the cultural reproduction of the ethnic community over the long run. However, instead of accomplishing these goals through strategies used by other Maya communities—such as adopting nontraditional crops for export production or developing cottage industries that would deplete valuable local forest land—CDRO's model sought to cultivate sustainable, explicitly local resources in order to use them as a source of cash, rather than sustenance. Specifically, CDRO proposed that its community members replace household corn production with the cultivation of native plants like chamomile, thyme, rosemary, aloe, and spearmint that residents would sell to CDRO as primary ingredients for the natural spa products.

Perhaps more interesting than what was *inside* the new products, however, was what was on the outside. Unlike earlier CDRO products, these cosmetics would bear no visible signs of their ethnic origins, circulating and accruing value on the basis of their universal appeal and commensurability with similar niche products (see Figure 5.1). Furthermore, rather than just stakeholders in

community development, the business model repositioned indigenous participants as shareholders in a corporate business and cultural entity.[10] In what follows, I describe these aspects of the model and their effects on ethnic identity
and corporate community.

To establish the new business model, CDRO recruited foreign technical
and market expertise in the hopes of professionalizing its production process.
CDRO's first-generation medicinal products had been designed by a doctor,
based on the logic that a local doctor was the most appropriate expert to oversee
the production of indigenous medicinal products. For the MABELI cosmetic
line, however, CDRO brought in a team of experts from France and Germany to
consult on how to produce and market its new cosmetic products for international sale. Consultants from these firms conducted an ethnomedical/botanical
study, an agro-ecological technical study, and a market study to determine the
types of plants available, their therapeutic qualities, and their market value.[11]
The marketing consultants in particular gave the organization ideas on how to
improve the quality of the cosmetic and to market it as a spa product that might
run just under $10 a bottle. Based on these recommendations, CDRO developed
a product name for this line made up of the Spanish acronym—MABELI—
that reflected the four product types included in the brand: *medicina* (medicinal), *alimentos* (health supplement), *belleza* (beauty), and *limpieza* (cleaning).
CDRO's own name, its indigenous constitution and orientation, and its location
were thus erased from the label, in many ways expunging the ethnic origins of its
production in pursuit of a new form of entry into the cash economy. The label
thus highlights the natural quality of the product, with the tag line "Natural Es:
Pureza del Bosque" (It's natural: From the Purity of the Forest). And lest the
cosmopolitan quality of these natural ingredients be overlooked, the products
are physically marked as part of a "Sistema Spa" (Spa system; see Figure 5.1).

In addition to this new type of product, the spa line also reflected CDRO's
efforts to remap where its products circulated and how they were to be consumed. Instead of purveying its products through neighborhood stores, tourist
booths, or community clinics, CDRO's director said that the organization had
approached the owners of the larger local supermarkets like Paiz and Dispensa
Familiar for retail space. Representatives from La Fragua, the owner of these
successful Central American supermarket chains, referred him to their parent
company, Walmart. Walmart and its subsidiaries thus presented themselves as
the biggest and most logical market for these products, both in terms of the local
circulation possibilities that they enabled as well as the possibility for "ramping

up" to a global distribution chain constituted by affluent Latin and North American shoppers. When I mentioned my alarm at the prospect of the Walmart collaboration to one of MABELI's administrators, she nodded her head knowingly, stating that she was well aware of Walmart's reputation. "The problem," she said, "is that we're working with La Fragua, and they're connected to Walmart." Resigned, then, to working both with these local affiliates and with their Walmart corporate representative, CDRO began selling the product throughout Guatemala in late August 2006. By 2010, the products were slated to appear on the shelves of Walmart subsidiaries in El Salvador and then expand to select stores in Costa Rica. Longer-term plans included the pursuit of Fair Trade contracts with European markets and North American Walmart suppliers.

Ecologically, the new community business model offered the promise of an environmentally friendly production strategy. Indeed, CDRO's director emphasized the need for ecologically sound and sustainable practices that started with local goods and methods so that development would come not just from profits, but also from their regenerative potential. Instead of introducing nontraditional export crops like the broccoli, lettuce, or snow peas currently cultivated by Mayan peasants in the fertile agricultural valleys of Tecpán, just outside of Guatemala City (Fischer and Benson 2006), CDRO's business model relied on *native* plants and herbs that grow naturally in this landscape, but that would now be actively and systematically cultivated on a larger scale. This strategy would allow residents to draw on natural resources in their midst. Importantly, this strategy would avoid the past errors of other development initiatives nearby, such as FUNDAP, a local cooperative in neighboring Nahaualá that had used forest products to create cottage industries in furniture production. That initiative produced short-term profits for its participants, but quickly deforested the surrounding communities, leaving them in worse shape than before. CDRO's business model was explicitly set up to conserve its valuable communal forest as a crucial source of material and cultural patrimony.

For community residents, however, the new business model was promoted first and foremost on the basis of its anticipated economic benefits, which could be reaped in exchange for foregoing access to household corn production. CDRO had secured evidence of the nature and extent of these anticipated benefits by way of a pilot study it conducted in 2005 with ninety households located across ten CDRO affiliate communities. This study indicated that while residents could grow only one crop of maize per year on their small plots, planting chamomile enabled three separate harvests. Furthermore, this

3:1 difference in yield translated into a fivefold increase in market value for the crop; in other words, while one harvest of corn was valued at US$59, three crops of chamomile were valued at $263 (Ballasteros-Coronel 2006). CDRO's study thus claimed that producers could make more money per square foot cultivated, with this new income enabling the *purchase* of corn in the market- place in order to satisfy participants' household consumption needs. In 2006, when CDRO officials first explained this project to me, the low price of corn in the marketplace bore out the logic of these economic forecasts and seemingly neutralized the risks of abandoning household corn production. As further evidence, a story on MABELI in a local newspaper cited community resident Pascualina Ana Vásquez, who noted, "With the income obtained from a por- tion of the chamomile, I have managed to sustain my family for eight months. With corn, it was not the same" (Ballasteros-Coronel 2006). The article goes on to note how families involved in the project now had income to purchase meat more frequently and to send their children to school—activities constrained by the meager fruits of corn production. As these examples suggest, the new initiative positioned community development and business development as symbiotic processes oriented toward reproducing the material means of com- munity existence. It literally sought to cultivate and maintain rural, indigenous community life as the seed for local development.

At the center of this ambitious project was a new organizational structure. MABELI was set up as a corporation with maximum authority embodied in the General Assembly of Shareholders. Individual community producers had the option of becoming members through payment of a fee or discounts from transactions with MABELI. By this initial investment, they would acquire cor- responding shares through which they become integrated into the business (CDRO 2005:44). CDRO would maintain a majority share in the corporation, both as a reflection of its role as the founding entity and also as a means of preventing appropriation of the initiative by wealthier investors. Therefore, individual producers had multiple ways of accessing economic benefits, once through their cash income and secondly as shareholders invested in the collec- tive profits of the initiative.

Rather than just raising individual incomes, however, the new spa venture was carefully designed to operate as a collective enterprise serving the maxi- mum number of indigenous community residents; therefore, CDRO's efforts sought to ensure that this initiative "incorporated" the entire community. To accomplish this, the new cultivation methods were designed specifically for application in the small farmstead plots that dominate that landscape. This orientation made participation in the project both possible and attractive for a larger number of residents, while also ensuring that the project did not benefit only the largest landholders. Landless community members could gain economically from the system by working as employees, a status that also gave them the opportunity to participate as shareholders. Interestingly, CDRO emphasized women as the target population for this project, noting that they frequently were the ones left without land or other income-generating opportunities. Furthermore, CDRO documents singled them out as being more efficient, responsible, and receptive to business due to their household managerial experience. As noted in the newspaper quote above, women raved about the new initiative for its ability to help them "sustain" their families in ways not possible with corn, a representation that reiterates the important role that women hold in managing the household economy (see also Chapter Six).[12] Clearly, then, the "new" business model embodied traditional collective values and divisions of labor in that it counted on household production and women's efficient, "surplus" labor as important production inputs.

Finally, to further ensure this connection between the new business model and ethnic community development, CDRO's plan called for the active integration of proceeds from the spa cosmetics and local development efforts. Specifically, it argued for linking income-generating activities like this to the development institutions and services already operating in the community—for example, health or education programs administered through local development councils. In this way, the organization hoped to move beyond simply increasing individual incomes and instead create an integrated economic, social, and cultural process (CDRO 2005:45).

As this description of the new business model suggests, CDRO's efforts sought not only to maintain the material basis for cultural reproduction in ways other than corn, but also to reproduce the social collectivity. This initiative reflected the twinning of ethnic community and corporate business structures in order to ensure both economic development and cultural reproduction as mutually reinforcing processes. It thus begs the questions of not only how these two institutional forms come together, but also what is at stake for its shareholders.

Visibility and Value: Repackaging Identity for the Market

In both cases described thus far, ethnic difference has served as an important resource for entrepreneurial initiatives, even as the content and form attributed to that ethnic difference has been continually reconfigured. CDRO's previous development efforts had formulated and projected the indigenous community as an authentic, collective ethnic development agent vis-à-vis its culturally coded products such as Maya medicines, jams, and artwork. These commodities were visibly labeled as ethnic products from a particular rural community and thus served as fetishized essences of those local, indigenous relations. Indeed, their economic value derived specifically from the authentic identity and traditions that the jams or medicines were purported to distill. Unfortunately for CDRO community members, however, these initiatives necessarily reflected certain limits in terms of their circulation and profit potential. The commodities themselves were plagued by somewhat rudimentary production processes that, while crucial to authenticating the products' indigenous roots and craftsmanship, also made them suitable only for local consumption and precluded them from international sale by failure to comply with global trade standards. As CDRO documents note, this meant that sale of the commodities was limited to tourists and other local consumers who could "come to them" (CDRO 2005). CDRO was similarly limited in terms of the price it could charge for these local products. Invoking a dependency-style discourse, CDRO administrators thus complained that these earlier initiatives required them to rely on the purchase of important value-added "finished" goods from outside of the community, while limiting community members to the production of raw or semifinished goods with low value and high price fluctuations in the market. Corn provided subsistence to mitigate these low profits and unstable market conditions; therefore, historically corn and commerce had worked together to reproduce both the material and symbolic foundations of ethnic community and identity. However, in the wake of CAFTA and corn's waning viability, CDRO needed a new strategy.

The new community business model sought to replace practices that had historically served as visible markers of ethnic difference—milpa cultivation and artisanal goods—with commodity forms that were more profitable in the market precisely because of their global circulation and nonethnic identity. CDRO organizers recognized that while the global demand for "ethnic" products of the type it had previously produced had risen substantially over the last decade and a half, this increasing visibility had come at a cost. As noted in Chapter Two, CDRO's own efforts to brand indigenous culture had drawn critiques from community development practitioners who equated CDRO's personnel and projects with capitalist interlopers rather than authentic community advocates. Furthermore, a strategy reliant on the commodification of culture also posed problems on the level of the global market. As Marilyn Halter (2000:66) has argued, "imported merchandise that gets categorized as ethnic chic . . . often results from escalating levels of worker exploitation. By the time global goods produced by local labor end up in the hands of cosmopolitan American consumers, the process can have been a decidedly inharmonious one." Therefore, CDRO was not interested in staking its development hopes on the global niche market for ethnic commodities. Instead, the new cosmetic line looked to cultivate new articulations of ethnic identity within the regional free trade economy.

For the Walmart venture, rather than crafting a shampoo or lotion that embodied ethnic difference vis-à-vis label images or ethnic marketing strategies, MABELI products were to bear no outward signs of ethnic difference. They were specifically designed to go "out" into the global market as natural spa products, to sit on the shelves of fluorescently lit, 200,000-square-foot megastores where they could reach a wider consumer base. Their content and quality, rather than their specifically ethnic origins, would allow them to be identified as higher-end, cosmopolitan products by shoppers from Mexico to Germany. Indeed, the bathtub scene in MABELI's promotional video described at the outset of this chapter illustrated this goal through the type of female consumer featured in the advertisement, the modern surroundings in which she was placed, and the way her bath was depicted as a distinctly recreational, leisure activity. CDRO was thus banking on the hope that these products would derive economic value in global niche markets from their commensurability, universality, and value-added qualities. In other words, the fungibility of the commodity form was to become the ultimate source of value. In some ways, this strategy resonates with ethnic corporate ventures worldwide that have increasingly sought to negotiate questions of inequality and rights in the market and the law (see M. Brown 2003; Povinelli 2002; Sawyer 2004). Jean Comaroff and John Comaroff's notion of "ethno-preneurialism" exemplifies this process, describing how indigenous groups have increasingly pursued successful business ventures that incorporated identity and commodified culture in their search for increasing choice, universal recognition, and entry into a global cosmopolis (2009:52). They show how this phenomenon builds on but intensifies and expands historical practices of "casino capitalism" pursued by Native American groups in the United States (2009). The fact that CDRO has sought similar ends through products that actively *elide* its communities' ethnic origins raises questions about how the meaning of ethnic identity and its relationship to the global market are being articulated through different entrepreneurial strategies. Furthermore, seeing CDRO's enterprise as part of a wider development initiative allows us to examine the geopolitical dimensions of this process—that is, how states, international organizations, corporations, and ethnic communities are invested in and/or have contested these reformulations of ethnic difference as sources of economic value.

The economic rationale behind CDRO's Walmart strategy pivoted on the Maya community's presumed comparative advantage in natural herbs and plants currently in high demand in niche cosmetic markets, as well as the community's ability to draw on "surplus" feminized household labor to subsidize the production process. This logic reflects important continuities in ethnic development tactics—for example, an insistence on local resources, production within the rural community, market-based commerce, and collective profit-sharing justified in terms of Maya values of mutual support. Nonetheless, while specifically Maya senses of self were clearly invested in the new products, that identity was relocated, moved out of the corn field and off of the product label into the future investments in cultural reproduction and economic development.

In this way, CDRO's old and new development strategies relied upon similar enterprising subjects working toward a consistent development end, even as each located and articulated ethnic identity in very different ways. Despite their new modes of production and circulation in the regional economy, the MABELI products did not reflect a transformation in their producers from a rooted, localized sense of self to an increasingly global or nonethnic one. Nor did they represent these communities' inaugural entrée into the market. Indeed, in many of these rural communities, residents returned from a day in the fields seated in pickup trucks purchased during labor stints in the United States or talking via cell phone with other relatives currently working in Houston. Moreover, they understood and frequently discussed the impact of transnational free trade agreements like CAFTA on the price of the corn they produced or the gas and utilities they consumed. For rural community members, transnationalism and participation in the market were thus long-standing, defining features of their everyday practice and development sensibilities.

The professionalization of production and emphasis on commodity commensurability that defined the new Walmart enterprise, however, represented an effort to renegotiate the terms of these residents' market participation in order to reproduce a specifically ethnic community. Through the MABELI spa line, CDRO sought to confront the unequal structure of the global post-CAFTA market in which these communities are embedded and to rearticulate the place of ethnic identity within it. For that reason, rather than a radical departure from its past practices, CDRO's tactic represented a continuation of the organization's deft institutional ability to appropriate new technologies in order to adapt to rapidly changing political economic contexts. In other words, the Walmart enterprise signaled not so much a displacement of the ethnic entrepreneur, but rather his or her *re*-placement within the new regional economy. This re-placement emphasized the *entrepreneurial* nature of the product rather than its ethnic particularity, precisely in order to maintain its producers' local identity and community.

First, this strategic reformulation of the ethnic entrepreneur was evident in CDRO's affirmation of the ethnic community as the moral and material ground for the production of Maya selves. In CDRO's affiliate communities, residents saw this territory not simply as the physical foundation for their collective livelihood, but also as the symbolic ground of a specifically ethnic community, tied together not just by physical proximity but also by a certain code of values and cultural practices grounded in this particular place. Therefore, CDRO and its community participants were ultimately looking to sustain the rural Maya community as the place where moral, cultural, and political subjects were grounded. Community here was significant not as a label, but rather as the place from which one speaks in the crafting of self. The place of community was significant because of the unique moral economy, which was perceived to anchor it (see Chapter Two)—a system of values that distinguished it from the logic of the market. Yet what is noteworthy is that in this post-CAFTA environment, the physical ground of community was the soil on which market relations were sown.

The Maya communities' own *ethnic* traditions formed the basis for the kind of *organizational and ethical* system promoted by the new corporate forms. Like a corporation, the ethnic community was recognized as a semiautonomous legal entity with its own legitimate authority and decision-making structures. Within that entity, Maya traditions of communal property and internal reciprocity— reinforced historically through corn production, among other means—have cultivated a corporate sense of identity and a history of collective enterprise as central features of ethnic community life. CDRO's *pop* or "woven mat" image stood as a powerful symbolic representation of this tightly woven social fabric and the collective ideology behind it. Cultural principles such as *apoyo mutuo* (mutual support) provided the basis for individual accountability and mutual trust within this corporate community model, supporting the community's autonomy and assuring the K'iche' mandate that "no one is left behind" (CDRO 1998). Practices of ethnic exclusivity in labor hiring practices further accentuated boundaries of collective enterprise, even in the context of high levels of economic stratification (Smith 1990a). Therefore, like a corporation, the ethnic community provided both an organizational and philosophical means of mitigating individual risk, while drawing on cooperative investment to promote collective benefits.

Given these convergences between the ethnic and corporate communities, CDRO saw the corporate business model and its partnership with Walmart as a suitable vehicle through which the community could relocate and reproduce itself within global niche markets, while simultaneously neutralizing the unequal effects of that same market. Rather than an exploitative, foreign form, the corporate model appeared familiar and even expedient for this task of ethnic development. Indeed, one case study of the MABELI cosmetic line validated the perceived complementarity of corporate forms and ethnic development when it described the MABELI project as a *social enterprise* "because it combines the productive and lucrative characteristics of a traditional company with the social sense and projection of the community" (Sanchez 2006:131). As this description implies, the social values and connection to community embodied in ethnic enterprise could be perceived as interchangeable with the global business ethic of corporate responsibility (see also Comaroff and Comaroff 2009).

By drawing attention to convergences between the moral and entrepreneurial aspirations of ethnic and corporate entities, my goal is not to reify the ethnic corporate community or to celebrate new forms of corporate morality. Instead, I am interested in how from very different angles and with very different interests, each of these actors is drawing upon similar forms of moral reasoning in order to address the problem of "how to live" in relation to the market (Collier and Lakoff 2005:30). In other words, how are specific community values being extended and invoked in business? How are corporate forms being abstracted and applied to community development? In his analysis of the metaphor of stakeholding, Sunley notes that "the idea of a *company as a community* often appears to substitute a normative community ideal for the realities of actual communities and hence neglects coercive relations and elite domination" (1999:2199; emphasis added). The community ideal—shared values, mutual

trust, transparency, sustainability—offers a flexible moral framework for negotiating and evaluating the relationship between corporations and other actors
in the global economy. It elides the significant class and gender inequalities that
we have seen define the ethnic community. Conversely, in the case of CDRO,
the idea of *community as a company* offers a tentative solution to the problem
of development in the changing global economy, even as it also elides the inequalities and risks that constitute corporate life.

CDRO's new community business model pivoted upon a corporate sense of
self and a shared, collective enterprise that positioned community residents as
shareholders in a common cultural destiny. The mutual intelligibility between
these terms as ethnic community precepts and corporate principles gives us
insight into the way that community morality and corporate forms are coming
together as a new "regime of living" in response to the ethical challenges posed
by the changing global economy in terms of its relation to ethnic identity and
local development. Will the appropriation of a corporate business form allow
the ethnic community to transcend its unequal position within the regional
free trade economy and thus mitigate the loss of the material and symbolic pil-
lar of ethnic community life—namely, corn? Will the invocation of community
values make Walmart a more conscientious and just stakeholder in the community development process? What is at stake in these new regimes of living?
It is to these questions and their implications for the ethnic entrepreneur that I
turn in the next chapters.

6 Accounting for Development
Debates over Knowledge and Authority

IN PREVIOUS CHAPTERS, I have detailed the diverse ways that ethnic identity has articulated with entrepreneurism within the space of global development policy and practice. In each of those varying configurations of the ethnic entrepreneur, knowledge has been crucial to defining the boundaries of ethnic identity and community as well as to marking the sources of development alternatives. In this chapter, I look more closely at these encounters in order to show which types of knowledge accrue value within contemporary neoliberal development paradigms, who is perceived to hold this knowledge, and why. In other words, what assumptions about knowledge are at work in the different forms of ethnic identity expressed in CDRO's community development method, in the UN's search for a pan-Latino diaspora, and in CDRO's Walmart enterprise? What kinds of convergences and contestations are evident in the relationship between the *local* knowledge assumed to define the indigenous community, the *translocal* knowledge embodied in migrants, and the *expert* knowledge that has guided ethnic community enterprise?

These questions of knowledge matter because of the important role that knowledge plays in the constitution of subjects, of political authority, and ultimately of power. Following Foucault (1980, 1990) and scholars who have built upon and extended his work on power-knowledge (Rose 1999; Dean 1999), I am interested in how the ways of knowing attributed to and invoked by the ethnic entrepreneur have been deemed authoritative and aligned with the goals of governance. In other words, given how neoliberal state and economic reforms have increasingly been enacted through localized, community-based development practice, those actors who can lay claim to certain kinds of knowledge can also lay claim to certain degrees of authority over community and even national development processes. In the varying configurations of ethnic entrepreneurship I have described throughout the book, ethnic subjects have been identified as embodying qualities and epistemologies associated with non-Western traditions as well as enterprising, technical, empirical forms associated with Western modernity. Nonetheless, as described in the previous chapter, the convergence between ethical business management strategies and indigenous corporate behavior was intelligible because of the conjoining of certain moral and technical forms of knowledge about markets and social relations in multiple domains. These convergences thus raise questions not only about the dynamic epistemological foundations of ethnic difference, but also about the changing forms of knowledge that govern development more generally.

In what follows, I revisit in turn community-level development politics, CDRO's institutional development initiatives, and migrant projects like the Digital Diaspora. While I use the terms *local/moral*, and *technical/expert* to discuss the various knowledge forms operating in these spaces, those labels are not meant to identify discrete bodies of knowledge, positioned in hierarchical (from particularistic to universalistic) and/or scalar (from local to global) relationship to one another. Instead, in each instance I highlight the assumptions and practices that position these forms as unique, and specifically ethnic epistemological stances. The scenarios thus underscore how diverse forms of knowledge increasingly come together to define the ethnic entrepreneur, rather than constituting discrete systems of knowledge that can be located exclusively in one or another kind of ethnic subject—such as *local* knowledge as the property of small-scale indigenous communities, and *expert* knowledge as the property of global elites. In other words, I argue that the tension between conceptions of local/moral versus technical/expert knowledge is crucial to articulating the meaning of ethnic difference and its relationship to development.

To understand these knowledge dynamics I again employ a micropolitics approach to identity. Specifically, this approach builds on a multisited, longitudinal study of diverse development actors working across multiple scales, and focuses on the practices, strategies, and forms of knowledge through which new subjects are produced and given value. Through this approach, we can appreciate both the changing forms of knowledge invoked to define ethnic communities, as well as the way preexisting class and gender inequalities operate to validate those forms. As such, a micropolitics approach provides insight into the specific strategies and practices through which power is enacted and embodied within certain subjects in the space of development.

Accounting for Local Knowledge

The ascendance of ethnic development initiatives during the 1990s pivoted on the assumption that they were informed not just by alternative methods or goals, as embodied by the *pop*, but also by a unique "local knowledge" that was both substantively different from Western ways of knowing and qualitatively more effective/efficient in terms of enacting development (Nygren 1996).[1] This assumption of an essential difference between ethnic, or "local," worldviews and Western institutions is not new, but rather echoes a dichotomy that has been identified by anthropological studies of development generally (Li 2007; Pigg 1997; Tsing 2005; Walley 2004) and by Latin American ethnic relations in particular (Smith 1990b; Urban and Sherzer 1991; Warren and Jackson 2002). Within this dichotomy, institutions such as the state have frequently been posited as vehicles for global capitalist penetration, while indigenous communities serve as an oppositional outpost for non-Western ways of being (see Escobar 1995). Yet, as we saw in the preceding chapters, what counts as "local" knowledge is not a foregone conclusion, but in fact a highly contested question within the very communities where it is presumed to reside. In what follows, I return to two Totonicapán Maya communities to examine debates over local knowledge in the context of meetings between council members and local authorities. These debates highlight not only the tension between what counts as local/ moral or expert/technical knowledge, but also shifts in who is seen to embody these diverse forms of knowledge and how they translate into authority over local development.

As I entered the San Pedro community hall in rural Guatemala early on a Saturday morning in 1999, I immediately sensed that this meeting would not be like the other events I had attended there (see Chapter Two). Because it was the weekend, the community hall was free of the shouting school children that usually filled this multipurpose center's inner salon. Instead, a nervous silence hung in the air, punctuated occasionally by the loud squeal of a chair being dragged across the floor. The seating was oriented toward the front of the room where a large stage had been mounted, housing an overhead projector and screen and a podium. As the hour progressed, several young council members and some of the CDRO main office representatives slowly took their seats along the right side of the room. At about nine-thirty, the mayor and accompanying authorities, each wielding his ceremonial cane, solemnly exited their upstairs office and proceeded down to the inner hall. They took their seats along the left side of the room. When they were settled, two young community members initiated what, indeed, proved to be an unprecedented meeting.

The meeting brought together the two entities responsible for community development—the local council (affiliated with CDRO's program) and the political authorities—each of whom represented different sources of social and political authority.[2] The meeting commenced as a council member came forward to ritually introduce the parties and moderate the event. Speaking in K'iche', he noted that the purpose of the meeting was to reach a consensus on community development issues. The council member then proceeded to call up a series of council members to describe the council's activities. One young college student placed several flowcharts onto the overhead as he explained in Spanish the status of the community's microcredit funds, procured from CDRO. He highlighted the source of the revolving funds, the amount of credits allocated to community members, the interest received on those loans, and the status of the council's overall account. An older gentleman with an architectural background used table graphs to explain the various phases of construction for the community hall, including the purchase of materials, the justification for structural design, and the building's overall space allocation.

While these men talked, another council member walked around the room, passing out a spiral-bound report that summarized the information for the meeting's participants. The materials included computer-prepared summaries of the council's organizational structure, a systematized classificatory schema highlighting areas of institutional focus as well as the scope/function of specific offices, and detailed spreadsheets enumerating program beneficiaries and budgetary allocations. This was exactly the kind of documentation that the council, or any local development organization, would submit alongside grant applications. It evidenced a universally recognizable, rationally organized institution with rigorous, empirically proven evaluative mechanisms that projected the accountability required by neoliberal norms. I wondered immediately about the significance of these materials for the unevenly literate population in attendance at the meeting.

When the council's presentations ended, a prolonged debate commenced about the council's leadership of community development efforts. The community authorities immediately took issue with the council's data because, for them, the empirical, rationalized nature of the council's evidence raised a red flag. Although the authorities were suspicious of the supposed self-evidence of the council's "facts," they were even more troubled by the introduction of this mode of argumentation into the debate. Far from demonstrating transparency, for them the reliance on rationalized classificatory schema, empirical audits, and enumeration reflected a powerful association with Western modernity (Hacking 1982) that seemed to only confirm the council's distance from the forms of knowledge that defined the indigenous community. The fact that the council was made up of more privileged community members—primarily the successful merchants and their increasingly college-educated children—made this distance even more dubious. So, while council members deployed technical, professional data to indicate their development efficacy and transparency, the San Pedro authorities interpreted this form of knowledge as a sign that the council was an outsider motivated by an interest in privatizing and usurping resources that rightly belonged to the community as a whole.

The authorities countered the council's right to lead by insisting on the custom of community consensus and the role that age, lineage, ritual prestige, and personal virtue play in structuring authority within that process. Rather than disembodied, objective, empirical facts and transparency as governing principles, the authorities reiterated the importance of an embodied epistemology constituted through responsible, virtuous behavior within a history of collectivism and ritual service. By demonstrating the correct morals, a community member was entitled to respect. Indeed, Eckern (2003:278) has argued that "No other concept better summarises Mayan morals than this word [respect], and it can be said to condense the official ideology of the Mayan polity." It was adherence to this particular set of rules of conduct and the wisdom derived from it that operated as the means for establishing authority and evaluating the effectiveness of development actions. Based on this configuration of moral authority, the authorities argued that *they* were the only entity fit to supervise and administer local development resources. In citing this Maya system of values and customs as the basis for their power, the authorities were invoking a tradition of local governance that situated particular embodied forms of indigenous knowledge and practice—such as consensus and ritual prestige—as timeless, authentic foundations for indigenous authority.

Of course, these representations elided the fact that the local political structure was itself the product of a dynamic relationship between local and state governance, as well as transformations in the social meaning that residents applied to those arrangements.[3] According to local historians, the authority of the community mayor was only a relatively recent development, and one that evolved from a long chain of other authority structures.[4] Consequently, the forms of knowledge and practice that authorities summoned as the basis for local authority were themselves a reflection of historically situated shifts in the forms of governance. The neoliberal context was significant here both as a unique moment within this historical trajectory as well as for the particular way that it framed the debate about indigenous knowledge for development, in terms of who or what was seen to embody it and how it was juxtaposed to noncommunity forms of authority and governance.[5]

In response to the authorities' challenges, the council members attempted to redefine what counted as legitimate local knowledge to more closely reflect the basis of their authority within the broader development community. First, they argued that they had developed a *systematic* understanding of community needs through their community diagnostics and program audits. To illustrate this point, council members frequently referred back to the documented data and reports. They presented these texts as written "facts," the authority of which hinged on both their apparent neutrality as well as their uninterpretability by this unevenly literate audience. Council members would simply point to the tables and say, "See? Every penny is accounted for." In doing so, they were invoking the hegemonic interpretation of numbers that may act to "(1) establish expertise and authority, (2) make knowledge impersonal, (3) portray certainty and universality, and (4) contribute to resolving situations for doubt, conflict, and mistrust" (Zaloom 2003:259; see also Poovey 1998; Strathern 2000). Rather than drawing on a history of public service, they were using this accounting of their labor and material successes in order to highlight their individual morality, virtue, and, thus, authority as development agents. This epistemological stance reflected the council's growing material and professional power as a development broker with the ability to rationalize local knowledge and parlay it into essential resources from state and international development institutions.[6] After all, the council's success in the development arena was based on its ability to speak for the indigenous community and, simultaneously, to embody certain forms of knowledge that were recognizable and authoritative according to neoliberal conventions— specifically, enumerated empirical data and rationalized evaluative mechanisms.[7] The council's strategy thus sought to produce a "research effect" that presented artifacts of scientific knowledge as conveyors of value (Elyachar 2005a:415).

The San Pedro debate underscores the contentious relationship between multiple, situated forms of knowledge and authority within the indigenous community. This tension was productive in that it authorized new types of knowledge and written modes of expression—such as development proposals, professional budgets, and technical reports—as well as privileged new types of development actors—namely, younger professionals rather than older men with a long history of community service, social prestige, and accumulated respect. Nonetheless, the legitimacy of these new forms had to be subjected to scrutiny and debate in order to determine whether they could be effectively resituated within community morality or whether they represented outsider expertise that was deemed detrimental to community culture and development interests. The council argued that its "facts" reflected its accountability, but the authorities pressed the council to specify not just the fact of accountability, but also the referent: namely, *to whom* was the council accountable?

In addition to stressing the contingent nature of local knowledge formations, this example draws attention to the importance of extant class differences between council members and authorities in determining the legitimacy of each body's claim to authority. However, lest this example appear to simply illustrate a predictable tale of modernization, whereby a traditional local knowledge is gradually replaced by modern forms of bureaucratic expertise, in what follows, I present a snapshot from a similar debate in a neighboring Maya community, San Miguel. In the subsequent case, we can see how valued forms of knowledge and the subjects who were seen to embody them shifted in response to growing migration from the rural communities and changing gender paradigms within development policy more generally. These shifts reveal not just the role of class inequality but also of gender differences in structuring legitimate forms of knowledge and authority for development.

In the summer of 2006, I accompanied CDRO representatives to a meeting between the local council and local political authorities in the neighboring community of San Miguel. Given the less developed infrastructure in San Miguel, the meeting that I attended there lacked the pomp and circumstance of the San Pedro event. Indeed, this community was just initiating the construction of a large community hall comparable to the Pixib'al Ja in San Pedro. All parties to the meeting entered the single-story cement-block, multipurpose salon somewhat unceremoniously, having just finished a pickup game of soccer in the outside pitch. The authorities quickly moved to one side of the dimly lit room and placed their ritual canes in racks on the tables in front of them. They then filed into chairs scattered behind the highest elected officials—the mayor, vice mayor, and secretary—who served as spokesmen for the authorities as a whole, as evidenced by the occasional collective nods and noises of approval from the other officials seated behind them.

The council members, who were much fewer in number, took their seats directly across from the authorities in folding chairs lining the opposite wall. The council was constituted primarily by women, dotted with a just a handful of older men. This demographic denoted a radical departure from the makeup of the San Pedro council, which was composed predominantly of male community elites. As such, it raised for me important questions about the role of gender in shaping development agency. After all, here it was women, rather than community class elite, who seemed to embody authoritative development agents and ethnic entrepreneurs relative to male community authorities.[8]

CDRO representatives had been called to the 2006 San Miguel meeting by their affiliate council to clarify information about the community microcredit program, administered through Banco Pop.[9] As the meeting commenced, the CDRO official rose and spoke briefly (in Spanish) about the mechanics of the Banco Pop loan. His authority on this subject derived both from his respected reputation as an educated, K'iche' professional as well as from the fact that he represented the institutional source of the funds in question. He then resumed his seat and left it to the local council to explain the benefits of this process. The task of explaining the financial implications of the loan fell not to one of the few gentlemen sitting among the council, but rather to one of the older women. All of the council members turned and deferred to this woman, who did not stand up to assume a position of authority but instead responded from her chair. Speaking simply and succinctly in K'iche', she explained the complex technicalities of the microcredit system to the authorities. In contrast to her council counterparts in San Pedro, she did not rely on professionalized reports or overhead projections that would reflect the masculine values of rationality, abstraction, technical competence, and disembodiment that are projected through global development practice (Radcliffe, Laurie, and Andolina 2004:407). Instead, to plead her case, she drew upon a sophisticated understanding of modern banking logistics and an eloquent translation of its technicalities for this diverse audience. Therefore, her authority pivoted as much on her ability to represent this complex data through traditional oratory forms and K'iche' language as it did on her mastery of the details. Notably, the CDRO official nodded approvingly throughout her explanation.

The councilwoman's financial prowess reflected the impact of a growing number of microcredit programs in the rural communities of Latin America and the centrality of women within them. International development institutions have frequently identified women as the primary targets of microcredit based on their connection to poverty and oppression; as such, they are seen as having the most to gain from both income-generating activities and the empowerment that microcredit is said to enable. However, women's centrality within micro-credit regimes also reflects particular financial knowledge, managerial skills, and moral authority that development actors have imputed to women.[10]

The Bangladeshi Grameen Bank provides a case in point. As of February 2008, the bank had 7.45 million borrowers, 97 percent of whom are women (Grameen Bank 2008).[11] While the Grameen Bank originally focused on women as "the poorest of the poor," its efforts have been similarly promoted on the basis of the specific kind of development subject that women are suggested to represent. As founder Muhammad Yunus himself has noted, "Given the oppor-tunity to fight against poverty and hunger, women turn out to be natural and better fighters than men" (Yunus 1994, cited in Rahman 2001:44). According to this view, women's privileged role within microcredit is premised on essential distinctions between male and female development subjects that make women superior borrowers. Anthropologist Aminur Rahman's ethnographic study of the Grameen Bank provides an analysis of exactly how gender differences in-form this woman-centered division of development labor. Specifically, Rahman (2001:24) argues that the bank "uses prevailing patriarchal norms and posi-tional vulnerability of women (immobile, shy, passive) for timely repayment and distribution of loans." In other words, women's reputation for being good managers comes, in part from being manageable and compliant themselves.

Echoing these larger development agencies, CDRO's own studies have simi-larly drawn attention to women's "natural" administrative and budgeting skills, positing them as products of women's day-to-day household management and juxtaposing them to men's engagement in income-generating activities outside of the home. At its annual general assemblies, CDRO administrators identified women as being inherently more responsible than men, spending money on fam-ily needs rather than on a drink with friends at a local cantina when given extra cash. According to these representations, women's aptitude for finances thus de-rived not only from more technical experience with household management, but also from better economic judgment about what was best for the family.

Returning to San Miguel, the authorities' initial response to the council-woman's lecture on the mechanics of microcredit suggested an effort to dele-gitimize her knowledge on the basis of gendered hierarchies of male authority within community development politics. Specifically, the men reacted with somewhat boyish giggling and talking among themselves. This response high-lighted the fact that what was at work here was not simply a struggle between the council and the elected authorities as two distinct bodies of local governance, but also an interaction between men and women over the gendered nature of development knowledge and authority (see also Chapter Three). Eventually, however, when the councilwoman returned each skeptical retort about the util-ity of the microcredit fund with an expert summary of its mechanics and finan-cial benefits, the authorities were left silent.

In this exchange, the local authorities attempted to assert their influence as traditional community leaders in order to justify their control over commu-nal funds. They wanted to see the money spent on a ritual community event that would ultimately bolster their own prestige and social status as benevolent elected officials. The council, through its female spokesperson, invoked both fi-nancial expertise and also the embodied morality and indigenous authenticity of the Maya woman, in order to argue their case for a longer-term approach. As the meeting drew to a close with no further protestations by the authorities, it was clear that the council spokeswoman had effectively thwarted any efforts to lay claim to the microcredit funds.

This case illustrates how the gendered structure of microcredit projects fa-cilitated women's claims to expert knowledge and, thus, a degree of authority within community development efforts. The councilwoman's successful enact-ment of feminine authority over a patriarchal model of community leadership in many ways represented a significant break from the gendered forms of com-munity development that I have described previously. As Little (2003, 2004a) notes, these particular gender patterns are not the norm in Maya communities where women, as artisanal producers and business managers, exert consider-able control in both household and neighborhood politics; however, they are reflective of a more general gendered division of development labor in other ethnic communities in Latin America (Bourque and Warren 1981; Montoya, Frazier, and Hurtig 2002). The councilwoman's newfound authority was based on the growing acknowledgment of women's expertise as financial agents—an expertise derived both from women's "natural" qualities as household manag-ers and also from women's banking knowledge within microcredit projects.

In the next section, we see CDRO similarly invoking local, cultural knowl-edge as the basis for its own technical expertise as a development institution, even as the value of that knowledge shifts in line with the organization's changing interlocutors. Therefore, these next examples further illustrate both the contradictions and the convergences between disparate sources of knowledge as they come together to redefine ethnic identity and its relationship to entrepreneurism within the space of development.

From State to Corporate Authority

During the 1990s, CDRO gained prominence for the way its efforts to enact ethnic development coincided with national projects of postwar democratization and decentralization. In particular, CDRO's emphasis on *poder local* (local power) sought to displace the role of the state in local development; however, that philosophy actually dovetailed with state devolution and privatization processes, as well as with Maya revitalization efforts to cultivate greater cultural and political autonomy for indigenous communities. For many of the same reasons, CDRO's formulation of local knowledge resonated with international development agencies looking to promote participatory, community-based, and sustainable development alternatives (DeHart 2008).[12]

One of the ways that CDRO articulated its difference from the Guatemalan state and other more conventional development projects was through its effort to represent Mayan epistemology in opposition to Western ways of knowing. In CDRO's *U'kuj wuj,* or institutional founding document, the organization described the source of Maya knowledge in distinct contrast to Western liberalism: "[CDRO's] global focus is based on the Maya worldview, which is different from the liberal Western vision that separates out problems and studies them in a specialized way, thereby losing sight of their interrelatedness as causes and as effects" (CDRO 1998b:18).

In this guiding philosophy, Maya culture was described as steeped in a pointedly non-Western cultural logic (Fischer 2001). In epistemological terms, Mayans' holistic understanding of cause and effect reflected a radically different way of knowing than the positivist, scientific method used in the West. Nonetheless, rather than providing a challenge to the status quo, CDRO's integral, holistic approach complemented neoliberal state reforms by validating the transference of development responsibility from the state to the local community (see Chapter One). In this way, CDRO's formulation of Maya knowledge accentuated a convergence, rather than a contradiction between a local, ethnic epistemology and neoliberal development norms.

Guatemalan media portraits of CDRO's general advisor, Benjamín Son Turnil, illuminate this convergence and its implications for national development. A newspaper interview with Son Turnil in 1997, provocatively titled "We Could Replace the State"[13] based on one of Son Turnil's suggestive quotes within the interview, portrayed him as a savvy development professional and a spokesperson for local Maya culture. Both the interview title and Son Turnil's responses throughout the article actively promoted CDRO as a possible substitute to the state, based on the distinct locus of change (the community rather than the state) and the development knowledge (Maya rather than Western) that CDRO represented.

The interview text was accompanied by a photo of a relaxed Son Turnil sitting in a chair of his somewhat austere, unembellished office (see Figure 6.1). The article introduction, run alongside the picture, noted:

> Economist and Social Worker Benjamín Son Turnil would pass unnoticed by any urban dweller. He is a simple, discreet, quiet man, but he embodies a philosophy and wisdom that he has translated into practice with his Maya K'iche' people of Totonicapán ... With that work, he has sought to change the appearance of this department, which is characterized as one of the poorest in the country. (Camposeco Cruz 1997:6)

In this introduction, Son Turnil is identified as a professional trained in the social sciences, and economics at that. His legitimacy as a development expert

Figure 6.1 Benjamín Son Turnil, CDRO's general advisor. Source: Author, 2006.

thus derived in part from his universal, scientific knowledge. Nonetheless, the interview also attributed Son Turnil's notoriety to his ethnic particularity—his ability to "embody a philosophy" that he had applied to strategies among "his Maya K'iche' people of Totonicapán." Therefore, Son Turnil personified the conjoining of both local and global expert knowledge forms, as well as the valuable ability to operationalize that knowledge into effective development policy. Like the council members in San Pedro or the women microcredit agents described above, it was the embodiment of these diverse forms of knowledge by the ethnic entrepreneur that allowed Son Turnil to make the claim that CDRO could do the job of development better and more efficiently from the state:

> [W]e are no longer are afraid to say that we could replace the state. This substitution wouldn't be an eminently political discussion although it has certain political content. We believe that it is more a discussion related to the *efficiency* of the projects and of the institutions that can fulfill their objectives. It is a discussion related to decentralization, a space that opens for us and we would be willing to take advantage of it . . . What's more, the government is there to administer resources and its obligation is to do so efficiently. (Camposeco Cruz 1997:6; emphasis added)

Son Turnil's assertion makes the question of who is to do the work of development an issue of competency and expertise, rather than of political persuasion or rights. CDRO would be a more proficient agent of development than the state because of its combined cultural knowledge and on-the-ground development expertise, facts that had already led international development institutions and the Guatemalan state itself to recognize CDRO as a model for ethnic development (Chapter Two). In arguing CDRO's merits in this way, Son Turnil echoed state and development agency efforts to depoliticize development and to frame it as simply a technical adjustment (Ferguson 1990; Mitchell 1991).

A 2006 discussion I had with Son Turnil about CDRO's relationship to the Maya movement further illuminated the situated formulation of local knowledge that undergirded both CDRO's ethnic development program and its claims on state power. In that conversation, Son Turnil explained CDRO's unique aptitude for development by citing the organization's lack of political affiliation—a dig at other Maya leaders who had been integrated into the Guatemalan state bureaucracy and a reiteration of the tendency to define Maya community in opposition to politics (Eckern 2003:274). In place of civil service experience, CDRO was distinguished by its strident emphasis on everyday development concerns in the rural communities. In other words, it was the organization's grounding in the ethnic community, which Son Turnil identified as a nonideological and epistemologically discrete space, that explained CDRO's superior development know-how.

These efforts by CDRO to define an authoritative vision of authentic indigenous knowledge indexes the situated nature of local knowledge, emphasizing its rearticulation in relation to shifting understandings about what was valuable about Maya culture and how it could be productively applied to addressing emerging development dilemmas. In his commentaries about other organizations, Son Turnil authorized his own formulation of authentic local knowledge as an epistemologically distinct, politically neutral, and yet notably efficient foundation for development. The difference between indigenous and Western knowledge thus justified the replacement of the state by community development programs.

One of the most surprising things about CDRO's Walmart spa initiative in 2005, then, was the organization's apparent rejection of localized, ethnic knowledge of the type Son Turnil described in favor of more specialized, foreign forms of knowledge. After all, the Walmart venture relied on outside "experts" to professionalize the production process and to develop a commodity that would elide its rural, indigenous origins in order to accrue more value within a global niche market. I argue, however, that rather than an abandonment of local knowledge, CDRO's spa cosmetic initiative demonstrates a shifting context for defining the legitimacy and value of the ethnic entrepreneur. Specifically, the spa line highlights a move away from efforts to establish the merits of indigenous local knowledge vis-à-vis national development politics (such as replacing the state) toward an attempt to establish the value of the ethnic community vis-à-vis profitable participation within the global market.

Working with a consultative group consisting of cosmetic firms (Henkel from Germany and Mane from France), image creation and branding experts (Punto & Aparte Publicists), and market positioning/product placement experts (UNIDEAS), CDRO hoped to gain important market knowledge that would provide a sustainable basis for regional development (CDRO 2005:30–31). In doing so, CDRO moved away from previous efforts to profit from the K'iche' communities' explicitly local, indigenous forms of expertise, in the form of artisanal medicinal products or textiles and other *típica*, or indigenous, crafts. It also departed from the organization's long-held objection to using "foreign" development experts. What it wanted to convey through its new product line and professionalized marketing process was a savvy knowledge about how to compete in the new regional free trade reality.

CDRO's collaborators in this process were part of a burgeoning global industry devoted to making a science of the market. As Zukin (2006) describes, this industry is constituted by firms specializing in market research—including surveys, focus groups, and other diagnostic tools—which seek to apprehend patterns in consumer activity that make an objectified market "knowable" to producers in new ways. This kind of research, Zukin argues, has been credited with producing new truths about both the market and consumers. It was research of this kind that had convinced CDRO to market its cosmetics as exclusive "natural spa products" (see Figure 5.1) rather than advertising their exotic ethnic roots, as consumers were said to care more about a product's ingredients than its geographic or cultural origins.

Studies by Marilyn Halter (2000) and Arlene Dávila (2001) have provided compelling analyses of the rise of marketing firms that specialize in niche ethnic markets, teaching producers how to package and circulate their goods in ways that resonate with culturally specific practices of particular communities. Dávila, for example, documented the work of Hispanic marketing consultants who she claims play a central role in producing a homogeneous, monocultural Latino consumer niche. Halter further explains how industry experts often authenticate their objective knowledge about a specific cultural group of consumers by invoking their own ethnic difference (104–5). Together, these studies demonstrate the important combination of cultural knowledge about specific ethnic group practices and values, as well as technical knowledge about market trends more generally for corporate profitability.

In CDRO's case, the move toward professionalization and expert knowledge does not mean that ethnic identity and local knowledge have been defined in opposition to foreign or objective expertise. Instead, CDRO recruited "outside" expert consultants for the Walmart initiative as a means of furthering the project's main goal, which was reproduction of the forms of knowledge, practice, and identity that are produced in the rural ethnic community. As such, global expert knowledge was ultimately enlisted to *sustain*, rather than wholly replace, local knowledge forms. This tactical choice reflects CDRO's recognition of the shifting context in which ethnic community development was located. While CDRO's earlier efforts sought to distinguish and validate ethnic local knowledge in relation to the dominant logic of state decentralization and democratization, this later initiative was responding to the growing power of corporate models in the global marketplace as the definitive framework for establishing legitimacy and value (Comaroff and Comaroff 2009).

Knowing Networks

Like the cases noted above, the Digital Diaspora project was similarly constructed upon assumptions about what kind of knowledge diasporic individuals possessed and how that knowledge could be put to work for development. In particular, project participants were presumed to embody local knowledge not just about a single community, but also about multiple locations; they simultaneously held valuable knowledge about the United States, its markets, and its technology, along with crucial insights into Latin America, its people and its needs. As such, like their ethnic, or "local," counterparts back home, diaspora development participants represented multiple but complementary forms of knowledge: namely, social capital and technical knowledge. They were to build on these diverse knowledge systems in order to function as intermediaries working across multiple social fields in the hemisphere. Their work would ideally develop human capital in Latin America according to the terms of the Millennium Development Goals, which included "Technical and entrepreneurial skills to adopt existing but underused technologies and scientific expertise to advance new knowledge" (UN Millennium Project 2005:13)

Because of their common experience of transnational migration and connections in multiple communities, projects such as the Digital Diaspora envisioned diasporic individuals not only as constituting part of a larger social network, but also as uniquely positioned to *build and expand social networks*. Take for example Akhtar Badshah and John Boateng, the main organizers behind the original Digital Diaspora idea. It took only a serendipitous encounter between Badshah and Boateng in Harvard Square to set in motion a process that would bring together important members of the African diaspora for the purpose of development (Chapter Four). Similarly, for the Latin America Digital Diaspora project, Digital Partners and UN organizers relied upon a snowball method of recruiting participants in the hopes of producing a "multiplier effect" that would not only capture significant members of the Latino diaspora, but actually bring them together as a coherent network of development agents.

Diasporic individuals' personal biography (gender, education, occupation) was one reason why they were perceived to be capable of creating these growing networks. Akhtar Badshah, for instance, brought to the Digital Diaspora initiatives a history of migration, an advanced education in the United States, development experience in the nonprofit sector, as well as paid consultant and corporate work, especially in the realm of information technology. In describing Badshah's fit for his subsequent position at Microsoft, Digital Partners board member Vijay Vashee noted "Non-profit groups worldwide knew or could quickly see that this guy was one of them." At the same time, Vashee said, "Microsoft's community affairs initiative needed someone with the types of national and international connections that Badshah brings to the job" (Bishop 2004). Therefore, just as Son Turnil's ethnic identity and essentialized local knowledge imbued him with a "philosophy and wisdom that he has translated into practice with *his people*," it was assumed that Latino participants in the Digital Diaspora would similarly be able to serve as cultural translators and network builders among *their* people in both the United States and Latin America.

Nonetheless, the Digital Diaspora members' social knowledge and capacity for networking was not simply a product of their ethnic or migratory background, but also a product of their class position as elites. As such, participants represented what Larner (2007:341) calls the cosmopolitan, "World Class Citizen" or "A-lister" subject that has become the coveted object of transnational development efforts. These participants were not representative of the experience of working-class migrants described in Chapter Three, but rather an exclusive kind of subject whose class status was seen to reflect important social and economic capital to be invested in development. What was needed was a more systematic way of capturing and channeling economic flows across these diverse constituencies in a way that would promote development. Diasporic individuals' network-building capacity and elite social capital would allow them to do exactly that.

In addition to this social capital, Digital Diaspora participants embodied important technical, expert knowledge that was crucial to the technology industry in particular and the communications market in general. Like the young college students who presented complex graphs and statistics at the San Pedro meeting described above, diasporic individuals' cultural knowledge and networking skills were valuable for their convergence with empirical, professional knowledge. As software engineers, CEOs, marketing representatives, or lawyers—Latinos in the Digital Diaspora represented important industry-specific knowledge that could be systematized and operationalized in regional development initiatives. The exact functionality or application of this diasporic knowledge or the technologies they represented were not as important as the idea of connectivity—both social and technological—as an important step in the development process. Migrants' knowledge was central to establishing new market connections between cottage industries in Latin America and consumer markets in the United States. In all of these diverse capacities, diasporic subjects were thus perceived as a force that could institutionalize regional, technical, and universal knowledge and experience, linking them through cyberspace. In this way, Latinos quite literally personified a bridge across the digital technology divide.

The Digital Knowledge Networks (DKN) analyzed and supported by UNESCO provide a compelling example of how these premises from the Digital Diaspora project have evolved and been translated into contemporary initiatives. Beginning in the late 1990s, DKN projects in Colombia and South Africa served as case studies for examining the nature and durability of diasporic networks. Based on their experiences and extensive further studies of more than one hundred projects, the UNESCO DKN acknowledged diasporic individuals' capacity for building "knowing networks" of like-minded and similarly positioned expatriates, as well as for "managing knowledge" through an information infrastructure (UNESCO n.d.). The potential of this "knowing network" was succinctly encapsulated in the following assertion by the DKN:

> Migrants abroad know how to contact others who share their national identity; they know how to work out collective procedures for doing things with one another; and finally, they know how to use information infrastructures of Internet in order to accomplish their collective goals for their countries of origin.[14] (UNESCO n.d.)

One area where the DKN diverges from the Digital Diaspora project is in the former's operating assumptions about the relationship between the diasporic individual's translocal connections and corresponding social knowledge. Rather than assuming pan-Latino identification with a *regional* homeland in Latin America, as the Digital Diaspora did, the DKN projects have emphasized *national* connections between diasporic individuals and their "countries of origin." Recent studies have stressed how DKN projects "brought [expatriates] back into the national sphere" and constructed the social identity upon which diasporic mobilization might occur (UNESCO n.d.; see also Meyer 2007). For this reason, the picture of diasporic identity painted here is "more proactive, turned to the future, than retrospective and based on memory" (Meyer and

Wattiaux 2006:9). This formulation of diasporic identity—and the knowledge production on which it is based—in many ways mirrors the relationship between identity and knowledge that we saw in CDRO and its affiliate council's ethnodevelopment efforts. As CDRO's director, Son Turnil forcefully argued in Chapter Two, local ethnic development was not about holding on to the past, but about the continual reconfiguration of ethnic identity in the present, especially as a tool for development. For that reason, CDRO could justify its recruitment of foreign experts for the Walmart project as simply another way of integrating multiple, situated forms of knowledge as complementary components of ethnic development. Both CDRO and the Digital Diaspora projects thus highlight the dynamic, productive role of knowledge within subject formation, and the coupling of cultural and technical knowledge as crucial ingredients of development agency.

The Micropolitics of Knowledge

This chapter has explored how diverse ethnic subjects—college-educated indigenous council members, female microfinance authorities, Latino professionals, working-class migrants, and ethnic development organizations—were aligned with bodies of knowledge that were deemed essential to and valuable for development in multiple locations. I have argued for a micropolitics approach in order to examine what constitutes these various forms of knowledge and why they were deemed valuable for development. In the three cases described here, I have shown "local knowledge" itself to be a dynamic, contested field in which professionalized, empirical, and expert forms of knowledge played constitutive roles. For example, in the rural Guatemalan communities examined here, both feminine forms of banking expertise and masculine, service-based prestige sat in tension as legitimate sources of local knowledge. In CDRO's development efforts, a non-Western epistemology, empirical measures of efficiency, and foreign market expertise all commingled to constitute the contours of ethnic community know-how for development. For migrants, experience in multiple cultural, political, and economic spaces as well as varying types of technological expertise were assumed to constitute the basis for their uniquely translocal knowledge. Importantly, then, the ethnic entrepreneur represents the subject who could productively embody these tensions in a way that is valuable for development.

And just as the local knowledge assumed to reside within ethnic entrepreneurs reflects multiple, wide-ranging sources and forms, the global, expert knowledge positioned as its foil relies on culturally specific knowledge about particular communities. Therefore, development institutions privileged community-specific, local knowledge as an important ingredient of global development strategy. Additionally, the particularistic knowledge of specific cultural communities—be they indigenous communities or Latino consumers—turned out to be central to crafting effective market strategies.

Despite these convergences, the ethnographic encounters described in this chapter highlight how these diverse forms of knowledge were produced through and were reflective of preexisting forms of inequality. For example, both class and gender inequality figured prominently in debates over who held the "right" kind of knowledge for development: indigenous elites and council members versus elected political authorities; migrating males versus women left behind; diasporic professionals versus market experts.

A focus on micropolitics is thus an important analytical tool for discerning the contingency of these relationships between forms of knowledge and authority and the social actors to which they are linked. In the cases at hand, this approach is illustrative of the specific forms of knowledge assumed to reside within the ethnic community and how those forms interface with principles privileged within neoliberal development practice. By asking about how shifts in governance bring into question forms of knowledge and authority within the community, we gain a more nuanced sense of the effects of this transformation. In the ethnographic encounters described here, we can see how forms of knowledge associated with neoliberalism do not represent simply a monolithic, "menacing" hegemonic force that intruded upon, eroded, or simply replaced a more authentic indigenous form of knowledge. While these neoliberal norms certainly have played a central role in defining ethnic community realities, their effects are far from assured. Ironically, these shifting formulations and their embodiment in specific kinds of subjects could just as soon provide economic value and status to a certain constituency's views as it could mark that group as culturally distant and morally bankrupt. Furthermore, these constellations of power-knowledge are themselves highly unstable and subject to frequent revision within the space of development practice.

7 Conclusions

IN EACH OF THE INITIATIVES analyzed in the book, we have seen how the deployment of new forms of knowledge and practice within the space of development made visible new actors and posed new ethical problems for those same actors. Indigenous communities and Latino migrants emerged not just as objects of state or global development policy, but rather as potent agents of social and economic transformation in their own right. Their development agency was premised on the newly identified value of their previously marginal cultural identities, knowledge, and practices in relation to historically and geographically specific configurations of the market. The ethical dilemma they faced was not *whether* to participate in the market—to be entrepreneurial, to be economically successful, to acquire financial expertise—but rather *how* to live with and participate in the market in ways that were complementary with other dimensions of their social lives and identities (see also Elyachar 2005b). Resolving this tension required situated forms of "moral reasoning" that, while specific to these particular subjects, could be reflective of "provisional linkages that structure common problems of living for actors" (Collier and Lakoff 2005:35), in that they called upon new subjects to do the work of development in effective, efficient, and moral ways.

In the experiences of both CDRO and Digital Diaspora, I have examined how ethnic difference became a valuable resource for development, especially as it was embodied in the refigured development agent of the ethnic entrepreneur. Working through the ethnic entrepreneur, community-based strategies were privileged as the most efficient, effective, transparent, and sustainable means of achieving development, given their perceived compatibility with neoliberal norms such as decentralized, privatized, and market-oriented enterprise;

rationalized, bureaucratic forms of knowledge and expertise; and individual responsibilization and self-care. In all of these scenarios, the ethnic entrepreneur embodied important tensions and possibilities for ways of living in relation to the problem of development.

Recognition of the ethnic entrepreneur at this juncture was based on a reassessment of the qualities associated with ethnic difference and their potential utility for development efforts in Latin America. Both Latino businesspeople in the United States and indigenous community residents in Guatemala were marked as valuable ethnic subjects because of the enduring bonds of solidarity that were assumed to define their relations, the unique cultural knowledge they could bring to the development process, and their embeddedness in local communities. The positive reappraisal of these qualities contrasted with cultural determinist theories that had posited ethnic difference as an obstacle to development and indigenous and migrant subjects as embodiments of underdevelopment (Harrison 2000; Harrison and Huntington 2001). The redefinition of ethnic identity as a valuable tool for development was, nonetheless, neither the product of radical value change on the part of ethnic actors nor the product of discursive shifts on the part of hegemonic development institutions. Whether in debates between Juan García and CDRO, or in the halls of the United Nations, these subjects defined ethnic difference through tense negotiations over class and gender inequalities, as well as social location. In each instance, ethnic authenticity and community insidership were traits to be proven, rather than assumed. These debates showed the actual content of ethnic difference to be contentious and contingent, rather than primordial and rigid. The rearticulations of ethnic identity that the debates produced were not simply important reflections of the dynamic and situated nature of culture and identity, but rather political and moral projects in and of themselves.

On the one hand, the ethnographic examples that I have presented appear to represent vivid illustrations of how ethnic development strategies have served to imbricate people in Western modes of modernization marked by expanding market relations and technical forms of expertise. As such, they ostensibly validate postulations of neoliberalism as a monolithic, hegemonic arm of global capitalism that increasingly seeks to infuse the market into every realm of human existence (see Harvey 2005; Comaroff and Comaroff 2000). After all, CDRO's Banco Pop extended the reach of modern financial institutions into the rural Maya communities and reproduced bureaucratic knowledge and audit procedures as the modus operandi for indigenous development techniques. The Digital Diaspora sought to expand the market for ICT products throughout Latin America and to transfer business acumen and technology expertise to its citizens. And CDRO's community business model staked its fortunes on the cultivation of niche products to be sold internationally by none other than Walmart!

On the other hand, protagonists of both the CDRO and the Digital Diaspora projects were able to access legitimacy and development resources as well as negotiate power differentials with neighbors, nation-states, and donors through their claims to ethnic difference. No longer an ethnic minority, Latino participants in the Digital Diaspora were potent translocal agents courted by multinational institutions who saw them as the keys to hemispheric development (Chapter Four). Similarly, no longer an organization composed of marginal rural peasants, CDRO was lauded as a "pioneer" capable of replacing the state and embodying a philosophy from which the entire development industry could learn (Chapter Two). CDRO's new community business model exemplified an important transformation in the meaning of ethnic identity, especially in terms of the reterritorialization of identity that it represented in relation to a changing regional free trade economy. CDRO's efforts to sell cosmetic products was premised on the idea that abandoning corn in order to sell more profitable local products in international markets would sustain the social and economic lifestyle that defined the community as Maya K'iche'. This definition indexed a move away from an emphasis on corn production as a defining characteristic of ethnic identity, toward an accent on the preservation of a rural, indigenous lifestyle with market-based, sustainable production strategies as simply a means to that end. Therefore, shifting to the production of other local crops did not represent "selling out" as much as it meant buying into a new configuration of ethnic identity—namely, one that pivoted on the reproduction of the rural indigenous community as a site of cultural and political reproduction (see also Fischer and Benson 2006) and one enacted through new forms of ethnic entrepreneurship.

In Chapter Five, I invoked Collier and Lakoff's (2005) notion of "regimes of living" as a means of making sense of the entanglement of corporate forms, community morality, and profit-seeking activities in the new NAFTA/CAFTA regional free trade economy. While CDRO's collaboration with Walmart appeared to represent not only a further marketization of community life, but also a business relationship of the most exploitative kind, CDRO officials perceived the initiative as a means of negotiating the structural constraints on cultural and political autonomy in a post-CAFTA landscape. For its part, CDRO pursued its market-based development strategies with an eye toward "correcting the economy" rather than just participating more fully in it. This stance echoes critiques by Nancy Fraser, who has argued that recognizing cultural difference does not reflect a transformation in institutionalized patterns of subordination and may, in fact, work against it; therefore, recognition and redistribution struggles must be tied in order for identity politics to be meaningful and transformative (2000:113). CDRO's efforts to build a value-added, sustainable, and equitable basis for cultural reproduction attempted to achieve just that kind of redistributive function, albeit through the market. By noting this, I do not mean to romanticize CDRO's market-oriented efforts. Clearly, these articulations of identity through the market are always precarious, with local communities shouldering the enormous risk of economic failure. Nonetheless, to fail to recognize the political intentions behind CDRO's economic strategies would be to further naturalize essentialist constructions of both ethnic difference and an all-encompassing market without regard for their heterogeneous forms and effects (Gibson-Graham 1996).

Similar kinds of predicaments existed for both the working-class migrants and professional Latinos targeted by diasporic development programs. Latin American migrants were recruited for transnational development programs for many of the same reasons that they were increasingly targeted by anti-immigration activists. Their labor in the United States was crucial to the national economy; however, their presence was critiqued as a violation of ethical norms of national sovereignty and citizenship. Their contributions to the U.S. economy justified demands for rights and cultural belonging in the United States (Coll 2010), even as their ostensibly intimate connection to family and communities "back home" in Latin America marked them as ethnic others. Their migrant identities made them legitimate and lucrative vehicles for transnational transfers of private capital, while the frequent association between Latin American workers and undocumented migration posited them as criminals (Dávila 2008; Inda 2006; Mahler 1995). In all of these dimensions, Latino emigrants embodied complex ethical problems in relation to hemispheric development and the role of the market within it. And yet, many members of the Digital Diaspora initiative volunteered to participate on the basis of their desires to bridge the digital divide and enable more equitable hemispheric development possibilities. For many of them, fulfilling a moral obligation to coethnic kin and opening new technology markets were not contradictory goals, but rather complementary, mutually reinforcing ends. Taken together, the CDRO and Digital Diaspora examples thus provide vivid examples of how differently situated ethnic entrepreneurs sought to resolve the problem of how to live in relation to a historically specific configuration of global market forces.

Because of these convergences, the kind of moral and political debates represented by CDRO's collaboration with Walmart or the Digital Diaspora's coupling of multinational corporations and Latino professionals provide a window onto related ethical dilemmas that we see taking place globally, even as they reflect different arrangements between identity, development, and the market. For example, we can see evidence of these dilemmas in the commodification and marketization of indigenous African culture as a survival strategy (Comaroff and Comaroff 2009), the dispossession of Egyptian social networks and survival practices of the poor in the name of the market (Elyachar 2005b), the recruitment of individual professional talent for Chinese national development (Hoffman 2010), the invocation of community participation as a vehicle for consolidating "foreign" control of local resources in Tanzania (Walley 2004) and the empowerment of women in the service of state authority in India (Sharma 2008), to name just a few examples. In all of these cases, the "friction" produced by unequal, unstable, and heterogeneous development encounters can lead to new arrangements of power and culture (Tsing 2005:5). Therefore, what is needed is a methodological and analytical approach that can capture the multiple places and encounters in which development and identity politics play themselves out. I argue that an anthropology of development provides just the tools for that task.

Through a multisited ethnographic analysis, my study has sought to highlight the diffuse nature of state development activity, the spatially dispersed manifestations of the ethnic entrepreneur, and the disparate sites in which development politics are produced and negotiated. This approach contrasts with studies that have focused on the "politics of recognition" for ethnic groups within a specific national context, especially in terms of the ambivalent openings proffered by the intersection between multicultural identity politics and state-specific processes of neoliberal decentralization (Appadurai 2004; Postero 2007; Povinelli 2002; Sawyer 2004; Speed 2005).[1] Evidence of the ambivalent effects of state recognition politics can certainly be seen in CDRO's changing political fortunes. By 2006, CDRO's tenure as the poster child for ethnic development had worn a bit thin. The 1999 election of conservative Alfonso Portillo as Guatemala's president and the triumph of his Guatemalan Republic Front

(FRG) fellow candidates at the local level initiated an antagonistic climate that crippled CDRO's efforts both materially and politically. Several state contracts for local health and social service provision were retracted, and the government tried to set up an alternative non-governmental organization to take over the task of local development in Totonicapán. The widespread celebration of CDRO's development prowess chronicled in the previous chapters had made it a vulnerable target for political persecution and competition for resources. As further evidence of this antagonism, local conservative party members began vandalizing CDRO vehicles, which they identified by the *pop* insignia emblazoned on the doors. CDRO eventually removed all of the logos from its cars, preferring to lower its visibility in the countryside in order to avoid negative exposure. In this case, privileged recognition by the state worked against CDRO, exposing the need for real structural reform, rather than just regime change. CDRO's decision to produce nonethnically marked spa products signaled a larger operational shift away from the "branding" of Maya culture within a specific sociopolitical space toward a search for ways to restructure their relationship to the global market. It thus underscores the need for a more expansive methodological and analytical framework to understand the implications of the emergent ethnic entrepreneur.

A multisited anthropological study of development offers us a critical view of the production and negotiation of ethnic subject forms within the development practice across multiple social fields. Especially in light of the contemporary transnational migration flows and regional free trade pacts that define the region, both individual ethnic subjects and entire communities do development work across national borders and stake their claims both to legitimacy and to resources in multiple places. Through a multisited study, we can see the diverse opportunities and challenges posed by the increased recognition of ethnic subjects as entrepreneurial development agents in such diverse spaces as rural indigenous communities in Latin America, U.S. urban communities and labor markets, and the halls of the United Nations. In these locations, ethnic subjects face unique predicaments over how and whether to put their ethnic difference to work for development.

In addition to a multisited method, I have employed what I called a micropolitics approach that focuses on the actual practices of governing and their relationships to different subjects in order to make sense of these complex, uneven, and shifting development effects. Through this analytical lens, indigenous organic intellectuals like Benjamín Son Turnil of CDRO, enterprising regional merchants like Juan García in San Pedro, dynamic community leaders like Catalina Tzoc in Santa Cecilia, and savvy Latino business professionals like George González in the Digital Diaspora could all be perceived to hold important keys to translocal development efforts, given their ability to embody authoritative forms of ethnic identity. Nonetheless, through their debates, we have seen how these diverse actors' claims to ethnic authority were based on heterogeneous and even competing notions of what and who counted as ethnic. Therefore, the micropolitics lens allows us to discern how diverse epistemological forms and practices work through heterogeneous subjects and structures of inequality as part of new arrangements of governance that privilege local, community-based institutions. This approach has sought to make visible the complex and sometimes contradictory effects that these new arrangements produce for differently situated subjects.

For example, despite the potentially exploitative relationship between Walmart and CDRO established by the natural spa enterprise, the stakes of this initiative were distributed among different members of the indigenous community. The MABELI line of products and the nontraditional crops that go into them represent exactly the kinds of "productive," household-income strategies that privileged rural indigenous women. Through the cosmetic enterprise, then, Mayan women were literally responsible for turning the rural community into a fertile ground for producing economic value and development within a broader context of regional free trade and dwindling access to land, even as this new arrangement undoubtedly exposed them to new kinds of risks. Therefore, rather than looking to CDRO's initiative for evidence of ethnic community submission or empowerment, a micropolitics approach allows us to interrogate the nature and stakes of these new arrangements from the vantage point of differently situated actors engaged in specific practices and strategies on the ground.

In the end, however, the predicaments faced by ethnic entrepreneurs in their various forms are even more pressing than the somewhat optimistic CDRO and Digital Diaspora development initiatives have suggested. The devastating international financial crisis that unfolded over the course of 2008 has made the question of how to live in relation to the market a major dilemma for global civil society and states alike. Some of the initial symptoms of that crisis were forcefully made visible by the biofuel-food crisis facing indigenous corn producers in Guatemala and Mexico (Chapter Five). They have also manifested in a dramatic decline in income for noncitizen Latino migrants in the United States since 2007, a subsequent decline in new migration from Latin America to the United States, and a steep drop in remittances back home to Latin America (Kochar 2008; Lopez, Livingston, and Kochar 2009; see also Bank of Mexico 2009). These transnational dynamics will no doubt require new strategies, new types of knowledge, and new alliances on the part of ethnic subjects as they seek practical ways to pursue development in the context of shrinking economic opportunities abroad, dwindling state supports, and tenuous international aid. In the cases I have discussed here, pan-Maya social movements in Guatemala and pan-Latino initiatives in the United States were shaped as much by contentious expressions of community, subnational, or class difference as they were by convergent articulations of pan-ethnic solidarity. One of the questions that this current political economic climate raises is whether the time is ripe for a new brand of ethnic entrepreneur—one that can bring together a broad array of previously marginalized subjects in order to more qualitatively transform the unequal structural relations on which the problem of development rests.

Notes

Chapter One

1. K'iche' is one of twenty-one official Maya language groups in Guatemala.

2. As Laurie, Andolina, and Radcliffe (2005:472) argue, development-with-identity strategies treated "indigenous culture as a flexible and dynamic resource, as the basis for creative thinking outside the standard 'box' of development solutions."

3. See in particular the research on immigrant economies done by Portes and Rumbaut (1996) and Zhou (2004).

4. In their early form, critical development studies tended to be highly discourse oriented in nature, neglecting a more grounded, ethnographic understanding of the way that certain ideas were debated, contested, and reconfigured through practice. Furthermore, this work tended to fetishize the role of international institutions like the World Bank as being the monolithic source of development discourse. Finally, theorists like Escobar (1995) sought to resolve the problems of development by arguing for an abandonment of the development project and the initiation of a utopian postdevelopment world defined by local knowledge.

5. The "Chicago Boys" working with Pincohet's regime in Chile during the 1980s provide a case in point. They were a team of Chilean economists who received postgraduate training in the United States at institutions such as the University of Chicago and Harvard during the 1970s. In their work for the Chilean government, they applied the Chicago School of Economics principles to guide the decentralization of the state and the liberalization of the economy, deregulating the economy and privatizing essential government services. Similar technocratic influence was also evident in the neoliberal regimes of Mexico and Brazil, among others.

6. NAFTA is a comprehensive regional trade agreement signed by the United States, Mexico, and Canada in 1994 that sought to promote freer flow of goods and

investment across national borders. CAFTA is a regional trade agreement between the United States and the Central American countries of Guatemala, El Salvador, Honduras, Nicaragua, and Costa Rica. The Dominican Republic was added to the treaty in 2004. Although ratified by the United States in 2005, the treaty remains to be ratified by the Costa Rican government. MERCOSUR is a regional trade agreement between Argentina, Brazil, Paraguay, and Uruguay signed in 1991

7. These shifts were not specific to Guatemala, but have been defined as central precepts of neoliberal rationalities of rule. See specifically Brenner and Theodore (2002), W. Brown (2003), Massey (1994), and Rose (1996, 1999) for more analysis of the diffuse, localized nature of neoliberal arrangements of power and decision making.

8. See Calderon and Szmukler (2004) for analyses of similar processes in Brazil and Bolivia. In the same volume, Davis (2004:355) highlights the importance of the Guatemalan case relative to Mexico, Ecuador, and Peru's efforts to negotiate decentralization, poverty reduction, and indigenous political participation.

9. Indeed, classic modernization approaches to development clearly recognized the role of culture within development; however, they frequently saw it as a reflection of certain development stages (Parsons 1982; Rostow 1960). In other cases, culture was viewed as a deterministic variable, explaining development failure or success in terms of the presence or failure of particular cultural orientations (see De Soto 2003; Harrison 2000; Harrison and Huntington 2001).

10. A long history of anthropological critique has sought to problematize this assumption of a primordial, isomorphic local culture, focusing on the multiple, hybridized identities that the ethnic community produces through its very complex interactions with translocal economic, political, and cultural forces (see Appadurai 1996; Comaroff and Comaroff 1993; García Canclini 1995; Nash 2001; Tsing 1993, 2005; Weismantel 2001). Rather than seeing essentialist discourses of community as reflections of a natural local identity, many scholars have also highlighted the increasing stakes of articulating communal identities for legitimating and achieving specific political ends (Chatterjee 1993; Jackson 1995; Spivak 1996; Warren 1998). Nonetheless, as Gupta and Ferguson (1997:13) note, "identity neither grows out of rooted communities nor is a thing that can be possessed or owned by individual or collective social actors. It is, instead, a mobile, often unstable relation of difference."

11. See Elyachar's (2005b) study of the informal economy in Cairo and Coutin's (2007) study of Salvadoran transnational politics as further cases in point.

12. See Huntington (2004) for an argument about Mexican culture in particular and how it constitutes a threat to the Anglo-Saxon foundations of American culture. See Bedolla (2005), DeGenova and Ramos-Zayas (2003a), Inda (2006), and Stephen (2007) for critiques of the racial and cultural politics behind this construction of Latino identity.

13. See Hale (2004, 2005, 2006) on neoliberal multiculturalism for an examination of some of the trade-offs and conundrums introduced by this convergence.

14. For example, Gabbert traces the diverse uses of ethnicity to refer to particular national identities (for example, the Irish), as well as tribal identities; to explain community self-identification as well as imposed, stigmatized representations. See also Warren (2001) on structuralist and symbolic formulations of ethnic identity that emerged specifically in Guatemala community studies.

15. By approaching this problem of identification as an ethnic one, I do not seek to contradict studies that view these communities in terms of racial formations; instead, I am interested in the way that particular kinds of difference are defined as ethnic and thus link their subjects to particular kinds of projects and communities.

16. One area where discussions about the relationship between the two fields has taken place is in the realm of the humanities. See, for example, Poblete (2003) for a discussion of the political and institutional bases for the ongoing distinctions between and consolidation of Latino/Latin American Studies.

17. Throughout the book, I use the term "Latino" rather than "Hispanic" to reference a broad community of people who have varying degrees of connection to Latin America and who have been subject to an experience of racialization or discrimination in the United States as a result of their cultural difference.

18. According to U.S. Census data, Hispanics represented 12.6% of the total population in 2000, compared with 12.7% black (Asian 3.8%, Other 2.5%). However, by 2010, they were projected to represent 17.8%, compared with the black population of only 13.8% nationally. Therefore, Hispanics reflected not only the largest minority population, but also the fastest-growing community. In certain parts of the country, notably California and the Southwest, Hispanics have quickly approximated 30–50% of the total population. California Hispanics reached 35.5% in 2005. A proliferating body of studies has focused on how Latinos negotiate racism (DeGenova and Ramos-Zayas 2003b), illegality (Coutin 2005; DeGenova 2005; Inda 2006), and processes of cultural belonging or citizenship (Coll 2010; Flores and Benmayor 1996; Rosaldo 1994) in order to transcend their political and social marginalization within the U.S. national context.

19. Studies of diasporic communities (Afro, Jewish, Chinese, Lebanese) are also relevant (Siu 2005; Perera 1994), especially in countries like Brazil or Cuba with a longer history of slavery or immigration. However, the study of "racial formations" so prevalent in the United States has tended to be reserved for studies of Afro-Latino populations, rather than serving as a more universal template for understanding relations across distinct groups in Latin America. Greg Grandin's (2000) study of Maya nationalism in Guatemala is a notable exception.

20. Again, see Charles Hale's (2004, 2005) critique about whether democratization has provided for increased opportunities for ethnic community participation

and inclusion, or whether it has merely served as a means of neutralizing opposition and reentrenching traditional lines of power.

21. For example, according to Barth (1969), ethnicity represents the maintenance of group boundaries in relation to an Other. Consequently, ethnic identity does not derive from an ancient or essential quality, but is articulated vis-à-vis interfaces with other groups. As an example, despite a trenchant, melting-pot ideology in the United States, a white, Anglo-Saxon identity often serves as the default "all-American" prototype. In most parts of Latin America, on the other hand, a Hispanized mestizo (mixed Spanish and Indian) identity would be the norm against which many indigenous or Afro-Latino populations would be evaluated and labeled ethnic. Therefore, a Guatemalan mestizo who might be perceived as an ethnic subject in the United States in relation to the white norm could simultaneously embody the unmarked category or nonethnic norm in his home country. While this subject might have some choice in how he chooses to identify in these two settings, his social identity in each place would also largely be determined by such attributes as his surname, phenotype, class status, and first language.

22. I provide a more extensive genealogy of Maya community studies in Chapter Two. For studies of Maya cultural production and revitalization in particular, see Fischer (2001), Fischer and Benson (2006), Hendrickson (1995), Little (2004a), and Nelson (1999). For studies of the impact of state violence, see Carlsen (1996), Carmack (1988), Manz (2004), Sanford (2004), and Wilson (1995), among others.

Chapter Two

1. By invoking the "moral economy," I am abstracting from E. P. Thompson (1971) and James Scott's (1976) somewhat distinct conceptualizations of a system of group relations regulated by customary rights and obligations. I follow more contemporary derivations of the concept that would allow us to think about the moral economy both as a reflection of the economy of values or norms that define a group in a specific moment (Fassin 2005), and as the relation of those values to the problem of the "market" rather than to the problem of patron-client exploitation and peasant subsistence production per se (Edelman 2005).

2. For more on the turn toward "participatory" development strategies, see Keating (2003) and Lemke (2001b).

3. See Lucero (2006), Martinez and Bannon (1997) and Stavenhagen (2004) as examples of studies commissioned by the World Bank to analyze indigenous culture and its relationship to development. See also the evolving terms of World Bank operational directive 4.20 (World Bank 2005a, 2005b), which sought to protect indigenous communities from the negative impacts of development.

4. For descriptions of the persecution of grassroots activists and indigenous organizations by the Guatemalan military, see Carmack (1988) and Manz (1988). For analyses of the different ways that Maya revitalization projects positioned themselves

relative to state politics, see Bastos and Camus (1993), Cojtí Cuxil (1991, 1994), Nelson (1999), and Warren (1998).

5. While mutual support is a fairly common feature within microcredit programs globally, CDRO's was significant because of the way that it positioned this form of social responsibility as a specifically Mayan cultural norm.

6. Indeed, Brysk (2000:277; see also 1994) argues that indigenous movements, like those seen in Guatemala, were "born transnational" because of the high level of multilayered connections that both enabled and supported their emergence as legitimate social and political actors.

7. By 2000, new shifts in international funding priorities away from Latin America (especially on the part of U.S.-based organizations) caused many to lament the end of an era and the disappearance of viable local strategies for development.

8. See Ferguson (1990) and Pigg (1997) for descriptions of how this mandate has shaped the formulation and execution of development projects worldwide.

9. This income came primarily from Banco Pop revenue.

10. The *Popol Vuh* is a sacred Mayan text that chronicles the history of the K'iche' people prior to and following the conquest of Guatemala.

11. Son Turnil's story also highlights the importance of ethnic artisanal production as a concrete source of economic development, and the potency of ethnic artifacts as markers of otherness desired by foreign tourists (see Little 2004a, 2003; Meisch 2002; Nash 1993; Stephen 2005; Wood 2008).

12. See, for example, Wagley (1949), Tax (1953), and Brintnall (1979) for germinal studies of modernization in Maya community life; see Grandin (2000) and Smith (1990b) for historical analyses of the relationship between Maya communities and the state; see Fischer (2001) and Little (2004a) for more contemporary studies of the relationship between Maya culture and global formulations of modernity; and see Cojtí Cuxil (1991, 1994, 1997) and Montejo (2005) for analyses of Maya movement articulations of Maya culture in relation to Guatemalan and Western cultures.

13. For more on this critique in relation to indigenous politics throughout Latin America, see Hale (2005), Postero (2007), Postero and Zamosc (2004), Sawyer (2004), and Yashar (2004).

14. See Wolf (1957) for the classic "closed corporate community" theory. See Chapter Five for a more sustained discussion of the convergences between corporate ethics and ethnic community morality.

15. See also Hale (2005), Jackson (1995), and Warren and Jackson (2002) for discussions of the politics of indigenous self-representation.

Chapter Three

1. Indeed, the economic crisis experienced in the United States in 2008—and the decline in the housing market in particular—had dramatic effects on the Mexican

economy. Mexico's Central Bank reported a 3.6% decline in remittances (from $26 to $25 million)—the first drop in remittances in thirteen years.

2. For example, the First and Second International Conference on Migrant Remittances, cosponsored by the World Bank, the Inter-American Development Bank, and other state representatives from the United Kingdom and the United States. The possibilities posed by international migration discussed at these fora are also documented in World Bank documents such as Richard Adams's (2003) analysis, "International Migration, Remittances, and the Brain Drain."

3. Carol Smith (1984) has used the case of Totonicapán to demonstrate the importance of commerce and textile production as supplements to traditional agricultural sources of income. She uses the importance of these multiple income strategies to destabilize traditional notions of the Latin American "peasant" and proposes "petty commodity producer" as a more appropriate economic classification for residents of the region. See Chapter Five.

4. The number of migrants from the rural communities is an issue of debate. While many local residents identified a 25 percent migration rate, CDRO argued that less than eight hundred residents from the *municipio* at large had migrated to the states. Despite the variation in these numbers, they do not rival the significantly higher numbers of migrants from areas such as Huehuetenango.

5. Mexico ranks third among the top remittance destinations in the world, following India and China.

6. Later in the same report, Kapur (2004:18) notes that this replacement of the public-public development transfers through foreign aid with private-private transfers between individuals and households has ambivalent effects. While personal remittances have an immediate poverty-alleviation impact, they do not alleviate "structural poverty," which may still require external financial resources as well as macroeconomic reforms.

7. This work has included studies of migrants within a given nation state, as in Li Zhang's (2001) analysis of how migrants from Wenzhou province were noted for their entrepreneurial prowess by their Chinese peers. It also includes transnational migrants, such as Lynn Meisch's (2002) work in Ecuador on Otavalo artisanal merchants and musicians who ply their wares in global markets.

8. "Transnational entrepreneurs are self-employed immigrants whose business activities require frequent travel abroad and who depend for the success of their firms on their contacts and associates in another country, primarily their country of origin" (Portes, Guarnizo, and Haller, 2002:287).

9. According to the report by the UN Secretary General (2006:49), migrants' entrepreneurship is facilitated by:

> their extended families, the multiplicity of children or siblings who can provide free or cheap labour, the financial opportunities provided by rotating credit associations run

by co-ethnics, the strength of social networks within the migrant community and reliance on relationships based on enforceable trust within that community. . . . Opportunities for entrepreneurship undoubtedly add to the dynamism of migrant communities and offer important avenues for the economic mobility of migrant entrepreneurs through the accumulation of wealth. Migrant entrepreneurs often generate increased trade with the countries of origin by selling goods produced in those countries.

10. For example, recent studies have repeatedly shown that Latino immigrants in the United States tend to be urban, to have more education, and to be economically better off than their rural counterparts (Pew Hispanic Center 2008).

11. Household subsistence plots, used mainly for cultivating corn and beans.

12. For further critiques of the gendered division of development labor, see CMMG (1995).

13. While upper-level Guatemalan state officials and diplomats have certainly played an important role in negotiating immigration laws that will accommodate their own migrant-citizens in the United States, community-level development projects have increasingly involved direct collaboration between migrant organizations and local municipalities. Given that local governments are not created equally, these translocal engagements thus reflect and reproduce uneven migration and development patterns across the national landscape, a process that accentuates unequal resource distribution and governance patterns within the nation-state generally (Caglar 2006). Therefore, while these public-private enterprises are often described as *transnational*, changing state forms and their development implications call for better understanding of the *translocal* processes at work.

14. Moya (2005:838), however, stresses the global existence of mutual aid societies, or HTAs, and casts doubts about the significance of North American exceptionalism as an explanation for their formation.

15. The Tres-por-Uno (three-for-one) program promises matching investments by municipal, state, and federal governments for every collective investment in community development initiated by migrant organizations abroad (López-Córdova and Olmedo 2005).

16. This differentiation is intensified as we look to questions of entrepreneurship, where studies have shown that immigrant enterprises abroad are "primarily the business of married males" (Portes, Guarnizo, and Haller 2002:288).

17. See for example, Chatterjee (1993), Mohanty (1991), Bourque and Warren (1981). For Guatemala, see Hendrickson (1995) and Nelson (1999). Through the use of traditional ethnic clothing, the inculcation of language and customs to children, and participation in specific community rituals, women are seen to both physically embody and also ensure the preservation of ethnic cultural difference.

18. One exception to this rule has been in areas of artisanal production and sales. Little (2003), for example, describes how Kaqchikel artisan vendors play an essential

and very public role in generating household income. He juxtaposes these artisans' gender power to K'iche' women's lack of authority in business decisions, due to their different relation to production (Little 2004a, 2004b)

19. Indeed, during 1998 and 1999, the Guatemalan countryside was literally dotted with small, colorful signs that announced the implementation of any number of state-sponsored development schemes, identified most commonly by their various acronyms (e.g. FIS, FOGUAVI, FONAPAZ). These schemes were usually administered in the form of short-term, small-scale infrastructure donations, such as the construction of a clinic or a schoolhouse, the extension of electricity or telephone service, or the receipt of stoves or roofing materials. They generally operated through an initial advertisement to eligible communities regarding the availability of certain types of funds. It was then up to the communities to organize, put together a proposal, and solicit the funds. The Fund for Social Investment (FIS)—the donor behind the stove project—was one of the largest state-directed, internationally funded initiatives of those associated with the Peace Accords. See MacLeod (1997) for further detail on the FIS internal organization, operation, and mandate.

20. Montoya, Frazier, and Hurtig (2002:8) call further attention to this dialectic relationship between gender and place, asking "how places create and constrain historically specific gender inequalities and how gendered social processes create specific kinds of places."

Chapter Four

1. UNESCO 2005. *http://portal.unesco.org/shs/en/ev.php-URL_ID=7815&URL_DO=DO_TOPIC&URL_SECTION=201.html* (accessed July 15, 2009). The original Digital Diaspora Network website on which this description was posted is now defunct.

2. Evidence of this assumption is articulated in the United Nations Development Programme's Human Development Report, titled "Making New Technologies Work for Human Development" (UNDP 2001). For a visual representation of the problem, see Figure 4.1, the cover of the March 2005 *Economist*, which features a young African boy holding what appears to be a rock to his ear, in the style of a cell phone. This *Economist* issue also features a critique of the Internet connectivity focus of the "digital divide" conversation ("The Real Digital Divide," 2005:11).

3. See Lisa Servon (2002) for an analysis of social inequality and public policy relative to technology gaps both within the United States and globally.

4. Official website of The Indus Entrepreneurs (TiE), http://www.tie.org (accessed June 29, 2009). TiE is now an international organization with roughly eight thousand members worldwide, organized in sixteen chapters located in the United States, Canada, the United Kingdom, and India.

5. Personal communication, Akhtar Badshah, February 23, 2005.

6. Africast, Inc., *http://www.africast.com*. (This webpage and URL, last accessed November 2, 2004, are now defunct and have been superseded by new URL, noted below.) In 2005, the Africast webpage shifted from an e-commerce portal to a site emphasizing "Global Africa Network" media, including a pan-Africa movie channel for streaming and cable connection (http://www.africast.tv/#home). John Boateng continues to work in an African global media firm formed in 2004 and its corresponding foundation.

7. See Larner (2007) for a description of how these same principles were used to mobilize New Zealand diasporic elites.

8. The inaugural event for the Africa project established a Social Venture fund to provide financial support for entrepreneurial activities using ICT in Africa. Afrishare, "a platform for sharing best practices and matching innovative projects with mentors and potential sponsors," was formed.

9. Digital Diaspora Network for Latin America and the Caribbean, http://www.ddn-latinamericacaribbean.org (accessed September 25, 2003). The website is now defunct, but a project description and broken link remain on UNESCO's webpage: *http://portal.unesco.org/shs/en/ev.php-URL_ID=7815&URL_DO=DO_TOPIC&URL _SECTION=201.html*.

10. Intel's People and Practices (PaPR) team was constituted by a group of social scientists working in concert with academic and private institutions to research diverse cultural formations globally with the goal of informing the development of new technology.

11. Dávila (2001:1) notes the similar, ironic projection of Spanish film star Antonio Banderas as the face and voice of U.S. Latinos by Spanish TV network Telemundo.

12. For more on the role of language, see works by Padilla (1985) and Zentella (2001).

13. For more on the history of U.S. civil rights politics, see Gracia and De Greiff (1998), Oboler (1995), and Suárez-Orozco and Páez (2001).

14. Studies by Alcoff (1998, 2005), Bedolla (2005), DeGenova and Ramos-Zayas (2003b), Dávila (1999, 2001, 2008), and M. Torres (1998) all provide rich analyses of the way that class and national affiliations have destabilized the consolidation of a unified Latino or Hispanic identity and community.

15. Julia Paley (2001) provides an especially astute analysis of this process as it shaped Chilean popular participation in the postdictatorship period. See also Sharma (2008) and Hoffman (2010) for studies of how this transformation of the state has shaped national development efforts in India and China, respectively.

16. In her study of ethnic marketing, Marilyn Halter (2000) notes how telecommunications and financial service firms have similarly become a consistent presence at Asian cultural events in California, both to express their cultural awareness and also to gain entry into important transnational markets.

17. This specifically neoliberal form of postnational Latin America can be distinguished from previous efforts to homogenize Latin America in the context of U.S. expansionist desires. According to Susan Oboler (1995:18), nineteenth- and twentieth-century narratives and policies constructed Latin America as a place of foreign others (relative to the normalized North) whose social status, race, and nationality were fused. See also Nicholas DeGenova and Ana Cecilia Ramos-Zayas (2003a) for a succinct genealogy of the shifting significance of *hispanidad/latinidad* within the history of the Americas.

18. Venezuelan president Hugo Chavez now regularly invokes this Bolivarian principle of unification in his efforts to construct a contemporary regional political and economic bloc.

19. Again, for studies of how these factors have shaped Latino identity politics, see DeGenova and Ramos-Zayas (2003b), as well as Oboler (1995), Portes and Rumbaut (1996), Suárez-Orozco, Suárez-Orozco, and Qin-Hillard (2003), and Zentella (2001).

20. For further analyses of the role of national identity, minority politics, and community in structuring diasporic politics, see Appadurai (1996), Basch, Glick-Schiller, and Szanton-Blanc (1994), Chatterjee (2004), Hall (1991), and Lionnet and Shih (2005).

21. These steps were to include establishing a Web platform for interaction between network members, holding a Digital Bridge annual meeting in Latin America, cultivating partnerships with institutions and corporations that could support the network, and establishing a Social Venture Fund to support specific projects (electronic communication to listserv, September 16, 2003).

22. Dávila (2001, 2008) provides a detailed portrait of how U.S. media and marketing have worked to cultivate the emergence of a Latino consumer niche in the United States.

23. Lionnet and Shih's (2005) framing of the relationship between minority politics and transnationalism is a helpful resource for thinking through the complexity of diasporic and minority identities at work here.

24. Elsewhere, Badshah noted that similar funds set up for the India and Africa networks have funded over two million dollars' worth of projects (see Verdegaal 2003).

25. See UNESCO (2005) for a summary of the project and a broken link to the original Digital Diaspora website.

26. Again, see Dávila (2001, 2008). Paulla Ebron (2002:190) also provides a compelling analysis of how Africa has similarly been constructed (and performed) as a singular political and cultural space. Her focus on the role of global capitalism and cultural commodities in producing "deep feelings" that mediate the relationship between African American "pilgrims" and their symbolic homeland is especially relevant to this conversation.

27. For further description of this process, see Dávila (2001) and González (2000).

28. See María de los Angeles Torres (1998) for an analysis of the evolving, but often tense relationship between Latino migrants and their home countries throughout the twentieth century.

29. While scholars have located the origins of the "Latino" concept in French imperial projects in Europe and Mexico, its salience as an anti-imperialist, political, and cultural identity in the United States is of utmost importance here and in the larger Latino imaginary. See DeGenova and Ramos-Zayas (2003a), González (2000), Oboler (1995), and Rodríguez (1998).

30. The preservation of translocal community identities is not simply an individual choice or the reflection of ethnic proclivities. Dávila (1999:181), for example, has argued that multicultural policies work to perpetuate the reproduction of a focus on origins or nationalistic identifications as a means of evaluating "appropriate" representations of Latinness.

31. See, for example, analyses by Edna Acosta-Belen (1998) or Mike Davis (2001). As Gerald Torres (1998:156) notes, "The pan-Hispanic idea is problematic because it requires those of us who were colonized by Iberian imperialists to begin, first of all, to conceive of ourselves as having an identity that overlooks or supersedes the various national cultures that give vitality to a specific ethnic identity."

Chapter Five

1. This commercial tradition has been intensified over the last two decades through high levels of male migration to the United States. During this time, women have emerged as important development actors mainly vis-à-vis microcredit enterprises. See Chapter Three.

2. Smith's (1990a:217) analysis of this phenomenon helps us to understand the structural dynamics that forge ethnic community solidarity based on residents' collective experiences of oppression. Nonetheless, those larger class inequalities do not necessarily foreclose the possibility of a moral community. As I have argued elsewhere, even the wealthiest community members frequently had to justify their place within the ethnic community through evidence of their compliance with a local moral economy based on reciprocity and collective solidarity (DeHart 2008).

3. See translation by Dennis Tedlock (1996). The *Popol Vuh* later became a prominent icon of Guatemalan national culture when it was taken up by Guatemalan Nobel Laureate Miguel Angel Asturias's award-winning novel, *Hombres de Maíz* (1981[1949]). Interestingly, Asturias's text addresses the tension between corn growers and commercial entrepreneurs as a way of critiquing capitalism and its corrupting influence on the Guatemalan national character.

4. Maya community members who have increasingly pursued commercial enterprises as an exclusive form of household production are often the subject of derogatory comments, marginalization, and suspicion, perceived as being morally suspect

and potentially linked to exploitative capitalist forces of privatization (Fischer and Benson 2006).

5. While white corn is cultivated primarily for human consumption in Mexico and Central America, yellow corn, the specialty of U.S. farmers, is used primarily for livestock feed. Trade proponents have pointed to this difference in production to buttress claims of the complementarity of regional free trade (Office of the United States Trade Representative 2005).

6. Within fifteen years of its implementation, CAFTA will eliminate tariffs on virtually all agricultural products.

7. While U.S. corn exports to Central America rose steadily from the inception of CAFTA until 2007, the first six months of 2008 revealed a 5 percent decrease in corn exports to the region, compared with the same period the previous year, due to the increased diversification of corn toward biofuel (ethanol) production. In Guatemala in particular, U.S. corn imports dropped by about 34 percent relative to the combined accumulated and outstanding corn export sales reported during the same period in 2007 (Foreign Agricultural Service 2008). These shifts responded to the dramatic variations in the value of corn in the global market as a result of the biofuel crisis. Between 2007 and 2008, U.S. corn exports to Central America saw a 33 percent increase in the value; however, by August 2008, the price of corn had plummeted 35 percent from its June 2008 high, reflecting the highly erratic commodity landscape in which it is located.

8. While not a central focus in this chapter, it is interesting to note not only the material implications of this new market environment, but also the ideological landscape it represents. What we see in this new configuration is food production pursued solely as a vehicle for international export instead of as a resource for household subsistence or even national development. Clearly, this is not the first time this predicament has presented itself; some would say that the history of global capitalism is defined by this very transition from Marx's theories of use-value to exchange-value.

9. These cases exemplify the push toward a cross-sectoral development strategy promoted by organizations such as the World Bank or the Inter-American Foundation as the only way to ensure economically viable, coordinated, and sustainable development efforts.

10. See Sunley (1999) on the concept of stakeholding and its relationship to business management theory. See Sadler (2004) on the way the stakeholding concept has reemerged within corporate social responsibility discourse.

11. According to CDRO administrators, consultants from the French cosmetics firm, Mane, "sniffed around" in the forest to identify which products would make good commodities that could be grown in the forest or domesticated at a later date. The hope was that, following on the heels of the proposed replacement of corn by herbal production, the communities might eventually be able to create additional consumer products from fruit and forest products.

12. It is important to note that both the emphasis on small, farmstead agriculture and the corporate structure of the cosmetic enterprise (having all producers and laborers invested as shareholders) were explicitly designed to stimulate total community participation and produce collective benefits for community members. Therefore, the new business model took what might have been considered some of the most significant sources of local poverty (such as landlessness, unemployment, and female-headed households) and made them the foundation for this enterprise.

Chapter Six

1. This view has also been promoted by scholars of the Maya movement. In the Guatemala case, MacLeod (1997:24) notes:

> For the Maya, in particular, the local assumes a transcendental importance as a space for becoming subjects, within their culture, their forms of social custom and their worldview. The local is a space of resistance as it is of cultural reproduction, and its consolidation and articulation is what permits [the Mayas] national projection."

2. Council members were elected by their fellow program participants. Nonetheless, as described in Chapter Two, despite the council's demographic diversity, its board of directors was constituted by middle-aged men like Juan García who were considered among the community's economic elites. Their class privilege enabled them to send their children to college and then draw upon their newly acquired technical knowledge (such as grant writing and accounting) to enhance the council members' pursuit of new development opportunities. The authorities, on the other hand, were elected to office as part of ritual service obligations associated with the civil-religious hierarchy, or *cargo* system (Cancian 1965, Eckern 2003).

3. A rich tradition of community studies in Guatemala provides a nuanced panorama within which to situate this focus on historically dynamic forms of local knowledge and authority within the indigenous community. See for example, Wagley (1949) and Tax (1953) for foundational studies of indigenous community culture and its relationship to Guatemalan society. See Grandin (2000) for a historical analysis of the relationship between Maya culture and Guatemalan nationalism. See Brintnall (1979) and Arias (1990) for studies of modernization debates in the context of cooperative production and Catholic Action activism. See Tedlock (1973) and Watanabe (1990) for studies of the significance of time and place in Maya culture. See Carlsen (1996), Carmack (1988), Manz (1988), Smith (1990b), and Wilson (1995) for state violence. See Fischer (1998, 2004), Fischer and Benson (2006), and Little (2004a) for the relationship between Maya communities and global capitalism.

4. For example, the current authority configuration could follow its genealogical roots from the *principales* (elders) whose authority was based on age, lineage, and spiritual knowledge through the *empirico* (literally translated as the "empiricist"), whose authority was based on his ability to serve as a liaison to the state civil registry

by providing an inventory of community births and deaths (Tzaquitzal, Ixchíu, and Tíu 2000:54–55; see also Asturias de Barrios 1998a, 1998b; Eckern 2003).

5. This perspective reflects Brass's (1991:33) argument that debates over power within ethnic communities are often articulated in terms of authentic insiders versus culturally different "alien invaders."

6. Richard Adams analyzed this articulatory function of "power brokers" as they translate interests from one "level" of power to another dynamic in his study of the national social structure in Guatemala. Importantly, however, Adams (1970:321) argued that a broker's power at each of the two levels "depends on the success of his operations at the other level."

7. However, in this case, the council's development success did not translate into greater authority within the community, as it did for the young Chimalteco brokers described by Watanabe (1990:194).

8. By 2009, CDRO administrators acknowledged that women constituted at least half, and often the majority, of the council members in participating communities.

9. As described in more depth in Chapter Two, CDRO deposits seed money with the community as part of an effort to create "communal capital" that, through loan interest, produces a collective nest egg out of which future local development projects are funded.

10. As United Nations Under-Secretary-General Anwarul K. Chowdhury noted, "Experience of the Least Developed Countries (LDCs) show[s] that microcredit and microfinance are effective tools of poverty eradication and empowerment of people, *particularly women*" (2004:2; emphasis added).

11. Data from the Grameen Bank website, http://www.grameen-info.org/bank/ index.html (accessed March 20, 2008). For more on the politics of gender and development, see Benería (2003), Kabeer (1994), Murphy (1997), Rai (2002), and Tinker (1990).

12. See Bastos and Camus (1993), Fischer and Brown (1996), and Warren (1998) for a discussion of the diverse organizational forms, goals, and identifications articulated within the Maya movement. Also, see Nelson (1999) for an analysis of the diverse and contentious meanings attributed to Maya activist and Nobel Peace Prize winner, Rigoberta Menchú within Guatemala.

13. "Podriamos plantear la sustitución del Estado."

14. Information technology has served as the platform for constructing these social networks and exchanging technical information. In the DKN projects, this kind of technology includes a public portal that enables exchange of information about the supply and demand of specific development initiatives. On the supply side, diasporic individuals can use the space to advertise particular skills or ideas that they hope to contribute to development efforts in their country of origin. On the demand side, development agencies can post project information, identify needs, and suggest col-

laborative opportunities for programs under way. In addition to the public space, the DKN includes a "private" space that is explicitly designed for posting by actors who are looking for help with particular projects. The private space was set up to enable assistance via online discussion and exchange of ideas, a repository of articles and reference materials, and a listserve "for building up a memory of on-going collective action" (DKN website). However, rather than relying on the more passive technologies (such as websites and e-mail listservs) that characterized earlier-generation projects such as the Digital Diaspora, the goal of these multiple media is to promote interactive technology that can do a better job of creating dynamic platforms for knowledge exchange and, thereby, of sustaining diasporic interest in network participation (Meyer 2007:19).

Chapter Seven

1. Many of these authors have taken up the question of recognition through the lens of citizenship in particular, situating the question of recognition within the problematic of state-civil society relations. For a fuller critique, see DeHart (2008).

References

Acosta-Belen, Edna, and Carlos Santiago. 1998. "Merging Borders: The Remapping of America." In *Latino Studies Reader*, edited by Antonio Darder and Rodolfo Torres, 29–42. Malden, MA: Blackwell Press.

Adams, Richard H., Jr. 2003. "International Migration, Remittances, and the Brain Drain: A Study of 24 Labor-Exporting Countries." World Bank Policy Research Working Paper No. 3069. Social Science Research Network, http://ssrn.com/abstract =636431.

Adams, Richard. 1970. "Brokers and Career Mobility Systems." *Southwestern Journal of Anthropology* 26(4): 315–27.

Africast Global Africa Network. Africast Global Media, Inc., http://www.africast.com (accessed November 2, 2004). This site has been superseded by http://www.africast .tv/#home; original link.

Alcoff, Linda Martín. 2005. "Latino vs. Hispanic: The Politics of Ethnic Names." *Philosophy and Social Criticism* 31(4): 395–407.

———. 1998. "Is Latina/o Identity a Racial Identity?" In *Hispanics/Latinos in the U.S.: Ethnicity, Race and Rights*, edited by P. De Grieff, 23–44. London and New York: Routledge.

Annis, Sheldon, and Peter Hakim. 1988. *Direct to the Poor: Grassroots Development in Latin America*. Boulder, CO: Lynne Rienner.

Appadurai, Arjun. 2004. "The Capacity to Aspire: Culture and the Terms of Recognition." In *Culture and Public Action*, edited by Vijayendra Rao and Michael Walton. Stanford, CA: Stanford University Press.

———. 2003. "Sovereignty without Territoriality: Notes for a Postnational Geography." In *The Anthropology of Space and Place: Locating Culture*, edited by Setha Low and Denise Lawrence-Zuniga. New York: Blackwell.

———. 1996. *Modernity at Large: Cultural Dimensions of Globalization*. Minneapolis: University of Minnesota Press.

Arias, Arturo. 1990. "Changing Indian Identity: Guatemala's Violent Transition to Modernity." In *Guatemalan Indians and the State: 1540–1988*, edited by Carol Smith, 230–57. Austin: University of Texas Press.

Asturias, Miguel Angel. 1981[1949]. *Hombres de maiz: Edición crítica*, 1st ed. Guatemala City: Fondo de Cultura.

Asturias de Barrios, Lina. 1998a. *La alcaldía indígena en Guatemala de 1821 a la revolución de 1944*. Guatemala City: Instituto de Investigaciones Económicas y Sociales, Universidad Rafael Landívar.

———. 1998b. *La alcaldía indígena, 1944 al presente*. Guatemala City: Instituto de Investigaciones Económicas y Sociales, Universidad Rafael Landivar.

Ayora-Díaz, Stefan Igor. 2007. "Translocalidad y la antropologia de los procesos globales: Saber y poder en Chiapas y Yucatan." *Journal of Latin America and Caribbean Anthropology* 1(2): 134–63.

Baker-Cristales, Beth. 2004. *Salvadoran Migration to Southern California: Redefining El Hermano Lejano*. Gainesville: University Press of Florida.

Ballasteros-Coronel, Mary. 2006. "Guatemala: Indígenas en la economía global." Notiteca Indígena Digital, 8 de noviembre, http://www.fondoindigena.org/notiteca_nota.shtml?x=10250 (accessed July 15, 2009).

Bank of Mexico. 2009. "Las remesas familiares en 2008," http://www.banxico.org.mx/documents (accessed June 29, 2009).

Barth, Fredrik. 1969. *Ethnic Groups and Boundaries*. New York: Waveland Press.

Basch, Linda, Nina Glick-Schiller, and Christine Szanton-Blanc. 1994. *Nations Unbound: Transnational Projects, Postcolonial Predicaments and Deterritorialized Nation States*. New York: Routledge.

Bastos, Santiago, and Manuela Camus. 1993. *Quebrando el silencio: Organizaciones del Pueblo Maya y sus demandas*. Guatemala City: FLACSO.

Barraud, Ariel and Germán Calfat. 2006. "The Effects of Liberalizing the Yellow Maize Market in Guatemala: A Partial Equilibrium Multi-Market Approach." Working Paper. Institute of Development Policy and Management. University of Antwerp.

Bedolla, Lisa García. 2005. *Fluid Borders: Latino Power, Identity and Politics in Los Angeles*. Berkeley: University of California Press.

Benería, Lourdes. 2003. *Gender, Development and Globalization: Economics as if All People Mattered*. New York: Routledge.

Bishop, Todd. 2004. "Microsoft Notebook: Philanthropies Chief has a Non-profit Pedigree." *Seattle Post-Intelligencer*, Monday, June 21. http://www.seattlepi.com/business/178715_msftnotebook21.asp (accessed August 10, 2009).

Bornstein, Erica. 2005. *The Spirit of Development*. Stanford, CA: Stanford University Press.

Bourque, Susan, and Kay Warren. 1981. *Women of the Andes: Patriarchy and Social Change in Two Peruvian Towns.* Ann Arbor: University of Michigan Press.

Brass, Paul. 1991. *Ethnicity and Nationalism: Theory and Comparison.* New Delhi/London: Sage.

Brenner, Neil, and Nick Theodore. 2002. "Preface: From the 'New Localism' to the Spaces of Neoliberalism." *Antipode* 34(3): 341–47.

Brintnall, Douglas. 1979. *Revolt against the Dead: The Modernization of a Mayan Community in the Highlands of Guatemala.* New York: Gordon and Breach.

Brown, Michael. 2003. *Who Owns Native Culture?* Cambridge, MA: Harvard University Press.

Brown, Wendy. 2003. "Neoliberalism and the End of Liberal Democracy." *Theory and Event* 7(1).

Brysk, Allison. 2000. *From Tribal Village to Global Village: Indian Rights and International Relations in Latin America.* Stanford: Stanford University Press.

———. 1994. "Acting Globally: Indian Rights and International Relations." In *Indigenous Peoples and Democracy in Latin America,* edited by Donna Van Cott, 29–51. New York: St. Martin's.

Burchell, Graham. 1994. "Liberal Government and Techniques of the Self." In *Foucault and Political Reason,* edited by Andrew Barry, Thomas Osborne, and Nikolas Rose, 19–36. Chicago: University of Chicago Press.

Burns, Andrew, and Sanket Mohapatra. 2008. "International Migration and Technological Progress." *Migration and Development Brief 4.* Development Prospects Group, Migration and Remittances Team, World Bank. http://74.125.155.132/search?q=cache: Wpg7F8hHUZUJ:government.gfmd2008.org/index2.php%3Foption%3Dcom_ docman%26task%3Ddoc_view%26gid%3D15%26Itemid%3D45+International+ Migration+and+Technological+Progress.%E2%80%9D+Migration+and+Develop ment+Brief+4&cd=2&hl=en&ct=clnk&gl=us&client=firefox-a (accessed November 12, 2008).

Bush, George. 2007. "President Bush's Remarks on the World Agenda." Aired May 31 on National Public Radio. http://www.npr.org/templates/story/story.php?storyId= 1057754 (accessed June 29, 2009).

Caglar, Ayse. 2006. "Hometown Associations, the Rescaling of State Spatiality, and Migrant Grassroots Transnationalism." *Global Networks* 6(1): 1–22.

Caldeira, Teresa. 2000. *City of Walls: Crime, Segregation and Citizenship in São Paulo.* Berkeley: University of California Press.

Calderon, Fernando, and Alicia Szmukler. 2004. "Political Culture and Development." In *Culture and Public Action,* edited by Vijayendra Rao and Michael Walton. Stanford, CA: Stanford University Press.

Camposeco Cruz, Eulalia. 1997. "Podriamos plantear la sustitución del Estado: Entrevista con Benjamín Son Turnil." *El Regional* (Quetzaltenango), 6. 18–24 de julio.

Cancian, Frank. 1965. *Economics and Prestige in a Maya Community: The Religious Cargo System in Zinacantan*. Stanford, CA: Stanford University Press.

Carlsen, Robert. 1996. *The War for the Heart and Soul of a Highland Maya Town*. Austin: University of Texas Press.

———, ed. 1988. *Harvest of Violence: The Maya Indians and the Guatemalan Crisis*. Norman: University of Oklahoma Press.

Cattlelino, Jessica. 2004. "Casino Roots: The Cultural Production of Twentieth Century Seminole Economic Development." In *Native Pathways: Economic Development and American Indian Culture in the Twentieth Century*, edited by Brian Hosmer and Colleeen O'Neill. Boulder: University of Colorado Press.

Chakrabortty, Aditya. 2008. "Secret Report: Biofuel Caused Food Crisis." *Guardian*, July 4. http://www.guardian.co.uk/environment/2008/jul/03/biofuels.renewableenergy (accessed September 7, 2008).

Chatterjee, Partha. 2004. *Politics of the Governed: Reflections on Popular Politics in Most of the World*. New York: Columbia University Press.

———. 1993. *The Nation and Its Fragments: Colonial and Postcolonial Histories*. Princeton, NJ: Princeton University Press.

Chowdhury, Anwarul. 2004. "High Representative's Statement on Microcredit." Second Committee of the 59th session of the General Assembly. http://secint50.un.org/special-rep/ohrlls/ohrlls/UNGA59/HR%27s%20statement%2015%20Nov%2004-item 89a-Eradication%20of%20Poverty.pdf (accessed August 7, 2009).

Christensen, Allen. 2007. *Popol Vuh: The Sacred Book of the Maya*. Norman: University of Oklahoma Press.

Cojtí Cuxil, Demetrio. 1997. *El movimiento Maya en Guatemala*. Guatemala City: Cholsamaj.

———. 1994. *Políticas para la revindicación de los mayas de hoy*. Guatemala City: Cholsamaj.

———. 1991. *La configuración del pensamiento político del pueblo maya*. Quetzaltenango: Asociación de Escritores Mayances de Guatemala.

Coll, Kathleen. 2010. *Remaking Citizenship: Latina Immigrants and New American Politics*. Stanford: Stanford University Press.

Collier, George. 1994. *Basta! Land and the Zapatista Rebellion in Chiapas*. Berkeley, CA: Food First Books.

Collier, Stephen, and Andrew Lakoff. 2005. "On Regimes of Living." In *Global Assemblages: Technology, Politics and Ethics as Anthropological Problems*, edited by A. Ong and S. Collier, 22–39. Malden, MA: Blackwell.

Comaroff, Jean, and John Comaroff. 2009. *Ethnicity, Inc.: On Indigeneity and Its Interpellations*. Chicago: University of Chicago Press.

———. 2000. "Millennial Capitalism: First Thoughts on a Second Coming." *Public Culture* 12(2): 291–343.

———. 1993. *Modernity and Its Malcontents: Ritual and Power in Postcolonial Africa.* Chicago: University of Chicago Press.

Consejo de Mujeres Mayas de Guatemala (CMMG). 1995. *Mujer maya, desarrollo y organización.* Guatemala City: Cholsamaj.

Cooperación para el Desarrollo Rural de Occidente (CDRO). 2005. "Resumen ejecutivo de la propuesta de desarrollo local—Sistema Totonicapán." Unpublished document. Totonicapán, Guatemala.

———. 1998a. Carta de CDRO a los miembros del consorcio. Unpublished correspondence.

———. 1998b. "U k'ux Wuj." Unpublished internal document. Totonicapán, Guatemala: CDRO.

———. 1997. "Saq Tzij." Informational Brochure. Totonicapán, Guatemala: CDRO.

———. 1995. "Saq Tzij." Informational Brochure. Totonicapán, Guatemala: CDRO.

Cordero, Mario. 2006. "Women Entrepreneurs." *Diario La Hora.* http://www.lahora.com.gt (accessed September 16, 2008).

Coutin, Susan. 2007. *Nation of Emigrants: Shifting Boundaries of Citizenship in El Salvador and the United States.* Ithaca, NY: Cornell University Press.

———. 2005. "Being En Route." *American Anthropologist* 10(7): 195–206.

Dávila, Arlene. 2008. *Latino Spin: Image and the Whitewashing of Race.* New York: New York University Press.

———. 2001. *Latinos, Inc.: The Marketing and Making of a People.* Berkeley and Los Angeles: University of California Press.

———. 1999. "Latinizing Culture: Art, Museums, and the Politics of U.S. Multicultural Encompassment." *Cultural Anthropology* 14(2): 180–202.

Davis, Mike. 2001. *Magical Urbanism: Latinos Reinvent the U.S. Big City.* New York: Verso.

Davis, Shelton. 2004. "The Mayan Movement and National Culture in Guatemala." In *Culture and Public Action,* edited by Vijayendra Rao and Michael Walton, 328–58. Stanford, CA: Stanford University Press.

———. 2002. "Indigenous Peoples, Poverty and Participatory Development." In *Multiculturalism in Latin America,* edited by R. Sieder, 227–51. New York: Palgrave MacMillan.

———. 1993. "World Bank and Indigenous Peoples." In *Denver Initiative Conference on Human Rights.* Denver, CO: University of Denver Law School. http://www-wds.worldbank.org/external/default/WDSContentServer/WDSP/IB/2003/11/14/000012009_20031114144132/Rendered/PDF/272050WB0and0Indigenous0Peoples01public1.pdf (accessed July 13, 2009).

Dean, Mitchell. 1999. *Governmentality: Power and Rule in Modern Society.* London: Sage.

"Decentralization: Latin American and Caribbean States Discuss Their Models." 1997.

Accountability: Newsletter of Financial Management Improvement in Latin America and the Caribbean, Phase 2, no. 14 (June): 1, 2, 4.

DeGenova, Nicholas. 2005. *Working the Boundaries: Race, Space, and Illegality in Mexican Chicago*. Durham, NC: Duke University Press.

DeGenova, Nicholas, and Ana Ramos-Zayas. 2003a. *Latino Crossings: Mexicans, Puerto Ricans and the Politics of Race and Citizenship*. London and New York: Routledge.

———. 2003b. "Latino Racial Formations in the United States: An Introduction." *Journal of Latin American Anthropology* 8(2): 2–17.

DeHart, Monica. 2008. "A Contemporary Micropolitics of Indigeneity." *Latin American and Caribbean Ethnic Studies* 3(2): 171–92.

———. 2003. "Local Power in 3-D: Development, Democratization and Decentralization in Guatemala." American Anthropological Association Annual Conference, November, Chicago.

———. 2002. "Latin America Area Survey: Interfaces between Social Practice and Technology." Research report submitted to Intel Corp., Portland, OR, September.

De Soto, Hernando. 2003. *The Mystery of Capital: Why Capitalism Triumphs in the West and Fails Everywhere Else*. New York: Basic Books.

Digital Diaspora Network for Latin America and the Caribbean, http://www.ddn-latin americacaribbean.org (accessed September 25, 2003). This website is now defunct; broken link available at http://portal.unesco.org/shs/en/ev.php-URL_ID=7815& URL_DO=DO_TOPIC&URL_SECTION=201.html.

Ebron, Paulla. 2002. *Performing Africa*. Princeton, NJ: Princeton University Press.

Eckern, Stener. 2003. "Visions of the Right Order: Contrasts between Mayan Communitarian Law in Guatemala and International Human Rights Law." In *Human Rights in Development Yearbook 2003*, edited by Lone Lindholt and Sten Schaumburg-Muller. Norway: Martinus Nijhoff, Nordic Human Rights Publications, pp. 265–90.

Edelman, Marc. 2005. "Bringing the Moral Economy Back in . . . to the Study of 21st-Century Transnational Peasant Movements." *American Anthropologist* 107(3): 331–45

Elton, Catherine. 2006. "Remittances: Latin America's Faulty Lifeline." Audit of Conventional Wisdom Series, MIT Center for International Studies, March. http://web.mit.edu/cis/pdf/Audit_03_06_Elton.pdf (accessed July 14, 2009).

Elyachar, Julia. 2005a. "Best Practices: Research, Finance, and NGOs in Cairo." *American Ethnologist* 33(3): 413–26.

———. 2005b. *Markets of Dispossession: NGOs, Economic Development and the State in Cairo*. Durham, NC: Duke University Press.

Escobar, Arturo. 1995. *Encountering Development: The Making and Unmaking of the Third World*. Princeton, NJ: Princeton University Press.

Fassin, Didier. 2005. "Compassion and Repression: The Moral Economy of Immigration Policies in France." *Cultural Anthropology* 20(3): 362–87.

Ferguson, James. 2006. *Global Shadows: Africa in the Neoliberal World Order*. Durham, NC: Duke University Press.

———. 1990. *The Anti-Politics Machine: "Development," Depoliticization, and Bureaucratic Power in Lesotho*. Cambridge: Cambridge University Press.

Ferguson, James, and Akhil Gupta. 2002. "Spatializing States: Towards an Ethnography of Neoliberal Governmentality." *American Ethnologist* 29(4): 981–1002.

Fischer, Edward. 2004. "The Janus Face of Globalization: Economic Production and Cultural Reproduction in Highland Guatemala." In *Pluralizing Ethnography*, edited by John Watanabe and Edward Fischer, 231–56. Santa Fe, NM: School of American Research.

———. 2001. *Cultural Logics and Global Economics: Maya Identity in Thought and Practice*. Austin: University of Texas Press.

Fischer, Edward, and Peter Benson. 2006. *Broccoli and Desire: Global Connections and Maya Struggles in Postwar Guatemala*. Stanford, CA: Stanford University Press.

Fischer, Edward, and MacKenna Brown, eds. 1996. *Maya Cultural Activism in Guatemala*. Austin: University of Texas Press.

Flores, Richard, and Rina Benmayor. 1996. *Latino Cultural Citizenship: Claiming Identity, Space, and Rights*. Boston: Beacon.

Foreign Agricultural Service. 2008. "U.S. Trade Exports—FAS Commodity Aggregations." FAS Online, http://www.fas.usda.gov/ustrade/USTExFAS.asp?QI= (accessed August 11, 2009).

———. 2007. "Guatemala Agricultural Situation: Guatemala Corn 2007." Global Agricuture Information Report #GT7002. February 20. Prepared by Karla Tay. http://www.fas.usda.gov/gainfiles/200703/146280330.pdf (accessed August 13, 2009).

Foucault, Michel. 1995. *Discipline and Punish: The Birth of the Prison*. New York: Vintage.

———. 1990. *The History of Sexuality: An Introduction*. New York: Vintage Books.

———. 1980. *Power/Knowledge: Selected Writings and Interviews*, edited by C. Gordon. New York: Pantheon Press.

Fraser, Nancy. 2000. "Rethinking Recognition." *New Left Reviews* 3(May/June): 107–20.

Freeman, Carla. 2001. "Is Local: Global as Feminine: Masculine? Rethinking the Gender of Globalization." *Signs* 26(4): 1007–37.

Freidel, David, Justin Kerr, and McDuff Everton. 1995. *Maya Cosmos*. New York: Perennial.

Gabbert, Wolfgang. 2006. "Concepts of Ethnicity." *Latin American and Caribbean Ethnic Studies* 1(1): 85–103.

Gálvez Borrell, Victor. 1998. *Experiencias de participación democrática y poder local en Guatemala*. Guatemala City: FLACSO.

García, Maria Elena. 2005. *Making Indigenous Citizens: Identity, Development and Multicultural Activism in Peru*. Stanford, CA: Stanford University Press.

García Canclini, Nestor. 1995. *Hybrid Cultures: Strategies for Entering and Leaving Modernity*. Minneapolis: University of Minnesota Press.

García-Navarro, Maria. 2005. "Successful Migrants Return to Help their Native Mexico." Aired February 18 on *Morning Edition*, National Public Radio.

Geertz, Clifford. 1963. *Peddlers and Princes: Social Development and Economic Change in Two Indonesian Towns*. Chicago: University of Chicago Press.

Gibson-Graham, J. K. 1996. *The End of Capitalism (As We Knew It): A Feminist Critique of Political Economy*. New York: Blackwell Publishers.

Glick-Schiller, Nina. 2005. "Transnational Urbanism as a Way of Life: A Research Topic Not a Metaphor." *City and Society* 1(7): 49–64.

Glick-Schiller, Nina, Ayse Caglar, and Thaddeus Guldbrandsen. 2006. "Beyond the Ethnic Lens: Locality, Globality, and Born-Again Incorporation." *American Ethnologist* 33(4): 612–33.

Glick-Schiller, Nina, and Georges Fouron. 2001. *Georges Woke Up Laughing: Long Distance Nationalism and the Search for Home*. Durham, NC: Duke University Press.

Goldstein, Daniel. 2004. *The Spectacular City: Violence and Performance in Urban Bolivia*. Durham, NC: Duke University Press.

González, Juan. 2000. *Harvest of Empire: A History of Latinos in America*. New York: Penguin Books.

Gordon, Colin. 1991. "Governmental Rationality: An Introduction." In *The Foucault Effect: Studies in Governmentality*, edited by Graham Burchell, Colin Gordon, and Peter Miller, 1–52. Chicago: Chicago University Press.

Gracia, Jorge, and Pablo De Greiff, eds. 1998. *Hispanics/Latinos in the United States: Ethnicity, Race, and Rights*. New York and London: Routledge.

Grameen Bank. 2008. "Grameen: Banking for the Poor." http://www.grameen-info.org/ (accessed June 19, 2008).

Grandin, Greg. 2000. *The Blood of Guatemala: A History of Race and Nation*. Durham, NC: Duke University Press.

Gupta, Akhil. 1998. *Postcolonial Development: Agriculture and the Making of Modern India*. Durham, NC: Duke University Press.

Gupta, Akhil, and James Ferguson. 1997. "Culture, Power, Place: Ethnography at the End of an Era." In *Culture, Power, Place: Explorations in Critical Anthropology*, edited by A. Gupta and J. Ferguson, 1–29. Durham, NC: Duke University Press.

Hacking, Ian. 1982. "Power and the Avalanche of Printed Numbers." *Humanities in Society* 5(3–4): 279–95.

Hale, Charles. 2006. *Más que un indio: Racial Ambivalence and Neoliberal Multiculturalism in Guatemala*. Santa Fe, NM: School of American Research.

———. 2005. "Neoliberal Multiculturalism: The Remaking of Cultural Rights and Racial Dominance in Central America." *Political and Legal Anthropological Review* 28(1): 10–28.

————. 2004. "Rethinking Indigenous Politics in the Era of the 'Indio Permitido.'" *North American Congress on Latin America* 38(2): 16–20.

Hall, Stuart. 1991. "New and Old Identities, New and Old Ethnicities." In *Culture, Globalization and the World-System: Contemporary Conditions of the Representation of Identity,* edited by A. King, 41–68. Minneapolis: University of Minnesota Press.

Halter, Marilyn. 2000. *Shopping for Identity: The Marketing of Ethnicity.* New York: Schocken Books.

————,ed. 1995. *New Migrants in the Marketplace: Boston's Ethnic Entrepreneurs.* Boston: University of Massachusetts Press.

Hamilton, Nora, and Norma Stoltz-Chinchilla. 2001. *Seeking Community in a Global City: Guatemalans and Salvadorans in Los Angeles.* Philadelphia: Temple University Press.

Harrison, Lawrence. 2000. *Underdevelopment Is a State of Mind, Updated Edition: The Latin American Case.* New York: Madison Books.

Harrison, Lawrence, and Samuel Huntington. 2001. *Culture Matters: How Values Shape American Progress.* New York: Basic Books.

Harvey, David. 2005. *A Brief History of Neoliberalism.* Oxford: Oxford University Press.

Hayden, Cori. 2003. *When Nature Goes Public: The Making and Unmaking of Bioprospecting in Mexico.* Berkeley: University of California Press.

Hendrickson, Carol. 1995. *Weaving Identities.* Austin: University of Texas Press.

Hodgson, Dorothy. 2004. *Once Intrepid Warriors: Gender, Ethnicity, and the Cultural Politics of Maasai Development.* Bloomington: Indiana University Press.

Hoffman, Lisa. 2010. *Patriotic Professionalism in Urban China: Fostering Talent.* Philadelphia: Temple University Press.

Hoffman, Lisa, Monica DeHart, and Stephen Collier. 2006. "Notes toward an Anthropology of Neoliberalism." *Anthropology News* 4(7): 9–10.

Holston, James. 2008. *Insurgent Citizenship: Disjunctions of Democracy and Modernity in Brazil.* Durham, NC: Duke University Press.

Huntington, Samuel. 2004. *Who Are We? The Challenges to America's National Identity.* New York: Simon & Schuster.

IADB. 2009. "IDB sees remittances to Latin America and the Caribbean declining in 2009." News Release, March 16. *http://www.iadb.org/news/detail.cfm?artid=5160&language=English&id=5160&CFID=365679&CFTOKEN=92626659* (accessed July 14, 2009).

————. 2008. "Remittances to Latin America and the Caribbean 2008." The Multilateral Investment Fund, http://www.iadb.org/mif/remesas_map.cfm?language=English&parid=5 (accessed July 14, 2009).

————. 2003. "Remittances continue to set records and exceed expectations," http://www.iadb.org/news/detail.cfm?language=English&id=2119 (last accessed July 14, 2009).

———. 2001. "Survey of Remittance Senders: U.S. to Latin America," http://www.re-vistainterforum.com/Bendixenfeb21_files/slide001.htm (accessed October 15, 2008).

Inda, Jonathan. 2006. *Targeting Immigrants: Government, Technology, and Ethics.* Malden, MA: Blackwell.

The Indus Entrepreneurs (website). "About TiE," http://www.tie.org/chapterHome/about_tie/viewInnerPagePT (accessed June 29, 2009).

Itzigsohn, J., C. D. Cabral, E. H. Medina, and O. Vasquez. 1991. "Mapping Dominican Transnationalism: Narrow and Broad Transnational Practices." *Ethnic and Racial Studies* 22: 316–39.

Jackson, Jean. 1995. "Culture, Genuine and Spurious: The Politics of Indianness in the Vaupes, Colombia." *American Ethnologist* 22: 3–27.

Jaramillo, Felipe, and Daniel Lederman. 2005. "DR-CAFTA: Challenges and Opportunities for Central America." Central America Department and Office of the Chief Economist Latin America and Caribbean Region, World Bank. 215 pp. http://siteresources.worldbank.org/LACEXT/Resources/258553-1119648763980/DR_CAFTA_Challenges_Opport_Final_en.pdf (accessed August 13, 2009).

Jurenas, Remy. 2006. "Agriculture in the U.S.–Dominican-Republic–Central American Free Trade Agreement." A Congressional Research Service Report for Congress: The Library of Congress, 26 pp. http://www.nationalaglawcenter.org/crs (accessed July 8, 2008).

Kabeer, Naila. 1994. *Reversed Realities: Gender Hierarchies in Development Thought.* London: Verso.

Kapur, Devesh. 2004. "Remittances: The New Development Mantra?" *G-24 Discussion Paper Series.* United Nations Conference on Trade and Development No. 29. http://www.unctad.org/en/docs/gdsmdpbg2420045_en.pdf (accessed August 10, 2009).

Kearney, Michael. 1996. *Reconceptualizing the Peasantry: Anthropology in Global Perspective.* New York: Westview Press.

Keating, Christine. 2003. "Developmental Democracy and Its Inclusions: Globalization and the Transformation of Participation." *Signs* 29(9): 413–37.

Ketkar, Suhas, and Dilip Ratha. 2007. "Development Finance via Diaspora Bonds: Track Record and Potential." World Bank Policy Research Working Paper 4311 (August 1). Development Prospects Group, Migration and Remittances Team. http://papers.ssrn.com/sol3/papers.cfm?abstract_id=1006322 (accessed June 29, 2009).

Khalifa, H. E. Sheikha Haya Rashed. 2006. "Closing Statement by the President of the 61st Session of the General Assembly." High-Level Dialogue on Migration and Development, United Nations, September 14–15. http://www.un.org/migration/gapres-speech.html (accessed November 10, 2008).

Kleymeyer, Charles. 1994. *Cultural Expression and Grassroots Development: Cases from Latin America and the Caribbean.* Boulder, CO: Lynne Rienner.

Kochar, Rakesh. 2008. "Sharp Decline in Income for Non-Citizen Immigrant House-holds, 2006–2007." Pew Hispanic Center Report. http://pewhispanic.org/reports/report.php?ReportID=95 (accessed November 13, 2008).

Landolt, Patricia, Lilian Autler, and Sonia Baires. 1999. "From Hermano Lejano to Her-mano Mayor: The Dialectics of Salvadoran Transnationalism." *Ethnic and Racial Studies* 22(2): 290–315.

Larner, Wendy. 2007. "Expatriate Experts and Globalising Governmentalities: The New Zealand Diaspora Strategy." *Transnational Institute of British Geography* 32: 331–45.

Laurie, Nina, Robert Andolina, and Sarah Radcliffe. 2005. "Ethnodevelopment: So-cial Movements, Creating Experts and Professionalising Indigenous Knowledge in Ecuador." *Antipode* 37(3): 470–96.

Lemke, Thomas. 2001a. "'The Birth of Bio-Politics'—Michel Foucault's Lecture at the Collège de France on Neo-Liberal Governmentality." *Economy & Society* 30(2): 190–207.

———. 2001b. "Participation." *Kulturkreis der deutschen Wirtschaft im Bundesverband der Deutschen Industrie* [Cultural Association of the Confederation of German In-dustry], edited by V. (Hg.), Ars Viva 10/02. Berlin: Kunst und Design.

Levitt, Peggy. 2001. *The Transnational Villagers*. Berkeley: University of California Press.

Levitt, Peggy, and B. Nadya Jaworsky. 2007. "Transnational Migration Studies: Past De-velopments and Future Trends." *Annual Sociological Review* 33: 129–56.

Li, Tania Murray. 2007. *The Will to Improve: Governmentality, Development, and the Practice of Politics*. Durham, NC: Duke University Press.

Light, Ivan. 1972. *Ethnic Enterprise in America*. Berkeley and Los Angeles: University of California Press.

Light, Ivan, and Edna Bonacich. 1988. *Immigrant Entrepreneurs: Koreans in Los Angeles 1965–1982*. Berkeley and Los Angeles: University of California Press.

Lionnet, Francoise, and Shu-mei Shih, eds. 2005. *Minor Transnationalism*. Durham, NC: Duke University Press.

Little, Walter. 2004a. *Mayas in the Marketplace*. Austin: University of Texas Press.

———. 2004b. "Outside Social Movements: Dilemmas of Indigenous Handicrafts Ven-dors in Guatemala." *American Ethnologist* 31(1): 43–59.

———. 2003. "Performing Tourism: Maya Women's Strategies." In "Development." Spe-cial issue, *Signs* 29(2): 527–32.

Lopez, Mark, Gretchen Livingston, and Rakesh Kochar. 2009. "Hispanics and the Eco-nomic Downturn: Housing Woes and Remittance Cuts." Washington DC: Pew His-panic Center. http://pewhispanic.org/files/reports/100.pdf (accessed July 16, 2009).

López-Córdova, Ernesto, and Alexandra Olmedo. 2005. "International Remittances and Development: Existing Evidence, Policies and Recommendations." Paper prepared for the G-20 Workshop on Demographic Challenges and Migration, August 27–28,

Sydney, Australia. www.iadb.org/.../i_INTALITD_OP_41_2006_LopezCordova_Ol medo.pdf (accessed November 12, 2008).

Lucero, José Antonio. 2006. "Indigenous Political Voice and the Struggle for Recognition in Ecuador and Bolivia." Background Papers: World Development Report. http://siteresources.worldbank.org/INTWDR2006/Resources/477383-1118673432908/Indigenous_Political_Voice_and_the_Struggle_for_Recognition_in_Ecuador_and_Bolivia.pdf (accessed November 12, 2008).

MacLeod, Morna. 1997. *Poder Local: Refleciones sobre Guatemala*. London: OXFAM.

Mahler, Sarah. 1995. *American Dreaming: Life on the Margins*. Princeton, NJ: Princeton University Press.

Mahler, Sarah, and Patricia Pessar. 2001. "Gendered Geographies of Power." *Identities* 7(4): 441–59.

Manz, Beatriz. 2004. *Paradise in Ashes: A Guatemalan Journey of Courage, Terror, and Hope*. Berkeley and Los Angeles: University of California Press.

———. 1988. *Refugees of a Hidden War: The Aftermath of the Counterinsurgency in Guatemala*. New York: State University of New York Press.

Martinez, Juan, and Ian Bannon. 1997. "Guatemala: Consultation for the Indigenous Development Plan. Listening to the Mayan Elders." World Bank: Central America Department, Latin America and Caribbean Region. http://www-wds.worldbank.org/external/default/WDSContentServer/WDSP/IB/1997/06/01/000009265_39712 29180601/Rendered/PDF/multi_page.pdf (accessed June 18, 2008).

Massey, Doreen. 1994. *Space, Place and Gender*. Minneapolis: University of Minnesota Press.

Meisch, Lynn. 2002. *Andean Entrepreneurs: Otavalo Merchants and Musicians in the Global Arena*. Austin: University of Texas Press.

Mendieta, Eduardo. 1998. "Hispanizing Race." In *Hispanics/Latinos in the United States: Ethnicity, Race and Rights*, edited by Jorge Gracia and Pablo De Greiff, 45–60. New York and London: Routledge.

Menjívar, Cecilia. 2006. "Family Reorganization in a Context of Legal Uncertainty: Guatemala and Salvadoran Immigrants in the United States." *International Journal of Sociology of the Family* 32(2): 223–45.

Meyer, Jean-Baptiste. 2007. "Building Sustainability: The New Frontier of Diaspora Knowledge Networks." Paper presented at the Center for Interdisciplinary Research conference, "Transnationalization and Development(s): Towards a North-South Perspective," Bielefield, Germany, May 31–June 1. (Center on Migration, Citizenship and Development Working Papers, No. 35.)

Meyer, Jean-Baptiste and Jean-Paul Wattiaux. 2006. "Diaspora Knowledge Networks: Vanishing Doubts and Increasing Evidence." *International Journal on Multicultural Societies* (UNESCO) 8(1): 4–24. http:www/unesco.org/shs/ijms/vol8/issue1/art1 (accessed July 16, 2009).

Mitchell, Timothy. 1991. "America's Egypt: Discourse of the Development Industry." *Middle East* 169: 18–34.

Mohanty, Chandra. 1991. "Under Western Eyes." In *Third World Women and the Politics of Feminism*, edited by C. Mohanty, A. Russo, and L. Torres. Indianapolis: Indiana University Press.

Montagne, Renee. 2008. "Agriculture Official: Energy Costs Drive Food Crisis." Aired June 10 on *Morning Edition*, National Public Radio. http://www.npr.org/templates/story/story.php?storyId=91342960 (accessed June 29, 2009).

Montejo, Victor. 2005. *Maya Intellectual Renaissance: Identity, Representation, and Leadership*. Austin: University of Texas Press.

———. 2004. "Angering the Ancestors: Transnationalism and Economic Transformation of Maya Communities in Western Guatemala." In *Pluralizing Ethnography*, edited by John M. Watanabe and Edward F. Fischer, 199–230. Santa Fe, NM: School of American Research.

Montoya, Rosario, Lessie Jo Frazier, and Janise Hurtig, eds. 2002. *Gender's Place: Feminist Anthropologies of Latin America*. New York: Palgrave Macmillan.

Moore, Donald. 2005. *Suffering for Territory: Race, Place and Power in Zimbabwe*. Durham, NC: Duke University Press.

Moya, Jose. 2005. "Immigrants and Associations: A Global and Historical Perspective." *Journal of Ethnic and Migration Studies* 31(5): 833–64.

Murphy, John. 2007. "DR-CAFTA: The Record So Far." U.S. Chamber of Commerce, Association of American Chambers of Commerce in Latin America (AACCLA). http://www.uschamber.com/ issues/index/international/ drcafta.htm (accessed October 15, 2008).

Murphy, Josette. 1997. *Mainstreaming Gender in World Bank Lending: Un Update*. Washington DC: World Bank.

Myers, Fred. 2002. *Painting Culture: The Making of an Aboriginal High Art*. Durham, NC: Duke University Press.

Nash, June. 2001. *Mayan Visions: The Quest for Autonomy in an Age of Globalization*. New York and London: Routledge.

Nash, June. 1993. *Crafts in the World Market: The Impact of Global Exchange on Middle American Artisans*. SUNY Series in the Anthropology of Work. New York: State University of New York Press.

Nelson, Diane. 1999. *A Finger in the Wound: Body Politics in Quincentennial Guatemala*. Berkeley: University of California Press.

Nygren, Anja. 1996. "Local Knowledge in the Environment-Development Discourse." *Critique of Anthropology* 19(3): 267–88.

Oboler, Suzanne. 1995. *Ethnic Labels, Latino Lives: Identity and the Politics of (Re)presentation in the United States*. Minneapolis: University of Minnesota Press.

Office of the United States Trade Representative. 2005. "CAFTA Facts: Meeting the

Needs of the Region's Rural Poor." CAFTA Policy Brief. http://www.ustr.gov/trade
-agreements/other-agreements/dominican-republic-central-america-united-states
-free-trade-agr-197 (accessed October 15, 2008).

Offit, Thomas. 2008. *Conquistadores de la calle: Child Street Labor in Guatemala City.* Austin: University of Texas Press.

Ong, Aihwa. 2006. *Neoliberalism as Exception: Mutations in Citizenship and Sovereignty.* Durham, NC: Duke University Press.

———. 1999. *Flexible Citizenship: The Cultural Logics of Transnationality.* Durham, NC: Duke University Press.

Orozco, Manuel. 2006. "Diasporas, Philanthropy, and Hometown Associations: The Central American Experience." Inter-American Dialogue, http://www.thedialogue .org/PublicationFiles/central%20american%20htas%20report.pdf (accessed July 14, 2009).

———. 2004a. "Mexican Hometown Associations and Development Opportunities." *Journal of International Affairs* 57(2; Spring): 31–52.

———. 2004b. "The Remittance Marketplace: Prices, Policy and Financial Institutions." Executive Summary. http://pewhispanic.org/files/reports/28.pdf (accessed November 12, 2008).

———. 2003. "Hometown Associations and Their Present and Future Partnerships: New Development Opportunities?" Inter-American Dialogue. A Report Commissioned by USAID. Washington, DC: USAID.

Padilla, Felix. 1985. *Latino Ethnic Consciousness: The Case of Mexican Americans and Puerto Ricans in Chicago.* Notre Dame, IN: University of Notre Dame Press.

Paley, Julia. 2001. *Marketing Democracy: Power and Social Movements in Post-Dictatorship Chile.* Berkeley and Los Angeles: University of California Press.

Parsons, Talcott. 1982. "Evolutionary Universals in Society." *On Institutions and Social Evolution, Selected Writings,* edited by L. Mayhew. Chicago: University of Chicago Press.

Partridge, William, and Jorge Uquillas with Kathryn Johns. 1996. "Including the Excluded: Ethnodevelopment in Latin America." In *Annual World Bank Conference on Development in Latin America and the Caribbean.* World Bank Latin America and the Caribbean Technical Department, Environment Unit, Bogota, Colombia, 39.

Payne, Leigh. 2000. *Uncivil Movements: The Armed Right Wing and Democracy in Latin America.* Baltimore: Johns Hopkins University Press.

Perera, Victor. 1994. *Rites: A Guatemalan Boyhood.* San Francisco: Mercury House.

Perry, Richard Warren. 2006. "Native American Tribal Gaming as Crime against Nature: Environment, Sovereignty, Globalization." *Political and Legal Anthropology Review* 29(1): 110–31.

Peterson, Kristin. 2001. "Benefit Sharing for All? Bioprospecting NGOs, Intellectual Property Rights, New Governmentalities." *Political and Legal Anthropological Review* 24(1): 78–91.

Pew Hispanic Center. 2008. "Statistical Portrait of Hispanics in the United States in 2006." http://pewhispanic.org/factsheets/factsheet.php?FactsheetID=35 (accessed November 13, 2008).

Pigg, Stacey Leigh. 1997. "Found in Most Traditional Societies: Traditional Medical Practitioners between Culture and Development." In *International Development and the Social Sciences*, edited by F. Cooper and R. Packard. Berkeley: University of California Press.

Poblete, Juan, ed. 2003. *Critical Latin American and Latino Studies*. Minneapolis: University of Minnesota Press.

Pollan, Michael. 2006. *Omnivore's Dilemma: A Natural History of Four Meals*. New York: Penguin.

Poovey, Mary. 1998. *A History of the Modern Fact: Problems of Knowledge in the Sciences of Wealth and Society*. Chicago: University of Chicago Press.

Popkin, Eric. 2005. "Pan-Mayan Ethnicity in the Guatemalan Transnational Community Linking Santa Eulalia and Los Angeles." *Current Sociology* 53(4): 675–706.

———. 2003. "Transnational Migration and Development in Postwar Peripheral States: An Examination of Guatemala and Salvadoran State Linkages with their Migrant Populations in Los Angeles." *Current Sociology* 51(3): 347–74.

Portes, Alejandro, and Robert Bach. 1985. *Latin Journeys: Cuban and Mexican Immigrants in the United States*. Berkeley and Los Angeles: University of California Press.

Portes, Alejandro, and Ruben Rumbaut. 1996. *Immigrant American: A Portrait*, 2nd ed. Berkeley and Los Angeles: University of California Press.

Portes, Alejandro, Luis Guarnizo, and William Haller. 2002. "Transnational Entrepreneurs: An Alternative Form of Immigrant Economic Adaptation." *American Sociological Review* 67: 278–98.

Portner, Claus. 2003. "Expected Impacts of CAFTA in Guatemala." New York: World Bank, http://wbln0018.worldbank.org/LAC/lacinfoclient.nsf (accessed November 30, 2007).

Postero, Nancy Grey. 2007. *Now We Are Citizens: Indigenous Politics in Postmulticultural Bolivia*. Stanford, CA: Stanford University Press.

Postero, Nancy Grey, and Leon Zamosc, eds. 2004. *The Struggle for Indigenous Rights in Latin America*. Brighton/Portland, OR: Sussex Academic Press.

Povinelli, Elizabeth. 2002. *The Cunning of Recognition: Indigenous Alterities and the Making of Australian Multiculturalism*. Durham, NC: Duke University Press.

Puppim de Oliveira, Jose Antonio. 2006. "Introduction." In "Corporate Citizenship in Latin America." Special issue, *Journal of Corporate Citizenship* 21(Spring): 17–20.

Radcliffe, Sarah, Nina Laurie, and Robert Andolina. 2004. "The Transnationalization of Gender and Reimagining Andean Indigenous Development." *Signs* 29(2): 387–416.

Rahman, Aminur. 2001. *Women and Microcredit in Rural Bangladesh: An Anthropological Study of the Rhetoric and Realities of Grameen Bank Lending*. Boulder, CO: Westview Press.

Rahnema, Majid. 1992. "Participation," In *The Development Dictionary: A Guide to Knowledge as Power*, edited by Wolfgang Sachs, 116–31. London and New Jersey: Zed Books.

Rahnema, Majid, and Victoria Bawtree, eds. 1997. *The Post-Development Reader*. London and New Jersey: Zed Books.

Rai, Shirin. 2002. *Gender and the Political Economy of Development*. Malden, MA: Blackwell.

Rappaport, Joanne. 2005. *Intercultural Utopias: Public Intellectuals, Cultural Experimentation, and Ethnic Pluralism in Colombia*. Durham, NC: Duke University Press.

Ratha, Dilip, Sanket Mohapatra, K. J. Vijayalakshmi, and Xu Zhimei. 2008. "Revisions to Remittance Trends 2007." World Bank Migration and Development Brief 5, Development Prospects Group, Migration and Remittances Team, July 10. http://siteresources.worldbank.org/INTPROSPECTS/Resources/334934-1110315015165/MD_Brief5.pdf (accessed June 29, 2009).

"The Real Digital Divide." *Economist*, March 12, 2005: 11.

Reilly, Charles. 1997. "Mayors, Mayans and Poets." *Grassroots Development* 21(1): 4.

———. 1995. *New Paths to Democratic Development in Latin America*. Boulder and London: Lynne Rienner.

Robicsek, F. 1983. *Maya Book of the Dead: The Ceramic Codex*. Norman: University of Oklahoma Press.

Rodríguez, Clara. 1998. *Changing Race: Latinos, the Census, and the History of Ethnicity in the United States*. New York: New York University Press.

Rodriguez, Richard. 2003. *Brown: The Last Discovery of America*. New York: Penguin.

Rosaldo, Renato. 1994. "Cultural Citizenship in San Jose, California." *Political and Legal Anthropology Review* 17(2): 57–64.

Rose, Nikolas. 1999. *Powers of Freedom: Reframing Political Thought*. Cambridge: Cambridge University Press.

———. 1996. "Governing 'Advanced' Liberal Democracies." In *Foucault and Political Reason*, edited by Andrew Barry, Thomas Osborne, and Nikolas Rose, 37–64. Chicago: University of Chicago Press.

———. 1991. "Political Power Beyond the State: Problematics of Government." *The British Journal of Sociology* 43(2): 173–205.

Rosenberg, Mica. 2007. "High Corn Prices Threaten Guatemalans with Hunger." Reuters. Wednesday, May 2. http:www.reuters.com/articlePrint?articleId=USN02299550 (accessed November 3, 2008).

Ross, John. 2004. "Tales of Corn Wars." *National Catholic Reporter*, Oaxaca, Mexico, April 16, p. 11.

Rostow, Walt Whitman. 1960. *The Stages of Economic Growth: An Anti-Communist Manifesto*. Cambridge: Cambridge University Press.

Rouse, Roger. 1991. "Mexican Migration and the Social Space of Postmodernism." *Diaspora: A Journal of Transnational Studies* 1: 8–23.

Sachs, Wolfgang, ed. 1992. *The Development Dictionary: A Guide to Knowledge and Power*. London and New Jersey: Zed Books.

Sadler, David. 2004. "Anti-Corporate Campaigning and Corporate 'Social' Responsibility: Towards Alternative Spaces of Citizenship?" *Antipode* 36(5): 851–70.

Sanchez, Gisela. 2006. "El potencial competitivo de Guatemala: Casos de éxito de empreses guatemaltecas competitivas," Guatemala: PRONACOM. http://www.centrarse.org/2007/biblioteca/El%20Potencial%20Competitivo%20de%20Guatemala.pdf (accessed July 15, 2009).

Sanford, Victoria. 2004. *Buried Secrets: Truth and Human Rights in Guatemala*. New York: Palgrave Macmillan.

Sassen, Saskia. 1999. *Globalization and Its Discontents*. New York: New Press.

Sawyer, Suzana. 2004. *Crude Chronicles: Indigenous Politics, Multinational Oil, and Neoliberalism in Ecuador*. Durham, NC: Duke University Press.

Schele, Linda, Mary Ellen Miller, and Justin Kerr. 1986. *Blood of Kings: Dynasty and Ritual in Maya Art*. New York: Norton.

Schmidheiny, Stephan. 2006. "A View of Corporate Citizenship in Latin America." In "Corporate Citizenship in Latin America," special issue, *Journal of Corporate Citizenship* 21 (Spring): 21–24.

Scott, James. 1976. *The Moral Economy of the Peasant: Rebellion and Subsistence in Southeast Asia*. New Haven, CT: Yale University Press.

Servon, Lisa. 2002. *Bridging the Digital Divide: Technology, Community and Public Policy*. Malden, MA: Blackwell.

Sharma, Aradhana. 2008. *Logics of Empowerment: Development, Gender, and Governance in Neoliberal India*. Minneapolis: University of Minnesota Press.

Sieder, Rachel, ed. 2002. *Multiculturalism in Latin America: Indigenous Rights, Diversity and Democracy*. New York: Palgrave Macmillan.

Silvey, Rachel. 2006. "Geographies of Gender and Migration: Spatializing Social Difference." *International Migration Review* 40(1): 64–81.

Siu, Lok. 2005. *Memories of a Future Home: Diasporic Citizenship of Chinese in Panama*. Stanford, CA: Stanford University Press.

Smith, Carol. 1995. "Race/Class/Gender Ideology in Guatemala: Modern and Anti-Modern Forms." *Society and History* 37(4): 723.

———. 1990a. "Class Position and Class Consciousness in an Indian Community: Totonicapán in the 1970s." In *Guatemalan Indians and the State: 1540–1988*, edited by C. A. Smith, 205–29. Austin: University of Texas Press.

———. 1990b. *Guatemalan Indians and the State: 1540–1988*. Austin: University of Texas Press.

———. 1988. "Destruction of the Material Bases for Indian Culture: Economic Changes in Totonicapán." In *Harvest of Violence*, edited by Robert Carmack, 206–31. Norman: University of Oklahoma Press.

———. 1984. "Local History in Global Context: Social and Economic Transformation in Western Guatemala." *Comparative Studies in Society and History* 26(22): 193–228.

Smith, James. 2006. "Guatemala: Economic Migrants Replace Political Refugees." *Migration Information Source*. http://www.migrationinformation.org/Profiles/display.cfm?ID=392 (accessed June 30, 2009).

Sombart, Werner. 1951. *The Jews and Modern Capitalism*. Glencoe, IL: Free Press.

Speed, Shannon. 2005. "Dangerous Discourses: Human Rights and Multiculturalism in Neoliberal Mexico." *Political and Legal Anthropology Review* 28(1): 29–51.

Spivak, Gayatri. 1996. *The Spivak Reader*, edited by Donna Laundry and Gerald MacLean. London and New York: Routledge.

Stavenhagen, Rodolfo. 2004. "Indigenous People in Comparative Perspective: Problems and Policies." Background Paper for Human Development Report 2004, United Nations Development Programme. http://hdr.undp.org/en/reports/global/hdr2004/papers/hdr2004_rodolfo_stavenhagen.pdf (accessed June 16, 2008).

———. 1986. "Ethnodevelopment: A Neglected Dimension in Development Thinking." In *Development Studies: Critique and Renewal*, edited by R. Anthrope and A. Krahl. Leiden, Holland: Brill.

Stephen, Lynn. 2007. *Transborder Lives: Indigenous Oaxacans in Mexico, California and Oregon*. Durham, NC: Duke University Press.

———. 2005. *Zapotec Lives: Gender, Class and Ethnicity in Globalized Oaxaca*. 2nd rev. ed. Durham, NC: Duke University Press.

Strathern, Marilyn, ed. 2000. *Audit Cultures: Anthropological Studies in Accountability*. London and New York: Routledge.

Suárez-Orozco, Marcelo, and Mariela Páez, eds. 2001. *Latinos: Remaking America*. David Rockefeller Center for Latin America Series. Berkeley and Los Angeles: University of California Press.

Suárez-Orozco, Marcelo, Carola Suárez-Orozco, and Desiree Qin-Hillard, eds. 2003. *New Immigration Reader; Interdisciplinary Perspectives*. London and New York: Routledge.

Sulko, H. E. Kastriot. 2006. Summary of Roundtable Proceedings: Multidimensional Aspects of International Migration and Development, Including Remittances. High-Level Dialogue on Migration and Development, United Nations General Assembly. *http://www.un.org/esa/population/migration* (accessed November 12, 2008).

Sunley, P. 1999. "Space for Stakeholding? Stakeholder Capitalism and Economic Geography." *Environment and Planning* 31: 2189–205.

Tax, Sol. 1953. *Penny Capitalism: A Guatemalan Indian Economy*. Washington, DC: U.S. Government Printing Office.

Tedlock, Barbara. 1973. *Time and the Highland Maya*. Albuquerque: University of New Mexico Press.

Tedlock, Dennis. 1996[1985]. *Popol Vuh: The Definitive Edition of the Mayan Book of the Dawn of Life and the Glories of Gods and Kings*. Revised ed. New York: Touchstone.

Thompson, E. P. 1971. "The Moral Economy of the English Crowd in the Eighteenth Century." *Past and Present* 50: 76–136.

Tinker, Irene, ed. 1990. *Persistent Inequalities: Women and World Development.* New York: Oxford University Press.

Torres, Gerald. 1998. "The Legacy of Conquest and Discovery: Meditations on Ethnicity, Race and American Politics." In *Borderless Borders: U.S. Latinos, Latin Americans, and the Paradox of Interdependence,* edited by Frank Bonilla, Edwin Meléndez, Rebecca Morales, and María Torres, 153–68. Philadelphia: Temple University Press.

Torres, María de los Angeles. 1998. "Transnational Political and Cultural Identities: Crossing Theoretical Borders." In *Borderless Borders: U.S. Latinos, Latin Americans, and the Paradox of Interdependence,* edited by F. Bonilla, E. Meléndez, R. Morales, and M. Torres, 169–82. Philadelphia: Temple University Press.

Tsing, Anna Lowenhaupt. 2005. *Friction: An Ethnography of Global Connection.* Princeton, NJ: Princeton University Press.

———. 1993. *In the Realm of the Diamond Queen.* Princeton, NJ: Princeton University Press.

Tzaquitzal, Efrain, Pedro Ixchíu, and Romeo Tíu. 2000. *Alcaldes comunales de Totonicapán.* Guatemala City: Secretaria de Coordinación de la Presidencia, Comisión de la Unión Europea.

United Nations, General Assembly. 2008. "International Migration and Development." Report of the General Secretary. http://daccessdds.un.org/doc/UNDOC/GEN/N08/456/78/PDF/N0845678.pdf?OpenElement (accessed July 14, 2009).

———. 2006. "International Migration and Development: Report of the Secretary General," http://www.un.org/esa/population/migration/hld/Text/Report%20of%20the%20SG(June%2006)_English.pdf (accessed July 14, 2009).

United Nations, INSTRAW. 2006. "Gender, Migration, Remittances and Development." Fifth Coordination Meeting on International Migration. http://www.un.org/esa/pop ulation/meetings/fifthcoord2006/P02_INSTRAW.pdf (accessed November 12, 2008).

United Nations, Millennium Project. 2005. "Investing in Development: A Practical Plan to Achieve the Millennium Development Goals." Report to the UN Secretary General. http://www.unmillenniumproject.org/documents/ (accessed November 13, 2008).

United Nations Secretary-General. 2006. "Address to the High Level Dialogue of the General Assembly on International Migration and Development" September 14, New York. http://www.un.org/migration/sg-speech.html (accessed July 14, 2009),

United Nations Development Programme (UNDP). 2001. *Making Technology Work for Development: Human Development Report.* Washington DC: United Nations.

United Nations Educational, Scientific, and Cultural Organization (UNESCO). N.d. "Digital Knowledge Networks." www.unesco.org/shs/migration/diaspora (accessed July 15, 2009).

———. 2005. "Digital Diaspora Network Latin American and Caribbean" http://portal
.unesco.org/shs/en/ev.php-URL_ID=7815&URL_DO=DO_TOPIC&URL_SECTION
=201.html (accessed July 15, 2009).

United Nations Information and Communication Technology (UNICT) Task Force.
N.d. "Two Task Force Initiatives." *Challenges and Partnerships: Opening Up ICT to
the World.* New York: United Nations.

U.S. Census Bureau. 2006. "General Demographic Characteristics—Population Estimates for 2006." http://factfinder.census.gov (accessed June 10, 2008).

Urban, Greg, and Joel Sherzer. 1991. *Nation-States and Indians in Latin America.* Austin:
University of Texas Press.

Van Cott, Donna Lee. 2000. *The Friendly Liquidation of the Past: The Politics of Diversity
in Latin America.* Pittsburgh, PA: University of Pittsburgh Press.

Van den berg, M.H.J. 2003. "Mainstreaming Ethnodevelopment: Poverty and Ethnicity
in World Bank Policy." *Review of International Social Questions.* Available at http://
www.risq.org/article17.html (accessed January 29, 2007).

Verdegaal, Jacintha. 2003. "U.N. Recruits Expats to Help Bridge Digital Divides." In-
terpress Service News Agency, September 29, http://www.ipsnews.net/interna.
asp?idnews=20368 (accessed June 30, 2009).

Wagley, Charles. 1949. "The Social and Religious Life of a Guatemalan Village." *American Anthropologist* 51(4): pt. 2.

Waldinger, Roger. 2007. "Between Here and There: How Attached Are Latino Immigrants to Their Native Country?" *Pew Hispanic Center Report.* www.pewhispanic.
org/reports/report.php?ReportID=80 (accessed June 30, 2009).

Waldinger, Roger, Eric Popkin, and Hector Aquiles Magana. 2007. "Conflict and Contestations in the Cross-Border Community: Hometown Associations Reassessed."
Ethnic and Racial Studies 31(5): 843–70.

Walley, Christine. 2004. *Rough Waters: Nature and Development in an East African Ma-
rine Park.* Princeton, NJ: Princeton University Press.

Walmart. 2008a. "Guatemala Fact Sheet." http://walmartstores.com/FactsNews/ (accessed
November 13, 2008).

———. 2008b. "Mercy Corps, USAID and Wal-Mart Forge Alliance for Guatemalan
Farmers." http://walmartstores.com/FactsNews/NewsRoom/8024.aspx (accessed November 13, 2008).

Warner, Melanie. 2006. "Wal-Mart Eyes Organic Foods." *New York Times,* May 12.

Warren, Kay B. 2001. "Introduction: Rethinking Bi-Polar Constructions of Ethnicity."
Journal of Latin American Anthropology 6(2): 90–105.

———. 1998. *Indigenous Movements and Their Critics.* Princeton, NJ: Princeton University Press.

Warren, Kay, and Jean Jackson, eds. 2002. *Indigenous Movements, Self-Representation,
and the State in Latin America.* Austin: University of Texas Press.

Watanabe, John. 1990. "Enduring Yet Ineffable Community in the Western Periphery of Guatemala." In *Guatemalan Indians and the State: 1540–1988*, edited by Carol Smith, 183–204. Austin: University of Texas Press.

Waterston, Alice. 2006. "Are Latinos Becoming 'White' Folk? And What That Still Says about Race in America." *Transforming Anthropology* 14(2): 133–50.

Weismantel, Mary. 2001. *Cholas and Pishtacos: Stories of Race and Sex in the Andes*. Chicago: University of Chicago Press.

Wilson, Richard. 1995. *Maya Resurgence in Guatemala: Q'eqchi' Experiences*. Norman: University of Oklahoma Press.

Wolf, Eric. 1957. "Closed Corporate Communities in Mesoamerica and Java." *Southwestern Journal of Anthropology* 13: 1–18.

Wong, Bernard. 1987. "The Role of Ethnicity in Enclave Enterprises: A Study of the Chinese Garment Factories in New York." *Human Organization* 46: 120–30.

Wood, William. 2008. *Made in Mexico: Zapotec Weavers and the Global Ethnic Art Market*. Bloomington: Indiana University Press.

World Bank. 2005a. "Indigenous Peoples," http://wbln0018.worldbank.org/Institutional/Manuals/OpManual (accessed June 18, 2007).

———. 1996. "Participation and Indigenous People." *World Bank Participation Sourcebook*. Washington DC: World Bank, pp. 251-54.

Yashar, Deborah. 2004. *Contesting Citizenship in Latin America: The Rise of Indigenous Movements and the Postliberal Challenge*. Cambridge: Cambridge University Press.

Yunus, Muhammad. 1994. *Banker to the Poor: Micro-lending and the Battle against World Poverty*. New York: Public Affairs.

Zadek, Simon. 2001. *The Civil Corporation: The New Economy of Corporate Citizenship*. Sterling, VA: Earthscan Publications.

Zaloom, Caitlin. 2003. "Ambiguous Numbers: Trading Technologies and Interpretation in Financial Markets." *American Ethnologist* 30(2): 258–72.

Zentella, Ana Celia. 2001. "Latin@ Languages and Identities." In *Latinos: Remaking America*, edited by M. Suarez-Orozco and M. Paez, 321–38. Berkeley and Los Angeles: University of California Press.

Zhan, Mei. 2009. *Other-Worldly: Making Chinese Medicine through Transnational Frames*. Durham, NC: Duke University Press.

Zhang, Li. 2001. *Strangers in the City*. Stanford, CA: Stanford University Press.

Zhou, Min. 2004. "Revisiting Ethnic Entrepreneurship: Convergences, Controversies, and Conceptual Advancements," *International Migration Review* 38(3): 1040–74.

Zlotnik, Hania. 2006a. "Migrant Entrepreneurship: An Overview." Presentation given at United Nations High Dialogue, Turin, Italy, June 28–30. http://www.un.org/esa/population/migration/turin (accessed November 13, 2008).

———. 2006b. "Statement to the Commission on Population and Development." New

York: United Nations. http://www.un.org/esa/population/cpd/cpd2006/CPD2006_ Zlotnik_Statement.pdf (accessed November 13, 2008).

Zukin, Sharon. 2006. *Point of Purchase: How Shopping Changed American Culture.* London and New York: Routledge.

Index